Hegel, Marx,
and the Laughing
Matter of Spirit

Hegel, Marx, and the Laughing Matter of Spirit

◆

R. A. Aumiller

NORTHWESTERN UNIVERSITY PRESS
EVANSTON, ILLINOIS

Northwestern University Press
www.nupress.northwestern.edu

Copyright © 2026 by Northwestern University Press. Published 2026.
All rights reserved.

Printed in the United States of America

10 9 8 7 6 5 4 3 2 1

Library of Congress Cataloging-in-Publication Data

Names: Aumiller, Rachel author
Title: Hegel, Marx, and the laughing matter of spirit / R. A. Aumiller.
Description: Evanston, Illinois : Northwestern University Press, 2025. | Includes index.
Identifiers: LCCN 2025038071 | ISBN 9780810149687 paperback | ISBN 9780810149694 cloth | ISBN 9780810149700 ebook
Subjects: LCSH: Hegel, Georg Wilhelm Friedrich, 1770–1831 | Marx, Karl, 1818–1883 | Spirit | Comedy
Classification: LCC B2929 .A884 2025 | DDC 193—dc23
LC record available at https://lccn.loc.gov/2025038071

Hegel, Marx, and the Laughing Matter of Spirit

◆

R. A. Aumiller

NORTHWESTERN UNIVERSITY PRESS
EVANSTON, ILLINOIS

Northwestern University Press
www.nupress.northwestern.edu

Copyright © 2026 by Northwestern University Press. Published 2026.
All rights reserved.

Printed in the United States of America

10   9   8   7   6   5   4   3   2   1

Library of Congress Cataloging-in-Publication Data

Names: Aumiller, Rachel author
Title: Hegel, Marx, and the laughing matter of spirit / R. A. Aumiller.
Description: Evanston, Illinois : Northwestern University Press, 2025. | Includes index.
Identifiers: LCCN 2025038071 | ISBN 9780810149687 paperback | ISBN 9780810149694 cloth | ISBN 9780810149700 ebook
Subjects: LCSH: Hegel, Georg Wilhelm Friedrich, 1770–1831 | Marx, Karl, 1818–1883 | Spirit | Comedy
Classification: LCC B2929 .A884 2025 | DDC 193—dc23
LC record available at https://lccn.loc.gov/2025038071

For Jan Sieber

in memory of our adventures in Lebanon

where we explored history as theater

and gave thanks to Dionysus

CONTENTS

Introduction
A Brief History of How History Became a Laughing Matter   *1*

Chapter 1
Twice-Two, or Tetradic Dialectics   *21*

Chapter 2
Comic Abortions and the Birth of Self   *45*

Chapter 3
The Birth of Community at the Comedy of the Cross   *63*

Chapter 4
Censoring Laughter   *85*

Chapter 5
A Young Hegelian Comedy   *97*

Chapter 6
Benjamin's Comedy of the Damned   *113*

Chapter 7
Antigone's Disappearance Act in Yugoslavia   *129*

Conclusion
History's Laugh Lines and Comic Resistance Today   *149*

Acknowledgments   *163*

Notes   *165*

References   *189*

Index   *197*

Introduction

A Brief History of How History Became a Laughing Matter

Hegel's philosophy has always created divisions among his readers. The fierce opposition between different camps of Hegelians is not like the inevitable disagreements that occur in scholarship on any other philosopher. The response to Hegel's thought enacts the very irreconcilable split he saw within Spirit. The divisions arising from the arguments concerning the correct reading of Hegel are performatively more correct than any single side of these debates. The split, the slit, the crack, the cleavage (*die Entzweiung*) cannot be avoided, although we try and fail to overcome it again and again. The question is then how to self-consciously stage the split. Will this stage play of Spirit be a tragedy or comedy?

The first split in Hegelian scholarship occurred during Hegel's own lifetime. On one side of the division were the Old Hegelians, who saw Hegel's philosophy as the weathered owl that swoops down to survey the end of history, *which is upon us*. Their opponents, the Young Hegelians, saw Hegel's philosophy as the fledgling cock that welcomes the dawn of a new stage of history, *which is upon us*. The tense opposition between "the Old" and "the Young" is already quite comical: two faces of Hegel knocking heads within the same historical crack. I will illustrate the situation for you in the form of two Hegelian haikus:

> Two Hegelians
> in a crack. Is this the end
> or the beginning?

> Neither sees that what
> one calls owl and one calls cock
> is the same damn bird.

The split between the Old and the Young Hegelians is often framed in terms of the former's defense of Hegel's philosophy as the ultimate expression of

Christian metaphysics and the latter's rejection of theological aspects of Hegel's thought in the name of revolutionary politics. Yet the Young Hegelians were neither united in their politics nor in their views on religion. Their disagreements concerning the relationship between religion and politics both drove their dialogue and divided them. The crack between the Old and the Young within the first-generation Hegelians immediately gave rise to another crack within the Young. Despite being split, the common factor that shaped the movement was the way they drew on Hegel's aesthetics as a lens to view modern life and revolutionary politics. Of all the moments in Hegel's extensive history of aesthetics, the Young Hegelians took inspiration from Hegel's analysis of the art-religion of the Greeks, giving particular attention to his dramatic portrayal of ancient comedy.[1]

In his grand accounts of the history of art, religion, and history, Hegel identifies ancient Greek drama as a historical moment when art grasped itself as something more than a representational object or creative production mirroring real life. Ancient drama highlights human activity as the subject for reflection and, therefore, had a special relationship to Spirit: a community's self-conscious reflection on the production of the political staging of its own social roles (a partial definition that will do for the moment). Drama exposes the theatrics of existence, placing aesthetic representation and reality in the same field. In a tragic framing of our social existence, we are the audience of our own lives, which we soberly watch unfold before us without fully recognizing ourselves as characters in the drama. By defending the rightness of their role, a tragic hero (on the stage, in society) often accepts blame and even takes credit for a societal disturbance that reflects a conflict belonging to all. Comedy invites the audience to participate in the drama, which no one can escape or individually alter. The conflict, personified in tragedy by the hero, is exposed in comedy as the result of a crack in the stage that rises beneath the hero's feet. Tragedy is traditionally coupled with fate, while comedy is coupled with the caprice of an individual character, often represented on the stage by a fool or scoundrel. Yet tragedy is tragic precisely for its overemphasis on the individual and the appearance of their guilt or integrity in connection with a specific action. Comedy is comic for exposing its own crack, offering a path toward agency or action that is fully negative, itself characterized by a split. On one side of the split, a comic character finds freedom in the insight that there is nothing substantial that can be done to alter a social script that damns them from the beginning to play the role of the fool (so why not play the role of the scoundrel?). In this case, as Hegel puts it in the *Phenomenology of Spirit*, "The self . . . plays with the mask which it once put on in order to act its part . . . [and] stands forth in its own nakedness and ordinariness, which it shows to be not distinct from the genuine self, the actor, or from the spectator."[2] On the other side, the chorus must set fire to the stage itself. Sometimes this movement is successful and results in the destruction of an entire way of life. Hegel ends his account of ancient comedy in the *Phenomenology of Spirit* by narrating the total collapse of the ethical system structuring Greek life. More often this movement to end and begin again fails, resulting in a minor disturbance within a social script.

Whether comedy results in total destruction or a glitch in the conventions belonging to the stage, Hegelian comic action lurks in an almost imperceptible stirring in the cracking open of the crack. In the *Phenomenology of Spirit*, Hegel remarkably identifies this stirring, a kind of movement of negativity within negativity, as the first emergence of "Self," who becomes a new protagonist of Hegel's drama.[3] The birth of Self in comic destruction is not a positive stage in itself. It can be seen either as a transition leading from one dramatic historical stage to another or as a kind of historical intermission. For Hegel, Greek comedy does not offer resolution but instead unlocks further drama. Ancient comedy opens onto what Hegel identifies in his *Lectures on the Philosophy of Religion* as "the divine drama" of Christianity.[4] This transition from "Art-Religion" to "Revealed Religion"—or from Greek drama to the drama of Christ—recurs within the *Phenomenology of Spirit* (1807)[5] and Hegel's public Berlin lectures on aesthetics (1820–29)[6] and the philosophy of religion (1821–31).[7] The unresolved drama of ancient Greek ethics continues to play itself out on the stage of Christianity. The mask representing the comic self is exchanged for the mask of Christ, the tragic-comic hero of the "new stage." This "higher stage" repeats the action of the former stage, unleashing deeper conflict that was present all along. The new beginning only deepens the contradiction that comic destruction appeared to defeat.

Each reader of Hegel has a favorite dialectical loop through which they read all the others. It's easy to get stuck in the spots where dialectic does not offer any satisfactory resolution or obvious path forward. Personally, I think these hiccups within the fluency of dialectical momentum are the most exciting. Dialectic, at times, ends on a moment of suspension, a curious property of *Aufhebung*, which repeats itself like a glitch in the smooth telos of historical progress. *Aufhebung*, as a narrative device in any experience and account of a conflict, is no more a new beginning than a termination, no more progress than paralysis, no more dramatic resolution than suspension. The Young Hegelians adopted a dialectical looping found in the crack between "Art-Religion" and "Revealed Religion" that captures the total collapse of an entire way of life and the moment of still darkness before the anticipation of a new beginning. They elevated this single historical transition (or moment of suspension) in Hegel's work to characterize the dramatic movement of history itself. The Young Hegelians specifically identified comedy as the internal motor of history—the work of the negative—and gave this historical comedy a second name: critique. Here we may add a second partial definition of Spirit: history's negative self-relation, when it grasps itself as such by coming to sense its own contradiction in a particular time and place.

As a political movement, the Young Hegelians barely lasted two decades: they came together in the first minor uprisings of the 1830s and dispersed after the grand failure of 1848. In the beginning, they collectively celebrated a series of minor revolts as the opening act of a great historical comedy. One of the newest and youngest members of the movement, Karl Marx, was responsible for introducing laughter into Young Hegelian revolutionary politics. In his first published essay, Marx responds to new Prussian censorship policies with an animated defense of the critical value of political affects, emphasizing audacity and humor.[8] The censorship promoted National Feeling (*das Nationalgefühl*), which it described as a *common sense* of decency and moderation, in the name of protecting free speech and civil discourse. Marx exposes National Feeling as the dark counterfeit double of Public Spirit (*der öffentliche Geist*). National Feeling dictates "common sense" by teaching its subjects ahead of time how they ought to feel (or, rather, not feel too strongly) about their individual and collective existence. Public Spirit, in contrast, is the emergence of unforeseen affects when individuals grasp themselves as a communal body in a specific place and time. Marx attributes a kind of critical laughter to Spirit when it seizes itself by the absurdity of its own political contradictions. Laughter does not only belong to critical philosophers and comedians who identify contradictions in their society. Nor can the philosopher's critique or comic's laughter on its own incite real political action. Revolution is born when a historical stage can no longer look at its own tragic contradictions with a straight face. *Revolution is history's laughter*.

Arnold Ruge, one of the founding Young Hegelians, was thrilled by Marx's Hegelian formulation of laughter as equally spiritual and critical and responded by introducing the concept of historical comedy.[9] Ruge only half joked when he claimed that it was due to "the gloominess, or, what is more accurate, the brutishness of feeling in the German spirit"[10] that its own revolution lagged behind countries like France, which had already experienced comic eruptions. As Ruge defined it, historical comedy is a growing shared sense that a particular stage can no longer sustain itself under the tensions of its own contradictions. Historical comedy is the self-relation of a crack on both a personal and an impersonal register. On a subjective level, individual actors begin to sense how the contradictions of a political stage simultaneously form their role and prevent their participation on that stage by splitting their subjectivity in two and pitting the sides against each other. On an impersonal, or objective, register, which is equally affective and sensational, history senses its own unsustainability at a particular stage. Materiality experiences an excess that overflows from a sense of lack that the tragic perspective refuses to fully acknowledge.

With the peasant uprisings—led first by the tailors (1830), followed by the pyrotechnists (1835), the Berlin arsenal riots (1846), and finally the potato farmers' revolt (1847)—the Young Hegelians sensed that Germany would soon erupt in its own historical comedy. As Ruge put it, "We will now be able to detect among ourselves the [emergence of a historical] comedy that unlike the *genre* comedy, does not destroy the shapes of the . . . bourgeois Spirit but that destroys Spirit's actual historical stages."[11] The Young Hegelians imagined that their own revolution would be a historical comedy that gives birth to itself in its own self-termination. By destroying the conventions of its own staging that alienate the individual from their self and communal body, comic destruction at once gives birth to the possibility of concrete self-relation of Self and Public Spirit. Although the Young Hegelians came together with the anticipation of a great historical comedy, the culmination of the uprisings resulted in the devastating failure of the March Revolution. This time, history repeated itself: first as comedy and then as tragedy, exposing the comic nature of the beginning as merely farce—the appearance of newness that repeats the contradictory contents of the old.[12] The Young Hegelians—having been silenced, kicked out of the university, sent into exile, and imprisoned—dispersed with their comic spirits thoroughly crushed.[13] Marx perhaps sarcastically mocked the old dream of comic revolution as "a happy separation with the past" when he reflected on the failure of the uprisings several years later.[14] The immense sacrifice demanded by the resistance appeared to be for nothing. Comic anticipation leads to nihilism when resistance arrives at the sensation that nothing changes. Double negation takes the form of real sacrifice that only results in loss, without synthesis or a new stage to propel the historical narrative forward into a new day.

The Young Hegelian political project was a complete failure. However, one of their most powerful legacies is their framing of history as occurring in theatrical stages. And yet, the Young Hegelians' dramatic rendering of history and its failure to overcome its own drama produced yet another enduring split within Hegel scholarship. Some understand the resilient split within Spirit, which finds new expression within the contradiction of each stage of history, as tragic. Others hear defiant laughter hissing out of the very crack of existence. Although the Young Hegelian movement passed away within two decades, it sometimes feels that more than two hundred years later the first generation of Old Hegelians—those grave defenders of the seriousness of Spirit—still guard the halls of the academy, handing out demerits to philosophers who laugh out of place. The Prussian censorship during Hegel's lifetime is at least partially responsible for the characterization of academic discourse as something that must prove its seriousness by watching its tone of voice and conducting itself in a way that is seemingly measured and impersonal. We might also blame Antigone, who inspires inexhaustible devotion in each new generation of Hegelians, for the prevailing tragic readings of Spirit.[15] Our Lady Tragedy is often upheld as Lady Philosophy herself.[16]

Despite the enduring alliance between academic philosophy and tragedy, the comic staging of Spirit has had a profound influence on nineteenth-, twentieth-, and twenty-first-century philosophy and history, stretching from Marxism to critical theory to feminist philosophy and psychoanalysis. I recount a historical comedy first conceived between ancient skepticism and

Greek drama that Hegel identifies as the birthplace of Self. In Hegel's narration, the same ancient drama is repeated in Christianity, giving birth to the comic Community (a new dramatic protagonist). This historical comedy escapes the pages of Hegel's writing and is fully played out on the world stage in the birth of nineteenth- and twentieth-century resistance movements, narrated by voices such as Marx and Benjamin.[17] I describe historical comedy as the split between each staging of history—or the splitting of each historical stage—that allows for the transformation of history through its own self-relation as it grasps itself by its crack. We might say that what makes history tragic or comic does not depend on the form of a historical stage but our relationship to the crack—or the cracking open or cracking up of the crack itself. The resurgence of new bursts of spiritual laughter occurs precisely in moments of historical disturbance, in which something stirs in Public Spirit. Historical disturbance takes the form of a total collapse of a way of life that forces us to begin again without knowing how. It also takes the form of a total collapse of a way of life that nevertheless preserves the contents of what appeared to come to pass. It takes the form of the persistence of a contradictory way of life in the repeated failure to put an end to an end.

Hegel, Marx, and the Laughing Matter of Spirit locates the eruption of historical laughter in different historical cracks within nineteenth- and twentieth-century Europe. I engage exiled philosophers, resistance fighters, and artists who self-consciously frame their engagement with their own political stage as a historical comedy: the Young Hegelians in response to Prussian censorship and in support of the peasant revolts of the 1830s and '40s; Walter Benjamin in response to the rise of fascism in twentieth-century Europe; and the Yugoslavian partisans in facing the seemingly impossible demand to begin again in the aftermath of the international defeat of fascism. Each of the philosophical and political movements highlighted in this narrative occurs on a razor's edge between triumph and defeat, capturing the audacity of those willing to sacrifice themselves for a new beginning and the devastation of the experience of defeat on some level: the failure of 1848 to shatter historical drama; the failure to escape the horrors of Nazism, the failure to sustain a new beginning and annihilate fascism in the birth and abortion of Yugoslavia. Each movement imagined itself as part of a great historical comedy that would bring an end to an oppressive stage of history. Yet the comedy-to-come passes away with a puff: the nonevent that doesn't occur or doesn't occur as anticipated. When the anticipated event on the horizon fails to arrive, something that is not always immediately detectable occurs. The nonevent is itself a double: the event that is aborted is accompanied by a phantom event that slips into existence in the shadows cast by collective uncertainty, despair, disappointment, and exhaustion. In some cases, this excess of communal affect, the only remainder of the failure to immediately implement material change, is itself the phantom event that may have unforeseeable reverberations.

In the failure to arrive as expected, historical comedy as a form of political engagement that dreams of radical social change undergoes transformation. The spirit of comedy persists through its own repeated failure, giving new breath to revolutionary resilience. I visit comic responses to historical world crises to experiment with new (or perhaps old) concepts and affects in response to the current world stage characterized by unrestrained global capitalism, the rise of new (or perhaps old) expressions of fascism, and the implementation of censorship that seeks to erase history and the existence of certain subjects from the present. The glaring contradictions of this world-historical moment express themselves locally and globally. Very few people can escape the overwhelming anxiety, depression, and exhaustion of the present moment that is layered with world crises threatening to erupt into irresolvable catastrophes. Those who continue to face the present with sobriety and moderation are the very defenders of tragedy. It seems that something has to give and a historical eruption could be horrific. It would almost be grotesque to characterize these times as comic. Yet laughter is often heightened when the situation for laughter is least appropriate.

Something stirs in the relationship between comedy and critical philosophy when the tragic structure of a political stage feels unalterable. Philosophy permits itself to be irreverent, audacious, frivolous, and even hostile when it has nothing to lose. The sense of having nothing to lose makes philosophy dangerous to the existing symbolic and political orders that perpetuate inequality and oppression. To challenge tragic injustice, critical philosophy must sometimes turn against the institutions that simultaneously sustain philosophy while holding it captive to the logic and style of the prevailing order. Renouncing the false promise of security, a promise offered by the same powers that place our thinking and being in contradiction, allows us to adopt new voices and morph into new forms. This book engages philosophers who find liberation in comedy when they are at their wits' end, battling corruption and persecution, and grappling with the seeming impotency of resistance. Comedy can no longer speak to contradiction in a way that is moderate and measured. In its opposition to tragedy, comedy doesn't always say or do something new. By mirroring tragedy back to itself, it allows absurdity to sink in and erupt to the surface. Under the influence of the spirit of comedy, philosophy gives witness to a tragic stage that can no longer hold itself together.

We take to the streets and occupy our universities to protest unbearable contradiction.[18] Everything pulls at the seams. And yet still nothing seems to change. What can be said when we've put everything on the line and do not achieve our revolution? I refuse to speak in my mother tongue, which has failed me, but I do not yet have a new language to rearticulate myself. How does one voice the experience of suspension? Suspension (my preferred translation of *Aufhebung*) describes the disorienting encounter with a kind of negativity that stirs within "what is" but also within "what is not." Negativity stirs within the cracks of contradiction. In the experience of suspension, we can't yet identify what is taking place in the world and within ourselves. Attempts to represent these experiences often feel abstract, because they don't make sense within our current way of grasping ourselves in a world that is changing even when it appears that nothing changes. I fully embrace this sort of abstraction in my commitment to historical materialism and radical political change because our transformed relationship to negativity can fundamentally disrupt our concrete relation to what is. A transformed relationship to the cracks that form us has the potential to produce an explosion. The following narrative meditates on nothing for the sake of revolutionary politics through four concepts, representing a protagonist, a dialectical method, two models of social and political change, and a mantra.

The Crack

This book dramatically stages "the crack" as the protagonist of a revolutionary politics at the service of the ongoing battle against inequality and oppression. The following narrative sometimes casts individual historical and fictional actors in the role of the crack: Antigone, Eve, Christ, Tito. Other times, oppressed groups enact the crack belonging to specific historical and political contexts: the proletariat, Jews, women and feminized individuals, Palestinians. Still other times the crack will be personified by nonhuman actors existing on the level of concept: Self, Community, Spirit. I occasionally capitalize the names of concepts when staging them as characters, allowing them to play out their comic caricature. Some characters/concepts are treated as comic duos to demonstrate the tension between their opposition and mirroring: Being and Nothing, Public Spirit and National Feeling, Spirit and Matter, Church and State. Philosophical concepts are often capitalized to represent their universal or absolute character. In this philosophical comedy, the capitalization exaggerates the defining features of a concept, exposing a crack in the Absolute. In other moments, the crack plays the Crack, exposing Nothingness standing forth in its own nakedness and ordinariness. Staging negativity at each of these registers—the subjective, the communal, the historical, and the ontological—is critical for contradiction to be grasped as personal and world historical.

Hegel's "totalizing" systems are structured by cracks or conflicts that propel his narrative forward. His grand narratives unfold through the dramatic action produced by the internal tension in each scene. The tension may appear to find some resolution at the close of one scene or historical era, but the old conflict resurfaces, expressing itself in the new scenario through the cracks in and between new characters/concepts and settings. The first three chapters of this book explore the movement of the crack in logic, history, and art and religion by analyzing specific characters in the *Science of Logic*, *Phenomenology of Spirit*, and *Lectures on the Philosophy of Religion*. Tragedy and comedy are moments in the latter two systems, which focus on aesthetics and religion. However, as I explore through my reading of the *Science of Logic*, they are also lenses through which one can read Hegel's systems and his philosophy.

There are different ways to interpret the cracks within Hegel's systems, which is to say, the cracks that Hegel identified in the world, especially as manifested in human life. Hegel's readers must reflect on several questions that prompt them to choose a side. These interpretive pathways are a bit like a choose-your-own-adventure story. The specific path you choose leads to further crossroads. This hermeneutical splitting has resulted in many plausible, incompatible Hegels. Each Hegelian camp claims to have found the pathway to the true Hegel. But there is value in allowing one's reading to be interrupted by a touch of doubt. The lure of the road untaken might seduce the curious reader to try to follow every combination of paths so as not to miss out on the adventures of an alternative reality. The movement of splitting cracks—within the characters/concepts—may lead the reader to occupy the space of the crack, in which they may entertain multiple timelines with contradictory conclusions.

The first crossroad questions whether Hegel's systems ultimately overcome the contradiction he identifies at every stage of history in every aspect of human life. Do his systems reflect the impossibility of achieving resolution and reconciliation once and for all? During Hegel's lifetime, as we will explore, this debate fixated on the character of Christ in Hegel's philosophy and for modern society. The irreconcilable split regarding whether Christ himself was the material embodiment of a spiritual split gives birth to the Right and Left Hegelians (a splitting before the Old and Young). The Right believed that Hegel believed Christ was the singular exemplar of unity between a human being and divinity; on a communal level, they thought this unity was embodied in the alliance between orthodox Lutheranism and the modern Prussian state. The Left, following David Friedrich Strauss, believed that Hegel's philosophy, if not Hegel himself, presented the character of Christ (God-man) as a historical and mythical representation of a contradiction that belongs to all human individuals and societies. The Right identified *a unity between two* as the quality of the exceptional state, whereas the Left identified *a crack within one* as the universal state of all beings.

Those who embrace the crack as a contradiction that necessarily constitutes every subject and society meet another crossroad: Is the crack in Hegel's systems deliberate? Does Hegel intentionally sabotage his project by designing his systems with cracks, or is he simply unable to achieve his professed desire to arrive at the Absolute? It's difficult to interpret Hegel's intention in light of the censorship that cracked down on the university toward the end of his lifetime. The political and religious authorities remained uneasy with Hegel's philosophy of religion despite the Right's desperate attempt to prove its compatibility with state ideology. I'm less interested in making an argument about the correct reading of Hegel and more interested in cracks that form my own social existence and the contemporary political stages that form our fractured, shared world today. The ambiguity within Hegel and post-Hegelian dialectics—resulting in so many contradictory camps of Hegelians—reveals different ways of dramatically relating to the same crack. My project goes beyond Hegel, employing comedy—which I define as a surfacing of the crack or contradiction—as a lens to grasp the contradictions within our political and social existence.

The first three chapters develop the crack through Hegel's concept of *die Entzweiung*. *Die Entzweiung* allows itself to be rendered in English in multiple ways: split, gap, rupture, severance, cut. *Die Entzweiung* may also be translated as slit, cleavage, crack—reflecting whatever corporeal crevice the translator favors or finds humorous. Spirit longs to grasp itself by its flesh. Yet, attempts to grasp *the matter of spirit* lead us to metaphors, which point to the body by pointing to a bodily lack that is constitutive of a body. Although some translators favor "cleavage," the word fails to capture the topological quality of a negativity that constitutes the body. "Slit," the derogatory slang word for the vulva, a metonymy for the mythical figure of Woman as lack, better captures the life-giving negativity within Spirit. I often lean into this metaphor when describing the thrill of self-relation as a kind of negative self-touch. One of my main protagonists, Nothing, grasps herself as Self by grasping a crack in her negativity. Although vulvas belong to individuals of any gender, and vulvas are not empty spaces but folds of flesh, I sometimes use the pronoun "she" to represent Nothing, since the feminine has been a site of reduction. I return to this same site to witness the birth of a fully embodied Self who grasps herself by her body and communal body. How is the binary—between Being and Nothing or masculinity and femininity—disrupted by this moment of self-touch? The Self is born from a slit but also gives birth to herself by coming into touch with a slit that forms her body and subjectivity. In addition to "slit," I like the term "crack"—the cracking up and cracking open—despite and because of its inappropriateness for four main reasons:

1. "Crack" evokes the long history of ass within philosophical comedy, allowing us to recall a series of (both pre- and post-Hegelian) philosophical comic episodes from Apuleius's *Golden Ass* to Nietzsche's ass festival.[19] "Crack" in this sense reveals an ancient alliance between comedy and philosophy.
2. The historical trajectory of dialectic may be understood as the telos of the crack. The appearance of progress is represented as stages of history or consciousness, each of which reaches a straining point, splitting into two. The fault line is always present but invisible in "the beginning" of each stage. Like a cheaply made appliance, periods of peace and prosperity, achieved through exploitation and inequality, contain a breaking point (*die Sollbruchstelle*). Development brings the fault line to the surface in

the deepening of the crack. A conflict experienced only by some in the beginning is felt by all at the breaking point.
3. The crack of Spirit allows us to at last answer the old riddle "what comes first, the chicken or the egg?," or, "where does the beginning begin?" One can look at the telos of the chicken and egg cycle as the drive to yield a new stage of life: the telos of the beginning that always begins again. But the telos may instead be understood from the (non)perspective of the crack or the cracking open. The beginning is not found in the position of the giver of life: the creator. Nor is the beginning in the first breath of being: creation. The beginning is instead in the cracking open. The beginning and the end are in the crack between the chicken and the egg. Hegel's teleology is inverted: the beginning is in the end, while the end is before the beginning. But solving one riddle only introduces new riddles. Is the crack both chicken and egg or neither chicken nor egg? What comes first—the metaphysical crack (immediately present in Being) or the ontological cracking open (Becoming)?[20]
4. Crack lastly evokes the curious role of Luther in Hegel's philosophy of drama. Luther saw all of creation as the excretion of the divine. To put it crudely, in the spirit of Luther, the holy (ass) crack within spirit is the negative condition for all organic matter. The character of Luther in Hegel's drama represents the crack between two stages of historical comedy: the first comedy is embodied by the death of the gods on Aristophanes's stage, the second by the crucifixion of Christ. In Hegel's anachronistic historical drama of drama, Luther enters the stage directly at the heels of ancient comedy. His despair reveals the persistence of unfinished drama that comedy had seemingly resolved. In the dialectic of comic laughter and Christian despair, two expressions of negativity, we witness the emergence of the ghostly birth of the subject, yet another shape of negativity: first as self, then as community.

Crack is one way of imagining a negativity that is ontological, historical, political, and the very constitution of our subjectivity. A philosopher who pursues negativity must rely on a series of mixed metaphors (the ass, the fault line, the egg, excretion) in the impossible attempt to grasp the indeterminate within thought, language, and existence. This book attempts to grasp nothing through metaphors that represent negativity in different forms and dialectical movements. It questions what kind of politics can arise from different ontological relationships to negativity, represented as a shattering, hissing, a glitch, a stutter. Figurative language, as a tool of speculative philosophy, enacts paradox. By attempting to bring us closer to something (in this context, closer to nothing), metaphor brings us further away. By attempting to make a concept clearer, figurative language makes it more abstract. It brings two together while holding them apart, simultaneously insisting in one breath, "This is like that" and "This is not that." (*This* cannot be *that*, because this is not equivalent to itself nor is that the same as itself.) The activity of dwelling within the unresolved suspension between affirmation and negation generates transformation. Hegel's systems are driven to render the crack as concept. The narrative, from one perspective, is a self-conscious performative failure. The repetition of the failure to grasp negativity as concept releases a certain subjective experience of overwhelming laughter or despair (despairing laughter), which punctures the narrative at critical moments. The "progress" of history is the despair of the reliable repetition of this failure. But is the despair of failure necessarily tragic?

The crack within Spirit may also be grasped as the crack between Spirit and Matter, as the title of this book suggests. From one perspective, Spirit may refer to an individual and communal act of self-relation that results in transformation; zoomed out, Spirit may take the appearance of a historical narrative about this transformation at one moment and across many eras and cultures. This historical narrative can be told from the perspective of individual actors who form a community through their relations (reconciliations) and nonrelations (conflict); however, the same story can and must be grasped through another perspective, the perspective of history itself as the protagonist of a coming-of-age drama, one who comes to a deeper self-awareness through a dialectic of self-doubt and newfound confidence as she attempts to grasp the changes in her material body (the human and more-than-human world). Spirit is her human body, but she is also an excess (of desires, emotions, certainty, doubt) that emerges from this materiality. I represent this spiritual excess as laughter: an embodied compulsion that emerges from what belongs to the body but cannot be contained by it.

For Hegel the relationship between Spirit and Matter is neither a simple opposition nor a simple unity. I would describe this dialectical relationship between Spirit and Matter as the constant process of "double grasping," playing off of one of Hegel's favorite concepts: the concept of the concept, *Begriff/begreifen*, which also may be translated as grasp/grasping. The double grasp is always a physical act (e.g., to grasp flesh) and an intellectual act (e.g., to grasp a concept). One might imagine the image of one hand grasping another by the wrist.[21] Which hand grasps which? Do the hands belong to two different bodies or one body? The unresolvable ambiguity captured in the image is central to Hegel's dialectics of power but also central to the matter of Spirit and the spirit of the matter. The terms in the double grasp also cross over each other. One might imagine one or two sets of hands belonging to one, two, or four bodies. Spirit must grasp itself by its flesh, while the flesh grasps itself as Spirit. This tickle-fest between Matter and Spirit results in bursts of laughter (can one tickle oneself?). As we will explore in detail, something always slips out of the grasp in Spirit's quest to know itself and be present to itself. The ongoing activity of self-relation is possible because it is never achieved or complete. This coming-of-age drama, which never progresses past adolescence, is played out in the self-relation/nonrelation of every individual and collective existence.

The Doubling of the Double

Crack can only be crack in its relationship to two sides. Each chapter repeats a similar line of dramatic action involving the complications of the crack. We begin with two opposing sides that are locked in conflict. The conflict is a split that simultaneously binds and separates the two sides. In order to overcome the conflict, it would seem that one of the sides must be defeated by the other. Then comes a twist! Each side is already in contradiction with itself. Each is already split into two or doubled. Rather than opposing each other, the two sides mirror each other in their (self)contradiction. In grasping one's own disjunction through the obvious contradiction in the other, there is the discovery of the impossibility of self-sameness.

I find inspiration in Hegel's dialectics, but my narrative unfolds according to its own rhythm based on the relationship between two sets of doubles. In my view, there isn't one true dialectical formula that drives history. Instead, the act of narrating our experience and history through different dialectical rhythms allows formerly invisible subjects to be counted or to count themselves within these narratives. I describe the dialectical process, by which two are revealed to be four, leading to the insight that one is already two (I am already two), "the doubling of the double" or "twice-two." The formulation begins with a double in the form of twins or the odd couple. The double multiplies or, rather, divides into two sets of two. In my tetradic formulation of dialectic, double negation does not resolve into a third positive term. Instead, double affirmation and double negation mirror each other and remain in suspension. What kind of movement can be generated from this repeated stalemate?

This introduction opens with the dynamic duo of "the Old" and "the Young," who represent "the End" and "the Beginning." Karl Michelet, a first-generation Hegelian, unsuccessfully attempted to ease the tensions between these two camps by offering a compromise. What if philosophy is *both* the owl *and* the cock?[22] My dialectical formulation adopts Michelet's both/and formulation, while demonstrating that every (both | and) is at once a (neither | nor). For this reason, attempts to find middle ground through relativism rarely leave anyone satisfied. I represent this formulation by revamping the ancient skeptical slogan "no more," originally used as an expression of undecidability.[23] The seemingly simple expression, intended to be a reduction, immediately pairs a negation (no) and a signifier representing excess (more). What is more, the two sides are immediately redoubled. The expression "Philosophy is *no more* an owl than a cock" simultaneously entails a double affirmation ("Philosophy is *both* owl *and* cock") and a double negation ("Philosophy is *neither* owl *nor* cock."). Equipollence is not merely the experience of being split between two equally compelling sides.[24] It is the experience of an irreconcilable paradox: (both | and) | (neither | nor). Because the crack is equally end and beginning, and end and beginning cannot logically be the same, the crack can be neither end nor beginning. Both are equally true. Because both are equally true in themselves and wholly opposed to each other, neither can be true. And yet, the paradox persists. We are stuck again in the space of suspension.

Chapter 1, "Twice-Two, or Tetradic Dialectics," introduces the doubling of the double, beginning with the originary ontological double: Being and Nothing. I develop my own formulation of tetradic dialectic by counting to four with the Ljubljana School of Psychoanalysis, especially through the comic philosophies of Slavoj Žižek, Mladen Dolar, and Alenka Zupančič. The Ljubljana School is known for synthesizing Hegel, Marx, and Lacan. One of the most innovative contributions of this (post-)Yugoslavian movement, in my view, is its restaging of dialectic through doubles and tetrads. Hegel reminds us at the end of the *Science of Logic* that dialectic may be counted to the beat of three or four.[25] These equally catchy dialectical rhythms make negativity dance to a very different tune. By giving structural emphasis to negativity, the Ljubljana School stirred up new comic disturbances in Hegelianism. Alenka Zupančič's *The Odd One In: On Comedy* identifies the ontological and political significance of comedy from a structural point of view.[26] Comedy is structured like a joke consisting of two narratives that cannot possibly belong to the same script; the simultaneous tension and ease of their paradoxical coexistence produce a comic effect. Zupančič's philosophical comedy stirred up questions now central to the so-called Next Generation Ljubljana School: What can the structure of comedy show us about how we are in the world? How can grasping our situatedness in the world through the framework of comedy produce a shift in our relationship to our own existence? How can even the slightest shift inspire a concrete eruption in what is?

My own comic dialectical rhythm follows these questions but is also set in motion by an insight found in Mladen Dolar's reading of the beginning of the *Science of Logic* in his essay "Being and MacGuffin."[27] We find that the ontological double is already, from the beginning, redoubled. As Hegel puts it, "Being, pure Being" is mirrored in "Nothing, pure Nothingness." An originary split in pure Being is repeated in pure Nothingness. Nothing is self-identical, which is to say, not even nothing is self-identical. My treatment places Being and Nothing on the analyst's couch to ask each a series of intimate questions about their traumatic infancy, their self-realization, and their (sexual) awakening. By exchanging a traditional triadic structure for a tetradic structure, the focus of dialectic shifts from the production of the third (the positive remainder of sublation) to the negative reproduction of the split itself. In subsequent chapters I argue that this split resurfaces at each historical stage in the form of political, social, and ethical conflict.

Chapter 2, "Comic Abortions and the Birth of Self," pauses at a moment of dialectical suspension in the *Phenomenology of Spirit* at the end of Greek "Art-Religion," the moment which later inspires Young Hegelian historical comedy. In chapter 1, I meditate on a negativity that stirs within negativity, generating a deeper experience of self-relation. The *Phenomenology* replays this movement through the relationship between art and philosophy at the end of ancient Greek ethical life. In parallel to the ancient alliance between tragedy and philosophy, Hegel highlights a counter-alliance between ancient comedy and Platonic skepticism: an aesthetic stage and philosophical stage that self-consciously abort their own contents, representing the inevitable collapse of an entire way of life. Building on Hegel's analysis of comedy and skepticism, I interpret Aristophanes's *Clouds* as a tribute to rather than a tirade at Socrates. In the ultimate comic act, Aristophanes directs his protagonist to set fire to the stage, to the horror of his audience, mirroring Socrates's own refusal to offer his interlocutors comic relief from their own contradictions that he brings to the surface. Hegel's production of Greek art-religion ends in a moment of darkness met by the comic poet's detached laughter and the skeptic's tranquility. In this strange moment, after the curtain has set and there is nothing left to say, we (audience members) witness something stirring in pure nothingness. At this heightened moment of drama, nothing seems to take place. But Hegel identifies a shadow of a shadow stirring in the nothing as the first emergence of Self.

Chapter 3, "The Birth of Community at the Comedy of the Cross," repeats and fully plays out the transition from Greek drama to divine drama through tetradic dialectics, replacing Being and Nothing with another dramatic duo: Tragedy and Comedy. Rather than ending historical drama, the drama represented by ancient tragedy and comedy is repeated in the drama of Christianity. By locating a redoubling of tragedy and comedy in the incarnation and crucifixion, I question, "What changes when nothing changes?" The repetition of the double is also a repetition of the split between two (which is also the split within one). I argue that with the repetition of the split, there is a shift in perspective. This shift represents the transformation of negativity itself while the self that emerges from the rubble of ancient life finds its body in the formation of an ethical community who fully grasps its shared guilt. The birth of the Community at the crucifixion inspires comic-anguish—a mixture of relief and horror—with the realization that the conflict that we thought we crucified with the criminal belongs to us all. The split identified in the tragic hero (first in Antigone, then in Christ) is revealed to be constitutive of all.

Historical Comedy

The second half of this book moves from Hegel to post-Hegelian political philosophers who enact a contemporary comedy in response to their own historical crisis. Hegel located comedy as an aesthetic double of a specific historical moment in the past. The philosophers and artists in the second half of this book grasp themselves as comic protagonists in such a historical moment. Some studies of comedy primarily question why a situation or joke is funny. In my analysis, comedy is not merely about humor but about a movement that brings a concealed or repressed contradiction to the surface. Laughter, likewise, is not only a response to what we find funny but a kind of eruption in response to tensions that can no longer be defended or ignored. Historical comedy considers laughter as a response to oppression, horror, disorientation, and loss. I sometimes analyze literal expressions of individual or communal laughter. But Spirit's laughter belongs to a stage when a community or entire historical moment cracks under pressure. This cracking point comes too late in the sense that an entire way of being in the world had to shatter for a communal realization of what was at stake. Comic release is also a sense of anguish in recognizing what cannot be retrieved: a reconciled community in which all individuals may freely play out their self-determined roles. Historical comedy grieves what was lost but also what was never born. The excess of communal affects that emerge from the crack in the stage simultaneously give birth to a new sense of self-relation that has already transformed history.

Kant describes laughter as an affect that is caused by the sudden deflation of heightened expectation.[28] Laughter is a compulsive response, reflecting an excess inscribed on the body. Kant's phenomenological description of an individual's experience of laughter finds historical and political expression in the Young Hegelians, who explore the subjective and objective side of the same outburst. From an objective perspective, the outburst belongs to the stage: history's attempt to grasp itself. One uncontrollable eruption in response to historical contradiction is revolution. Revolution—like laughter—is the embodied convulsion of history in response to the surfacing of a contradiction that constitutes its stage.

Chapter 4, "Censoring Laughter," and chapter 5, "A Young Hegelian Comedy," witness the birth of the Young Hegelian political movement in response to the Prussian censorship of emotions such as humor and laughter. The majority of Young Hegelians wrote from a place of exile when "being an academic" and "being a philosopher" seemed to be in conflict. State ideology had thoroughly permeated the university and other vital social institutions such as the church, media, and theaters. As Marx argues, censorship is both externally imposed by the state and internally reinforced by those who insist on the seriousness of rigorous scholarship, the civility of measured discourse, and reverence toward institutions that openly flaunt their own farcical production. One form of censorship targets what we are permitted to say. Another form of censorship teaches us from the time we are children how we should feel—or, rather, not feel too strongly—about the contradictory situation in which we find ourselves. Censorship teaches us, above all, to watch our tone of voice, even in our inner dialogues. The Young Hegelians and Marx are traditionally viewed as turning Hegel on his head by exorcising spirit from materiality. In the act of slashing Hegel's tires, Spirit leaks out, hissing like laughter as materiality becomes deflated. This chapter insists on the critical role of Spirit in Ruge's and Marx's dialogue about historical comedy, during a period when both still believed that revolution was not only possible but imminent and inexorable.

In chapters 2 and 3, Hegel looks backward, identifying comedy as a specific moment in the past. In chapters 4 and 5, the Young Hegelians locate Hegel's vision of comic destruction in the future on their own horizon. Chapter 6, "Benjamin's Comedy of the Damned," begins with Marx, who, several years after 1848, now looks backward, reflecting on historical comedy as a missed opportunity. I identify two models of revolution in these two temporal placements of historical comedy: (1) revolution as history's shrill laughter that shatters the articulation of a tragic stage of history, and (2) the repetition of failed revolutions as the comic slapstick of history (history's stumble, hiccup, stutter) through which the reproduction of tragic contradiction grasps itself as farce. The first model reflects the Young Hegelian failed vision of the comic destruction of everything established and familiar; the second model, which I locate in Marx's writings after 1848, appears as a recurring glitch within the repetition of the same. In *The Eighteenth Brumaire of Louis Bonaparte*, Marx connects the first model with the utopian dream of the revolution *to come*; he connects the second model with actual proletarian revolutions, which interrupt themselves and restart midsentence without reaching their punchline.

Chapter 6 traces a direct "laugh line" from Marx to Benjamin, whom I highlight as the principal heir to Young Hegelian historical comedy in the twentieth century. I locate a reiteration of these two versions of historical comedy in Benjamin's writings on comedy and revolution in response to Hitler's rise to power. Drawing directly on Hegel and Marx, Benjamin claims that Spirit is Matter's laughter, or, in my formulation, *the laughing matter of spirit*.[29] At times, Benjamin describes this comedy of spirit as the messianic end of history. Yet, more often, Benjamin's historical laughter is not shrill but ghostly: a barely perceptible stutter within the articulation of everyday time and speech. This second model reflects the dramatic movement of Hegel's Spirit: the self-conscious movement of history as it comes to grasp itself as such. Spirit is propelled forward while also circling back onto itself through the recurring moment of the negative. This repetition of the crack is the indestructible comic object that resurfaces with each dialectical turn. The hiccup or stutter regularly interrupts the straight lines of historical progress.

Marx stages the proletariat not on one side of a conflict but in the crack itself. Benjamin likewise develops a comedy set in the underworld, acted out by "the damned," those who have been determined to be nothing by the society they are born into. He associates the damned with the proletariat but also with the figure of the Jew and with the feminine. Benjamin's comedy of the damned calls for the ghostly revenge of those who have been determined to be nothing but return to haunt the space that denies them. This chapter brings together Benjamin's comedy of the damned with Sara Ahmed's philosophy of resignation as feminist resistance. In the meeting of Benjamin and Ahmed, I find a political spirit born from the vengeful laughter of those who recognize defeat in their beginning. How do those who have been determined to be nothing by their society gain agency precisely through their social status as the nothing (which is to say, as living embodiments of societal contradiction)?

Throughout this book and history, the character of Antigone represents an alliance between tragedy and philosophy. In chapter 7, "Antigone's Disappearance Act in Yugoslavia," Antigone plays the role of the protagonist in a Benjaminian comedy of the damned performed in the devastating aftermath of World War II. In my dramatic narrative, Antigone gets the last word through her silence. We circle back to Antigone to reveal her comic role in Yugoslavia precisely in her repeated failure to appear on the stage as expected. *Antigone* was reenacted on many European stages during and following World War II. Jean Anouilh's 1944 rendition staged *Antigone* in Nazi-occupied Paris. Brecht's 1947 production likewise portrayed Creon and the state as representing fascist Germany and Antigone as the tragic hero of the anti-Nazi resistance. The audience of the French and German productions fully identified with Antigone over and against Creon. The tradition of staging Antigone in postwar Yugoslavia allowed the audience to identify with both Antigone and Creon (alluding to Tito rather than Hitler), who belong to the same state. The conflict that initially appears to be between Antigone and Creon is revealed to belong equally to both. Antigone's split between her conflicting roles as sister and citizen is mirrored in Creon's split between his roles as sovereign and man. In the dramatic doubling of the double, the split in each is magnified. Dominik Smole's celebrated 1959 Slovene rendition, *Antigona*, stages Antigone in the position of the split. Antigone herself never appears on stage but haunts it in her chilling absence, which is repeated in four distinct moments. Each time Antigone fails to appear, nothing changes, and yet her absence becomes more unnerving. We realize only in the end that the entire play takes place after Antigone's apparent death. Antigone's silence speaks to the feeling of paralysis in the face of the task of reconciliation following World War II, which divided Yugoslavia between factions of fascist supporters and the partisan resistance. Her absence represented a sense of historical suspension following the war, one characterized by a split between the desire for peace and the desire for justice. In tragedy, Antigone is split between two roles but defends the contradiction that places her at odds with herself and her community. In comedy, Antigone returns as a kind of negativity stirring in the crack itself, which deepens and rises to the surface, unsettling the appearance of superficial unity.

Nothing Changes

It often seems that despite our tireless fights for justice and equality, nothing changes. Many of us come to sense this despair when we realize that our consent or lack of consent counts for nothing, when our testimonies of our own experience count for nothing, when violence that is done against our individual and communal bodies counts as nothing, even before the law. We find ourselves at a curious stage of history where our world leaders flaunt their farcical nature while perpetuating conditions that place many lives between tragedy and horror. Does comedy—as an art form and a model for political resistance—have the critical power to challenge leaders who make little attempt to conceal corruption and contradiction under a veil of seriousness? I seek to define the dramatic role of those who have been denied the gift of appearing as political actors in the process of disrupting a tragic stage that determines them to be nothing. This book reinforces the statement that nothing changes without succumbing to nihilism. I look to accounts of failed revolutions and new beginnings to locate a model of ongoing resistance through our failure to overcome tragedy. As Marx notes, although the great revolution never arrived as expected, the failed revolution of 1848 caused "all Europe [to] tremble at the June Earthquake." A certain kind of political action can only take place in the comic insight that we have already lost from the beginning. In the proletariat's cry, "I am nothing, but I must be everything!"[30]

Hegel, Marx, and the Laughing Matter of Spirit identifies political resistance in the model of comedy as the repetition of failed revolutions. It looks backward in defeat with Marx at the repeated failures of our acts of resistance. It looks upon the grotesque in comic-horror with Benjamin. It finds revelation in the flickering lives of those who cannot fully appear as political actors. And finally, it locates political action born from a position of absolute defeat, in the recognition that I have been determined nothing from the beginning. With the recognition of defeat, we laugh in the face of the oppressor, "I have been determined nothing, but you cannot destroy what is already nothing." I question how those who have been determined to be nothing (denied genuine voice and representation as political subjects) can gain agency precisely through their role *as* the nothing.

The rise of global fascism and xenophobia, the persistence of genocidal violence and racism, the deepening of economic disparity, and the implementation of destructive censorship laws suggest that despite our battles for justice and equality, nothing changes. History tragically repeats itself. And yet, I claim that with every failed revolt and act of resistance, nothing itself changes. Nothing is amplified in her repeated refusal to appear as expected. Nothing takes the form of the emancipatory event that fails to take place and the individuals who fail to appear as political subjects. Through the slapstick of history, which causes the reproduction of tragedy to stumble, nothing undergoes change as it increases in power. Nothing is both the object and agent of change. Nothing changes, but nothing really does change. *Hegel, Marx, and the Laughing Matter of Spirit* repeats the phrase "nothing changes" as a mantra until a confession of defeat becomes a battle cry for political resistance.

Chapter 1

Twice-Two, or Tetradic Dialectics

Marx somewhere remarks that history repeats itself first as tragedy, then as farce. But what he failed to mention was that tragedy and farce repeat themselves, first as tragedy, then as farce.

In the opening act of *The Eighteenth Brumaire of Louis Bonaparte*, Marx stages tragedy and farce as a historical duo, farce tripping directly into tragedy's historical footprint.[1] Marx states that although Hegel recognized that history repeats itself, he failed to see this historical doubling through the structures of tragedy and farce. Although Marx claims to make this addition to Hegel, we also might hear a bit of irony in his famous catchphrase. "First as tragedy, then as farce" has the ring of Abbott and Costello's "Who's on first? *Who's* on first!"[2] In the events of 1848, the Young Hegelians learned firsthand that what announces itself as a historical break with tragedy is often exposed as farce: tragedy wearing a comic mask. On a formal level, "first as tragedy, then as farce" appears on the historical stage as an odd couple like Abbott and Costello or Laurel and Hardy: a pair of opposites, one of which is always at the heels of the other. On the level of content, "first as tragedy, then as farce" is not the odd couple but identical twins, a mirroring of the same: Who's on first? *Who's* on first!³

Not only did Hegel himself already frame history as a theatrical production, he took the formulation of the historical double—tragedy and farce—one step further, multiplying "first as tragedy, then as farce" times two (2 × 2): first as tragedy, then as farce, now once more, *only this time comically*. Chapters 2 and 3 trace Hegel's drama of historical repetition in the most obvious place, his analysis of "Art-Religion" and "Revealed Religion," in which Greek tragedy and comedy are repeated in the drama of Christianity: first, in the tragedy of the incarnation, in which contradiction is attributed to one tragic hero; then in the comedy of the crucifixion, in which this very same contradiction is revealed as belonging to all. The tetradic dialectical repetition (2 × 2) that structures Hegel's dramatic rendering of ancient art and religion also structures an ontological drama in the opening of the *Science of Logic*. This chapter locates (2 × 2) in the redoubling of the original comic duo: Being and Nothing.[4] As Hegel frames it, Being and Nothing are already from the beginning redoubled: "Being, pure Being" and "Nothing, pure Nothingness." Four figures are already lurking within the original two.

Hegel points out at the end of the *Science of Logic* that if we insist on counting, dialectic can be counted in sets of three or four stages.[5] Why do we insist on counting? Who counts? Who does the counting, and who or what is (not) counted? What changes when we count differently?

In a triadic dialectical structure, the first term passes into its negative counterpart before returning to itself concretely as the third term. Counting to three renders dialectic as a waltz in which the positive term is transformed as it is spun through the mediation of its negative partner: Being–Nothing–Becoming. Yet, Hegel reminds us that dialectic can also be set to the rhythm of a four-step beat. Recounting a dialectical turn through a tetradic structure tells a new story using the same characters. Or rather, it tells the exact same story from the perspective of a figure who played a supporting role in the first staging. Tetradic dialectic shifts the focus from the transformation of the first term to the dance of the negative. The shift from three to four yields different kinds of affective relations between the same characters (concepts) and between the audience (readers) and these staged concepts. Even before we can grasp these concepts as concept, we begin to sway and snap our fingers to a new groove, relating differently to Being and Nothing. More important, Nothing begins to relate differently to itself as it takes center stage, learning to count itself as Being precisely in its nothingness (chapter 1). By counting to four, Nothing counts itself first as self (chapter 2), then as community, and only then concretely as self (chapter 3).

There are different ways to count to four with dialectics. I begin by counting to four with the Ljubljana School of Psychoanalysis, a school of Hegelians emerging in the dissolution of Yugoslavia who synthesized German idealism, Marxism, and Lacanian psychoanalysis. One distinct aspect of this school is its foundation in a tetradic reading of Hegelian dialectic. In the following, I touch upon several iterations of tetradic dialectic in the thought of three founding members of the Ljubljana School: Slavoj Žižek, Mladen Dolar, and Alenka Zupančič. By drawing on the different contributions of each, I arrive at my own tetradic rhythm, which I refer to as the dialectical doubling of the double. The following chapters play out this four-part dialectic on a historical, political, and subjective register.

This chapter applies psychoanalysis and aesthetics to an ontology that is without human actors (they will join us later). I'm interested in what kinds of affective relations and disjunctions emerge in changes that are structural, such as in the shift from triads to tetrads. I'm equally interested in what kinds of affective relations and disjunctions emerge when nothing changes, such as in the repetition of the formation of the double. Freud identifies the figure of the double as producing an uncanny effect.[6] As he argues, *das Unheimliche* traditionally describes an encounter with something quite strange, some form of sinister opposition that threatens to snuff out one's existence. But the chill that runs over my skin at the uncanny encounter is not due to the strangeness of this other but instead comes from a repressed familiarity. The stranger turns out to be my mirror image, although I may not recognize myself in their reflection. Freud positions the double not between tragedy and farce but between horror and comedy. As I explore in chapter 5 with Marx and Benjamin, the historical double of tragedy and farce slips into comic-horror with revolutions fought by ghosts and zombies. Freud puzzles over the double, recognizing that although in one context the double chills us, in another, it strikes us as comical. He concludes that the experience of standing face to face with our own double is chilling because we cannot recognize that this other is a repetition of something that has already occurred or is already present within myself or is nothing more than myself.[7] But when the double is reproduced (for example, in an aesthetic representation of the double on the stage or on the screen), we recognize something that was formerly too close for comfort. The "ghastly multiplication" of the double allows for a certain realization to come to the surface.[8] The uncanny incites a burst of laughter. Yet laughter does not always offer release. It is also a symptom of heightened tension as the site of dramatic suspense shifts. By appearing at a distance, what was once too close for comfort surfaces as inseparable from one's self.

In the spirit of Freud's analysis of the fragile line between the uncanny double and its redoubling, I identify the doubling of the double found in critical moments of Hegelian tetradic dialectic as producing a kind of comic excess that occurs with a shift in perspective. For the moment, I define the "comic" as a kind of shift in affective relations that occurs even though nothing appears to have changed. The effect of the comic is the emergence of new unpredictable affects as one grasps oneself differently. In my use, the comic effect indicates not simply humor but a response to paradox that comes too close to home, provoking any number of emotions. Laughter is one response to heightened tension and release. Perhaps we insist on counting precisely because the process of counting produces different kinds of affective relations. We can test this hypothesis by counting on one hand. It almost goes without saying that two provides greater pleasure than one, the loneliest number. Many also find two to be preferable to three, the tired trope of dialectic as a teleological waltz. Two seems to offer lightness, relieving one from her loneliness and lacking the complications of a third who comes in between. And yet we learn through Freud, and later through Marx and Benjamin, that the double (even the double of tragedy and farce) borders on something closer to horror than comedy. However, when the double is repeated, even when it is repeated in its exact same form, an affective shift takes place. In the following, I explore the comic effect of four in my staging of dialectic as the doubling of the double or, to borrow the title of a sketch by Laurel and Hardy, *Twice Two*.[9]

As a literary trope, the double may take one of two forms: a pair of opposites or a pair of twins. The trope of the odd couple, on one side, and the twins, on the other, appear to serve very different narrative functions. The forms may incite different kinds of affective responses from the audience. However, the form of the opposed double sometimes conceals the realization that the contents of the first figure are only reduplicated in the second. The "straight man" of the odd couple cannot see themselves in their counterpart, "the fool." The redoubling of the double, however, forces not only the audience but the original double on stage to confront what was already present but unrealized from the beginning. (Spoiler: this something will turn out to be nothing, nothing more than a split in each, which is also a split in nothing.)

To illustrate this redoubling within the opening of Hegel's *Logic*, I visit classic and pop-cultural representations of redoubled twins and odd couples. The chapter concludes by exemplifying my own formulation of tetradic dialectics in two short films by Laurel and Hardy in which the comic duo redoubles itself. The formula (2 × 2) produces comic excess through the dialectical redoubling of the uncanny double.

Counting to Four with the Ljubljana School of Psychoanalysis

An origin is often split between at least several contentious accounts. The beginning of Hegelian-Lacanianism in Slovenia is no different.[10] While some locate the beginning in Žižek's 1980 book, *Hegel in označevalec* (Hegel and the Signifier), others say that French psychoanalysis was first popularized in Slovenia by Rastko Močnik, a student of Božidar Debenjak, a Slovenian Marxist who introduced the Frankfurt School into Yugoslavian academic discourse.[11] After returning from Paris where he worked with Lacan, Močnik published a book in 1981, *Mesčevo zlato: Prešeren v označevalcu* (Moon's Gold: Prešeren in the Signifier), which reads Slovenia's most celebrated poet through a Lacanian framework.[12] A contemporary English translation of this work might be renamed *Everything You Always Wanted to Know about Lacan (But Were Afraid to Ask France Prešeren)*.[13] Močnik locates Lacan as already lurking within nineteenth-century Slovenian thought. His work suggests that the Romantic poet could only fully grasp himself as France Prešeren upon the arrival of Lacan to Slovenia nearly a century after his death. This paradoxical dialectical approach resonates in the work of two more of Debenjak's students, Dolar and Žižek, whose work demonstrates that Hegel could only fully grasp himself through Lacan. What is more, I would add, this meeting could only take place as it did in the birth and disillusionment of Yugoslavia.

The meeting of Hegel and Lacan in Yugoslavia allowed Hegel to recall his own laughter, which had been thoroughly stifled by reductions of dialectic to a teleology of positive progress by the late twentieth century. The Ljubljana School became internationally popularized, partly through Žižek's comedic performance style, which, for some, was a refreshing burst of irreverence within a genre that tends to take itself very seriously. Yet, the sense of humor that emerges from Hegel's dialectics can't be reduced to Žižek's comic delivery. Instead, the comic effect is a result of a structure that is recovered through the Ljubljana School's attention to the dramatic role of the negative, which trolls the positive production of progress. As Zupančič argues, comedy is not essentially a matter of style or humorous affect but is located in the persistence of a paradoxical structure. Or rather, comedy is the paradox of two contradictory structures or accounts that cannot logically coexist and yet persist in equal parts harmony and tension.[14] The overlying triadic and tetradic meters in Hegel's dialectics are a prime comic example of what Zupančič describes as "two mutually exclusive realities . . . articulated together, visible at the same time."[15] A triadic meter tells a story of progress and synthesis, while the tetradic meter tells a story of suspension and stuckness. Extending on or perhaps diverging from Zupančič's philosophy of comedy, I would add that the affects that erupt from each of these structures and their coexistence makes all the difference.

Žižek's first book, based on his doctoral thesis, which remains untranslated into English, engages a concept of difference found in Jacques Derrida, whose philosophy has inspired countless aesthetic movements that lean into the absurdity and irony of exposing the absent origin or original referent.[16] And yet, the philosophical comedy characteristic of Slovenian Hegelianism is quite different from postmodernism. Postmodernism and Hegelian modernism both challenge the traditional understanding of the relationship between authenticity and mimicry or original and reproduction, sharing the claim that everything that appears is equally appearance.[17] Yet they give rise to different structures of desire and affect, in how they insist on counting or losing count. Postmodernism finds comic relief in abandoning the desire for authenticity altogether. It represents a stage at which we are beyond our longing for an origin, resulting in a kind of unbridled repetition in difference. One can think of the early Looney Tunes episodes in which Elmer Fudd finally has the rabbit at the other end of his double-barreled gun.[18] Each time he thinks he's got the wascally wabbit, it pops up double. The rabbit continues to multiply, as rabbits do. Fudd is suddenly surrounded by hundreds of taunting rabbits, only to find that there was never an original Bugs but instead infinite *What's up, Doc?*s in difference.[19]

The production of unrestrained repetition without end tickles the humor of the absurdist. Postmodernism takes pleasure in losing count. But for this reason, it cannot register the comic structure of dialectical repetition, which foolishly insists on counting. In dialectical comedy, one multiplies or divides one into two. One's claim to oneness is upset by this precise doubling that echoes and parodies the first's claim to originality. The comic quality is in the disturbance of one's claim to be one or first. But the comic is equally in the persistence of the desire for unity and self-consistency, despite the repetition of this disturbance. We must admit to ourselves that we still long for authenticity to allow for the pain and pleasure of disillusionment again and again when such claims to originality are reliably, almost mechanically, overturned.

Postmodern repetition is unrestrained, without origin or end. Dialectic doubling, in contrast, is controlled and without release from the unfulfilled desire to identify the beginning of beginnings and to put an end to ends. Although the dialectician knows better, her desire to count beginning with one persists. What sustains one's desire to count herself as one? Dialectical comedy reveals that one has placed her faith in nothing. The subject's quest for unity is futile. Yet it doesn't present her desire for oneness as absurd. Rather, it is precisely her faith in nothing that teaches one to count oneself by counting (on) negativity.

Through a postmodern lens, Hegel's negativity appears to be in the service of positive production, and counting appears to be in the service of progress. As a result, Spirit has to fend off defenses of its tragic character and critiques of its comic lightness.[20] Judith Butler captures this common late twentieth-century French caricature of Hegel in their 1987 *Subjects of Desire*: "For Hegel, tragic events are never decisive. There is little time for grief in the *Phenomenology* because renewal is always so close at hand. What seems like tragic blindness turns out to be more like the comic myopia of Mr. Magoo whose automobile careening through the neighbor's chicken coop always seems to land on all four wheels."[21] Butler illustrates the way Hegelian dialectic had become understood (via Derrida, Deleuze, Foucault, and Lacan, for example) as a totalizing comedy, driving toward the moment of the recovery of the subject, who passes through the trial of the negative and returns to himself stronger than before. As Butler points out, the real comic-horrors of the negative are reduced to myopic bliss.

The dramatic plotline of the Mr. Magoo scenario is repeated in countless cartoons, frequently evoked by the Ljubljana School, which paradoxically embraces the familiar episode as characteristic of Hegelian thought. Rather than denying the French critique of Hegel, the same episode is retold by many philosophers within the extended Ljubljana School community to the delight of the audience, who never grows tired of the same joke, which produces new insight and laughter with each repetition. Several cherished examples are found in comic duos like Wile E. Coyote and the Road Runner, and Tom and Jerry. The story, which Butler uses to represent a critique of Hegel, is repeated by Slovenian Hegelians. Yet the stress is placed on a different beat. Mr. Magoo careens through the air without realizing his car has left the ground. In another version, the cat chasing the mouse runs off the side of the roof and temporarily runs in place with no ground beneath its feet. There is a pause, a moment of suspension, followed by a split second of panic. The character, still suspended in the air, looks down and realizes its fate. Žižek delivered one of the most well-known versions, two years after Butler's version, in his 1989 *The Sublime Object of Ideology*:

Twice-Two, or Tetradic Dialectics

> We all know the classical, archetypal cartoon scene: a cat approaches the edge of the precipice but she does not stop, she proceeds calmly, and although she is already hanging in the air, without ground under her feet, she does not fall—when does she fall? The moment she looks down and becomes aware of the fact that she is hanging in the air. The point of this nonsense accident is that when the cat is walking slowly in the air, it is as if the Real has for a moment forgotten its knowledge: when the cat finally looks down, she remembers that she must follow the laws of nature and falls.[22]

In one reading of dialectic through the story of Mr. Magoo or the cat and mouse, the subject lands on their feet, offering the audience comic relief. Another retelling of the same episode instead dramatically pauses at the moment of suspense: "*To be continued . . .*" Comedy is about resilience. As Zupančič writes,

> the comic universe is, as a rule, the universe of the indestructible (this feature is brought to its climax in cartoons, but is also present, in a more subtle way, in most comedies). Regardless of all accidents and catastrophes (physical as well as psychic or emotional) that befall comic characters, they always rise from the chaos perfectly intact, and relentlessly go on pursuing their goals, chasing their dreams, or simply being themselves. It seems that nothing can really get to them, which somehow contradicts the realistic view of the world that comedy is supposed to promote.[23]

The indestructible comic object can be seen as the subject. However, I would argue that the comic subject of dialectic is not the resilient protagonist who always lands on their feet. Instead, resilience is found in the return of the chasm that appears out of nowhere at the moment Coyote thought he had the Road Runner in his grasp (the moment the philosopher swore they had grasped their concept). The devastating fall that follows the reappearance of the precipice on our road to progress somehow manages to catch us off guard every time despite its regular recurrence. Dialectic highlights the resilience of the subject. Yet depending on how one counts, subjectivity is not necessarily located in the recovery, the return of the positive term to itself. It is also found in the return of the precarious crack that resurfaces in each episode. From the view, or (non)perspective, of suspension, the positive moment of resolution is exposed as farce. The ground is never really stable. The audience can never really relax because we know that disaster is always around the corner.

The cartoon episode depicting a moment of suspension over an abyss echoes a similar episode that recurs throughout the history of philosophy. Kierkegaard tells a story, later retold by Sartre, about the dizzy subject peering over the edge of the cliff, stunned by the possibility (freedom) of their own (self-)negation.²⁴ Nietzsche tells the same story with a different emphasis. The subject becomes self-conscious as they see themselves being seen by the abyss.²⁵ I like to imagine this same episode dialectically, from the point of view of the abyss, who sees herself being seen by the subject. In this moment of mutual suspension, I imagine a comic double take from both the subject and the chasm. In suspension before the fall, there is a double movement, or one realization grasped on both a subjective and objective register. The protagonist grasps themselves as nothing more than the chasm beneath their feet, their inescapable fate. A moment of pure terror. Yet in this same moment, from a different perspective, the (non)perspective, the chasm looks up and sees the protagonist come plunging toward it. A thrilling moment of ecstasy for the chasm. The protagonist grasps their own negativity. The chasm, in turn, grasps itself as the subject of the drama. The double grasp is like the plot of *Freaky Friday*, in which two characters change bodies in order to grasp something that was true about themselves all along.²⁶ In my reading, this moment of suspension, in which nothing comes into touch with nothing, is not in the middle of a dialectical turn, soon to be resolved when the subject lands on their feet or is reborn in the next episode. Suspension is a full dialectical turn that reveals the impossibility of its resolution. The rebirth of the subject does not occur at the end of the episode in the resolution of a synthesis; nor is the subject reborn when they confidently step forward into the position of a new thesis at the beginning of another episode. Recovery occurs when the abyss learns to count herself as subject by grasping herself by her negativity.

The characterization of the exchange between two sides of negativity depends on how one counts *Aufhebung*. Triadic dialectic equates *Aufhebung* with resolution while tetradic dialectic equates *Aufhebung* with suspension. The dialectical episode lands in a different place: on land or in the air. In the process of counting to four, negativity comes into touch with itself. In his 1991 essay "Why Should a Dialectician Count to Four?" Žižek pauses over the relationship between two kinds of negativity.²⁷ This was the same year of Slovenia's tumultuous break with Yugoslavia and exactly ten years after Močnik's book on Lacan and Prešeren. Although the Ljubljana School develops its tetradic structure in dialogue with Lacan,²⁸ Žižek's essay identifies this dialectical rhythm as grounded in Hegel's own thematization of quadruplicity. As Hegel states in the doctrine of the concept toward the end of the *Science of Logic*, dialectic may be grasped as a *quadruplicity* as much as a *triplicity*:

> If one at all cares *to count*, this *second* immediate is *third* to the first immediate and the mediated. But it is also *third* to the first or formal negative and to the absolute negativity or second negative; now in so far as that first negative is already the second term, the term counted as *third* can also be counted as *fourth*, and instead of a *triplicity*, the

abstract form may also be taken to be a *quadruplicity*; in this way the negative or the *difference* is counted as a *duality*.[29]

The "first" stage of negativity (the second term) has the appearance of being an external contradiction to the first term. However, this initial negativity is internal to the first term. There is already a disjunction or disturbance with the content of the first term despite its appearance of self-sameness. One is already two. Because this unity is abstract, it necessarily passes over into the form of its negative "other." Žižek maintains that there is a stage of negativity that is distinct from both the formal opposition of the first negation and the final resolution:

> Negativity must be counted twice: to negate the starting point effectively, we must negate its own "inner negation" in which its content comes to "truth" . . . This second, self-regulating negation, this (as Hegel would put it) otherness reflected into itself, is the vanishing point of absolute negativity, of "pure difference"—the paradoxical moment which is *third* since it is already the first moment which "passes over" into its own *other*. What we have here could also be conceptualized as a case of retroactive determination: when opposed to its radical Negative, the first moment itself changes retroactively into its opposite.[30]

The first negativity or contradiction only reveals itself retroactively as internal to the first term through the second formal stage of negativity. In other words, through the second negation, one appearance of negativity—in which two sides appear as external, radical opposites—is negated by a deeper expression of negativity. The second stage of negation marks the real movement of the negative, which was present from the beginning. On one level, nothing really changes, yet "it changes precisely in so far as it remains the same."[31]

In *The Odd One In: On Comedy*, Alenka Zupančič distinguishes between two kinds of historical repetition that correspond with Žižek's identification of two kinds of negativity.[32] Zupančič extends a tetradic reading of Hegel's dialectic to Marx's *Eighteenth Brumaire*, playing out a purely logical movement on a historical and political register. The first kind of repetition takes the form of a new stage of history that appears to break with the past but actually preserves the content of what it opposes in the guise of a new form. This is the repetition of the eighteenth- and nineteenth-century revolutions, which have the appearance of introducing a new formal stage of history but merely repeat and secure the content of bourgeois society. In contrast, there is a second kind of repetition that does not appear to be different from what comes before it in terms of its form. We find this repetition in Marx's analysis of the actual proletariat revolutions, which fail to initiate a new social and political order. However, this repetition draws attention to the internal contradiction in what it exactly reproduces. In Marx's terms, the first kind of repetition is a farce, the preservation of tragedy in the appearance of a comic break. The subtle shift of perspective offered by the latter's failure to produce a new stage reveals repetition's power to disrupt a symbolic order through its decentering movement. With this second kind of repetition "nothing changes." The same form is repeated and yet the repetition of the same form ultimately allows for a disruption.

It might seem that the first kind of repetition (a change in form that preserves the content of the old) is opposed to the second kind of repetition (a repetition in form that reveals something new about the old content). However, Zupančič considers the two kinds of repetition as two stages of one dialectical turn. Deleuze identifies mechanical repetition (*automaton*)—in which nothing really changes—as the lower form of repetition on which a more radical form of repetition can bring about something singular. Hegelian dialectic operates on the inverse. First, there is the appearance of radical newness in the formal movement from one and its negative double. Then, in the *automaton*—the exact reiteration of the first two figures—"something" new emerges. The transformation of content in the second repetition comes about precisely by revealing that the oppositional form produced by the first kind of repetition is the preservation of the old content. The concealed disjunction between form and content in the first stage is only revealed as such through a second stage of repetition, through which the disjunction is made visible.

One can read the tetradic movement linearly, as Hegel's philosophy is traditionally understood as the chronological unfolding of history. In the framework of the Ljubljana School, this unfolding is only realized retroactively through a repetition that is an inversion. History goes forward only by going backward. I find in Dolar's philosophy of the double the suggestion of a second nonlinear reading of the Hegelian tetrad.[33] Rather than moving horizontally (chronologically or retroactively), Dolar hints at a dialectical movement that spirals inward within the first internal split. Through Dolar's thought, we encounter the second meaning within the negative duality of "the negation of negation." The second negation belongs to the first negation. Dialectic reveals a deeper sense of negativity within the first split. In Dolar's words, "There is a gap in the Hegelian negative (of negation), lurking at the very same spot, not somewhere else."[34] Dolar's philosophy of the double locates a scission within the scission between two. This gap within the negative is the very site of subjectivity.

In the following, I retell the first movement of Hegel's *Science of Logic* through a four-part structure that both builds on and departs from elements of Hegel and the Ljubljana School. Hegel's explicit statement at the end of the *Science of Logic* about the four-part structure of dialectic is already implicit in the beginning: not only the beginning of the *Science of Logic*, but (from a speculative view) what might be grasped as the very beginning.

Twice-Two, or Tetradic Dialectics

Double It

A dramatic duo comes in two varieties: in the form of twins—two of the same—and in the form of the odd couple—a pair of opposites who are two in one. In both cases, the second figure of the set of two seems to relieve the first from her tragic nature. The spirit of gravity—represented by the first of the pair—appears to be elevated by the spirit of frivolity—introduced by the second. However, although two (at first) may seem more fun than just one, two can also be slightly creepy. We experience this feeling while in the presence of obsessive lovers who threaten to annihilate each other in their passion. Although two may have the tendency to lose their initial appeal, twice-two produces a comic effect. Let's consider the old Doublemint gum commercials with the unforgettable imperative: "Double your pleasure! Double your fun!"

The first commercial for Doublemint chewing gum aired in 1956. A woman sits in front of her vanity intently gazing into her reflection as she combs her hair. As she stands and turns away from her vanity, her reflection follows her. To her delight, her reflection is revealed to belong to another figure with her exact appearance and form (figures 1.1 and 1.2). Wrigley's Doublemint Twins are born in this moment when the lonely girl finds a perfect companion in her reflection that comes to life. The moment when one is revealed as two appears to be delightful. One will never be alone again now that she is two. When the 1980s rolled around, Wrigley decided that the twins weren't really all that fun anymore. The fantasy of the twins at first had sex appeal, but at the end of the day, there was something unsettling about the ultimately autoerotic nature of the girl who had only her reflection for companionship. Rather than imagining oneself erotically positioned between the two playful sisters, the viewer instead sees herself in the girl blowing bubbles alone in front of the mirror. Although one is revealed to be two, two are also still one. The original incompleteness of the one was merely doubled in two but masked by the appearance of completeness offered by the mirror image.

Just as minty-fresh was losing its flavor, Wrigley found its marketing solution within the tagline of their own slogan: "Come on and double it!" In the early commercials, silhouettes of two identical men appear in the background or foreground in the position that the audience occupies. The new campaign brought the boys to the same playing field as the girls, making all four figures objects of pleasure. The girls were redoubled in their male counterparts, finding lovers at last in the redoubling of the first autoerotic double. The original one's loneliness or fragmented nature is not overcome in the doubling of the twins. But as an audience, we can take pleasure in the absurdity of what was initially pitiful, if not creepy: the girl's mistaken sense of completion found in her reflection. In shifting her object of desire from her reflection to one found in the world, the first girl seems to overcome her isolation. And yet it seems all too obvious that the twin girls fall immediately in love with the twin boys

Figures 1.1 and 1.2. Joan and Jayne Boyd Knoerzer as Wrigley's first Doublemint Twins. Television commercial, 1959.

simply because they see themselves in their male doubles. The same may be said of the boys' attraction to the girls.

We might consider the development of the Doublemint girl who discovers a perfectly symmetrical companion in her reflection through what Jacques Lacan identified as the "mirror stage."[35] Lacan defined the mirror stage as an early prelinguistic stage in which the infant gains a sense of self through its identification with its reflection. Prior to recognizing itself in the mirror, the infant could only observe itself through fragmented, floating parts of its body (its hands or toes). When the infant shifts from a fragmented body image to an image of itself as a totality, it gains a permanent sense of self. This sense of self, however, is rooted in this "double" that is inverted and distorted in size. As the infant matures, it shifts from the spectral ego based on the mirror image to a social ego based on its dialectical grasp of itself through the other. These two phases of the ego—in which we grasp our self through the mirror image and in which we grasp ourselves through the other in the world—may appear to be opposed. Yet, Lacan claims that the individual will continue to relate to herself and her environment imperfectly throughout her life since there will always be a certain disjunction between her physical reality and the inverted double through which she grasps both herself and the world.

In the case of the Doublemint girl, the discovery of her double initially offers her a sense of completion, but her security quickly gives way to a sense of unease. To overcome this uneasiness, she seeks security not in her mirror image but in a form quite different from her own. And so, the twin girls are partnered with the twin boys. The disjunction between the two sisters, whose relationship ultimately leaves something to be desired, is also the disjunction between the first girl and herself. We might speculate that the uncanny nature of the second girl lies in the fact that she does not offer perfect symmetry because her actions are inverted. The uncanny nature would thus lie in this slight difference, this sense of something being slightly off. But we may also speculate that the uncanny nature of the second does not lie in difference but in sameness, as the first twin recognizes a crack in herself that is not filled but only magnified by the presence of her twin.

Wrigley's campaign found success in the familiar comic trope of the double-double, a trope that Shakespeare frequently employed in his comedies. The two sets of twins in *The Comedy of Errors*, for example, allow for "double the pleasure" by doubling the trouble with more possibilities for confusion, misidentifications, inversions, and the old "switch-a-roo."[36] But why does the first double become funnier in its redoubling? What does the doubling of the double do to the first double? My suggestion is that the dialectical process of doubling the double reveals something that was already true about the relationship of the first duo. Something or, more precisely, *nothing* new emerges in the relationship between the split in the first double and the doubling of the split itself in the second double. The addition of the boys, of course, does not fill in the gap between one and two (which is to say, between one and one) but rather represents a shift from the first girl's imperfect relationship with herself to her imperfect relationship with the world. In a sense, nothing changes in the doubling of the double. But in another sense, the first undergoes transformation. In the redoubling, the first one is able to recognize the disjunction in herself, not as something to overcome. Instead, in grasping the disjunction outside of herself as something that exists between the two brothers, she has the opportunity to recognize the disjunction as constitutive of her subjectivity. The uncanny thus may be experienced in a moment of comic relief.

Two Peas in a Pot

One is the subject of tragedy. As Antonin Artaud argues in *Theater and Its Double*, the content of tragedy is what is absolutely singular, what cannot be repeated or represented by another.[37] Hegel also defines tragedy by oneness, but for him, the oneness of tragedy is the joke of comedy: comedy is the process of exposing the oneness of tragedy as farce. The tragic figure sees herself from the start as an absolute singularity. Her ethical conviction pits her against the world. She is tragic, however, not because she must die at the hands of the world that refuses to see the rightness of her conviction. Her tragedy is instead in her one-sidedness: her inability to see that the ethical action demanded by her deeply personal conviction is also an impersonal product of the system that she believes she opposes. On the other side of the tragic hero is the one who protects the unity of the whole and demands the challenger's death. This one, opposed to the first one, fails to see that the transgression of the outsider is also demanded by the ethical system he protects. What appears to be the loneliest number is a logical absurdity because there are always two tragic heroes who mirror each other even in (especially in) their opposition. Tragedy can only see itself from the eyes of the hero on one of its sides. It tries to maintain the absurdity of its ultimate Oneness by killing the one who is identified as introducing conflict. The conflict, however, does not belong to the outsider—who is not an outsider at all—but belongs instead to the stage itself. Tragedy cannot see that the crack that divides one and one is what constitutes the stage. Tragic blindness is blindness to the perspective of the blind spot itself: the (non)perspective of the crack.[38]

The tragic perspective does not see that the figure of the double is always already lurking within one. Farce, to use Marx's terms, presents itself as comic relief but is as blind as tragedy to the crack within one. It sees tragedy as the loneliest one and attempts to relieve tragic alienation by providing one with a companion. And so, one becomes two either through a sister who is the same (as in the Doublemint gum commercial) or through a companion who is her missing half, her opposite who is not opposed but who makes her whole (a normative tale of girl meets boy). As we see in Aristophanes's myth of the circle people from Plato's *Symposium*, two of the same as well as two opposites hopelessly struggle to overcome their incompleteness by attempting to fill in the crack between them.[39] The twin, as I have already claimed, has the appearance of providing great fun for the loneliest one. The twin enters the private world of the one and shares the one's personal convictions and senses of pleasure that appear to be only one's own. Many comedies revolve around the playfulness of twins. However, although twins have been taken up as the subject of comedy, they are also the subject of horror (the twin sisters who haunt the halls of Overlook Hotel). In movies such as *The Parent Trap*, one finds great pleasure in the discovery of a lost other who is as familiar as herself.[40] But this same plot also produces a chilling effect when one discovers the other who is no different from oneself. The horror of *The Shining* does not lie in Jack's encounter with the ghosts from the past, but in his encounter with himself as his own split identity comes to the surface.[41]

The sense of horror lurking in the figure of the double is illustrated nicely by the 1992 film *Single White Female*.[42] The story opens with Allie Jones, who kicks her fiancé out of their apartment after she discovers he has cheated on her with his ex-wife. Allie's appearance of fierce individuality, represented by her definitive spunky red haircut, sets her up as the tragic hero. She maintains her independence although she is alone in the Big City, surrounded by predatory older male figures. Allie posts an ad for a roommate and finds relief from her isolation in Hedy Carson. When Hedy moves in the girls quickly become as close as sisters (Hedy mentions that her own twin died at birth). The girls complement each other in their differences. Each becomes the other's missing half. Sisterly giggles are exchanged as they fix their broken plumbing, raise a puppy, and swap clothing. There is, at first, an air of lightness when one becomes two and two are fused back into a one. However, the problem with the one-two-One formula is that in the process of joining two, one side tends to absorb the other into itself. The sister eats her twin. The film's tone changes when the girls go to a salon to get their hair cut. As Allie admires herself in the mirror, she catches a glimpse of Hedy descending the staircase of the salon, sporting Allie's signature red bob haircut (figure 2).

The scene is a dark double of the Doublemint gum commercial, in which the reflection comes to life. The lightness of sister play descends into horror as Hedy quickly takes over Allie's identity and eventually attempts to snuff out her existence altogether. We learn that Hedy, in fact, killed her real twin and now seeks redemption by repeating the murder. Allie begins to experience her relationship with Hedy as uncanny, not simply because Hedy is revealed to be something other than what she initially seemed (not a shy, sweet girl, but a serial killer), but because this other takes the form of something that is all too familiar, a figure who becomes indistinguishable from Allie herself. It becomes clear to both girls that there isn't room for two. Despite the appearance of fusion, there is still the first or the original who is threatened to be displaced by the secondary copy. But which one is which? In

Figure 2. Hedy (Jennifer Jason Leigh) mirrors Allie (Bridget Fonda). Barbet Schroeder, dir., *Single White Female*, Columbia Pictures, 1992. Courtesy of Columbia Pictures. All rights reserved.

the final scene, Hedy and Allie fight to the death. Which one is original and which one is the copy is of no matter. The victor will rise when one side of the double is destroyed.[43]

The trope of the odd couple produces a different dramatic tone than the trope of the twins. As we have seen, two of the same can be funny or horrifying depending on how the two-fused-in-one are staged. However, there is something inescapably comic about the difference between two opposites fused into one, as proven by great double acts such as George Burns and Gracie Allen. Even when the odd couple plays the villain, the comic chemistry of the duo shines through. The first figure of the odd couple, as in the case of the first of the twins, fits the mold of the tragic hero. The first is typically narrow-minded and stubborn, hotheaded, and quick to anger. He shakes his fist at the world, which he must conquer with his small-minded plans lest the world destroy him. He is blinded by his one-sidedness. Unto himself, this frustrated, isolated figure is not very funny at all, but instead rather pathetic.

And yet, when the spirit of gravity is paired with its opposite—the spirit of frivolity—the tragic nature of the first seems to be diffused. Figure one represents order, necessity, fate, and essence: both what is and what ought to be. Figure two, in contrast, represents play, possibility, contingency, and accident: both what may be and what is not. One is absolute, and one is not. At each step, the second figure trips up the fatalism of the first. At each turn, the seriousness and severity of the first is mocked by the silliness of the second. The tragedy of the first is constantly overturned by his comic double, who is the immediate repetition of his every movement. Like the broom-faced sweeper dog from *Alice in Wonderland*,[44] the comic double immediately sweeps away the tracks of tragedy.

But is the tragic nature of the first one really overcome by the comic cleanup man? Hegel saw Greek comedy on the ancient stage not as comic relief from tragedy but as a mirror of the tragic stage. As he puts it, the reconciliation on the comic stage of Greek history is superficial or abstract freedom.[45] On the ancient tragic stage, the grave hero steps before the chorus to defend the absolute rightness of her actions. She soberly utters, "It is. It must be. It cannot be undone." The tragic hero solemnly sacrifices herself in the name of her gods, which she represents. On the comic stage, we drag the gods onto the stage and make them represent themselves. We laugh as they are tortured and mocked and cry: "The gods are dead! All that was no longer is. It is not." The double in the form of the odd couple represents these two stages on one stage. The tragic utterance "It is" is met with the comic proclamation "It is not!"

Ontology as a Game of (Not) It

We children of the 1990s played an incredibly obnoxious game in which we would interrupt someone's speech yelling, "NOT!"[46] "NOT!" became popular in North America through the *Saturday Night Live* sketch "Wayne's World," later produced as a movie in 1992. The following year, the American Dialect Society selected "NOT!" as the word of the year. "NOT" became much more than a game. It was both our ethical duty and sick compulsion to scream "NOT" in someone's face the moment they opened their mouth. The comic double operates on this game of "NOT!" One says, "It is." Two responds, "Not." "It is."—"Not."

(It is | Not) | (It is | Not)
(Being | Nothing) | (Being | Nothing)

The immediate movement from the tragic one to the comic double reflects the first movement of Hegel's *Science of Logic*.[47] Following Hegel, we begin with what would appear to be the most fundamental category of thought:

pure Being without further determination. We begin with Being, but the moment we try to point to Being—to determine what it is that Being might be—we arrive at its negative double, Nothing. This is so since the content of pure Being—indeterminate immediacy—cannot be distinguished from the emptiness of pure nothingness. A radical change appears in the immediate movement from Being to Nothing—from the spirit of gravity to the spirit of frivolity—from the "It is" to the "It is not"—from tragic seriousness to comic laughter. However, insofar as these two stages appear as simply opposed (even as they appear on the same stage), the relationship between one and (not) one fails to show us anything new. The radical change in appearance is a mere repetition of the empty contents of the pure forms. Insofar as the two appear to be simply opposed, we miss the biggest joke of philosophy: according to logic itself, Being and Nothing cannot be the same, and yet we cannot logically distinguish one from the other.

We can understand this crisis as belonging to the logician who, to his embarrassment, cannot distinguish the form of pure Being from the form of pure Nothingness. But we can also imagine this identity crisis as belonging from the beginning to Being itself. From this perspective, the *Logic* begins with a depiction of the mirror phase of Being's "development." In other words, "the beginning" is in Being's repeated failed attempt to grasp its own identity as something that is whole and complete.

In one reading of this passage, Being appears in the form of the odd couple: Being and Nothing. Hegel redoubles the odd couple when he replays the movement from Being to Nothing backward, this time, starting from Nothing and arriving at Being.[48] It is as if Being passes by a mirror and is chilled by its missing reflection. Nothing likewise attempts to reflect on itself as pure nothingness and is startled by the image of its uncanny double, Being. Being and Nothing each try again to grasp themselves, but this time as an ontological compound of Being and Nothing. And yet even as a compound, Being and Nothing can grasp themselves imperfectly through a reflection that is inverted:

(Being | Nothing) | (Nothing | Being)

I first count to four with Hegel by beginning with the double in the form of the odd couple Being and Nothing, which is redoubled and inverted in Nothing and Being. I count this as a full dialectical turn within the first two paragraphs of chapter 1 of the *Science of Logic*.

However, there is a second way to count to four in these two paragraphs. We can begin with a duality composed of opposing forms or a duality that is two of the same form. The originary redoubling of the odd couple may also be read as the redoubling of twins. As Mladen Dolar points out in "Being and MacGuffin," "Being, pure Being" is already split by a comma and repeated:

> One could say: in the beginning there is *being* posited twice, or in the beginning there is a gap in *being*, a gap between the first and second *being*, splitting the *being* from itself, by the sheer cunningness of its grammatical structure . . . The minimal rhetorical device is precisely repetition, introducing redundancy, the surplus of rhetoric over "information." Saying something twice is redundant, it doesn't bring new information . . . But the rhetorical at this point has immediate ontological value, it is the rhetoric of *being* itself, which makes that *being* insist before ever properly "existing," it insists as a repetition and a cut. The minimal, for being pure, is a redoubled minimal.[49]

Being is already from the beginning its own double, even "before" Being loses itself in the image of its negative double. As I see it, this splice and repetition within pure Being allows Being to fold onto itself in an originary, although imperfect, self-relation. Being tries to reflect upon itself but can only grasp itself by the disjunction between itself and its double.[50] The first set of ontological twins is mirrored in the second set: "Nothing, pure Nothingness." Nothing appears as a radical negation of Being, but it is instead nothing more and nothing less than the repeated content of Being. The content of pure Being from this perspective is not nothing in the form of emptiness, but rather negativity in the form of the comma, the splice, the disjunction or the split.

(Being | Being) | (Nothing | Nothing)

In my interpretation, this originary crack or stutter in pure Being is heightened when repeated in pure Nothing. The only content of pure Being and pure Nothing is the stutter itself. The disturbance that causes Being to interrupt and repeat itself is mirrored in Nothing. The comma represents a stirring in Being that is mirrored in the stirring in Nothing: a negative glitch within indeterminate negativity. The difference between one and one in the case of the twins (Being and Being or Nothing and Nothing) and one and one in the odd couple (Being and Nothing or Nothing and Being) is only formal. In both cases, the redoubling of the double magnifies an active negativity—a repeated stutter or glitch—in the stillness of pure emptiness. The second ontological double magnifies something—or rather nothing—that was there from the beginning.

We are presented with an origin story that constantly interrupts itself and restarts: it is a beginning that does not require a full sentence (Genesis 1:3), but also requires more than a single word since *the word* is already repeated (John 1:1); it is at the same time less than a single word since it is no more than the gap between the repetition of nothing. In the beginning was the stutter. In the beginning was the glitch.

Nothing Changes

Comedy teaches us how to count to four: One, Charlie Chaplin; Two, Abbott and Costello; Three, the Three Stooges; and Four, the Marx Brothers.[51] But the comic dialectician begins with the double to count to four. To further illustrate this dialectical doubling of the double through comedy, I turn to the classic comic duo, Laurel and Hardy. Oliver Hardy was a 280-pound man who wore a bowler hat and suit that were slightly too small, while Stan Laurel was a slim man who wore a bowler hat and suit that were slightly too large. Ollie played the role of the serious man who was easily frustrated. He saw himself as the more intelligent of the two, although he constantly led the two into pitfalls. Stan, Hardy's easygoing sidekick, played the role of the simpleton. As Nabokov describes him, he was "wonderfully inept, yet so very kind."[52] While Ollie easily loses his temper, Stan easily bursts into tears. And yet Stan, who appears so fragile and naive, always seems to come out on top without even trying. His mere presence causes Ollie—the spirit of gravity—to self-sabotage. In every sketch, Ollie, thinking he knows best, forcefully pushes Stan out of the way and takes the lead. Ollie, of course, walks directly into disaster, while Stan remains unscathed.

The chemistry between Laurel and Hardy reflects the dynamics between the spirit of gravity and the spirit of frivolity. However, there are two Laurel and Hardy shorts that intensify the formula of the odd couple times two. Through an early experiment with overlaying film, the two play themselves and their doubles. *First as Tragedy, Then as Farce* is fully played out as *First as Tragedy, Then as Farce: Redoubled*. In the 1933 short *Twice Two*, Laurel and Hardy marry each other's sisters, also played by the duo, in a double wedding. In the opening scene, the men call their wives from work. The usual slapstick between Laurel and Hardy is mirrored in the antics between their female counterparts who are at home preparing an anniversary dinner. Hardy is squirted in the face with black ink while the female Hardy gets a cake in the face. Initially, the dynamic between Laurel and Hardy is only paralleled by the dynamic between the sisters. But the dynamic is complicated when the four sit together at the table (figure 3). Laurel sits across from the female version of himself (a replica in drag) and next to the female version of Hardy (his opposite in drag). Hardy likewise sits across from his female twin and next to his female opposite. The anniversary dinner begins with two sets of twins sitting at the table, each twin looking into his or her near reflection. But what emerges over the course of the dinner are four different combinations of the original odd couple: Laurel and Hardy, Hardy and Laurel, Laurel and Laurel, and Hardy and Hardy.[53] The traditional dynamic between Laurel and Hardy operates on a movement that oscillates to and fro from one to two to two to one, like an endless game of *fort-da* between Being and Nothing, a game in which nothing changes. The dinner table, which stages the double-double, also features a ping-ponging of bickering and slapstick between one

Twice-Two, or Tetradic Dialectics

Figure 3. Stan Laurel and Oliver Hardy, doubling as their wives. James Parrott, dir., *Twice Two* (MGM, 1933). Snap Entertainment Pictures / Alamy Stock Photo.

and one's opposite. The exchange is always between some version of Laurel and Hardy, but never the exact same combination of Laurel and Hardy. Even when nothing changes, the movement from one back to the other is not exactly the same. As Dolar puts it, "One cannot step into the same being twice."[54]

The 1930 short *Brats* is a rare instance in which Laurel and Hardy carry out the entire plot without the aid of any other actors. And yet the double is not alone on stage. Laurel and Hardy redouble themselves, this time playing both the roles of Stan Sr. and Ollie Sr. and that of their sons, Stan Jr. and Ollie Jr.[55] While their wives are out hunting ducks, the men are given the womanly task of watching the children. The scene opens with a game of checkers. Ollie is determined to win, although Stan has already captured a large stack of Ollie's red checker pieces. Like a game of "NOT" in which children negate each other's words almost before they leave the other's mouth, Stan jumps to make a move the moment Ollie's hand hovers over a checker piece. When Stan is distracted, Ollie quickly makes his play. Stan immediately captures two more pieces. *It is. It is Not. It is Not.* After pausing to look sternly into the camera, Ollie begrudgingly advances one of his pieces. *It is.* The spirit of gravity plays the spirit of frivolity at a game of checkers. This scene has a dark double in Bergman's *The Seventh Seal*, in which Antonius faces Death in a game of chess.[56] But Stan and Ollie do not play chess but rather a round of children's checkers, which Ollie nevertheless treats very seriously. The game is redoubled in the children's games, where the boys too go back and forth. In a game of building blocks, the boys take turns placing one block upon the other. The boys gain speed until Stan Jr.'s block lands on Ollie Jr.'s finger, resulting in a violent crash of the block tower (the crash is of course the telos of a game of building blocks). The formula seen in checkers and building blocks is repeated twice more: the boys take turns grasping the long neck of a glass vase placing one hand over the other's hand. This game predictably ends with the crashed vase. Finally, a game of tag is proposed, otherwise known as "It," which ends before it can begin. For a game of "It" immediately becomes a war of "Not it!"

Between one and two, there is a change in form but not in content, since *It* and *Not* are initially indistinguishable, but create what would appear to be a changeless movement to and fro. In the mirroring of this movement in the second double there is no formal change between one and two (the original Stan and Ollie) and one and two (the mechanical reproduction of the first in Stan Jr. and Ollie Jr.). What changes in the repetition between the first double and its exact duplication that produces a comic effect? My answer is nothing. Nothing changes in the dialectical redoubling of the comic double. *Nothing changes* in four ways:

1. Nothing changes in the movement from the first double to the second double. The change in form only reproduces the empty contents of each (Being, Being → Nothing, Nothing).
2. Nothing changes in form and content in the alternative formulation that repeats and inverts the same structure (Being, Nothing → Nothing, Being). Both the dialectical redoubling of the twins with the negative companions and the redoubling of the odd couple fail to bring about new content. Between Being and Nothing nothing changes.
3. Between Being and Nothing nothing changes. This is to say, nothing itself undergoes transformation. When the first duo is duplicated or mirrored in the second duo, the split (Hegel's comma) between the first duo is itself repeated in the second split between the second duo. The moment of the negative at first appears to be within the second figure, who diffuses the severity of the first one. However, when the double is repeated, negativity reveals itself to be between the two (which we see in the second two). What appears to be between two is already true of one.
4. Between Being and Nothing nothing changes. This is to say, the negativity that binds and separates Being and Nothing (and Being

Twice-Two, or Tetradic Dialectics 43

and Being) is the agent of change. The comma sets everything in motion. Nothing itself is in the position of the subject who in counting to three forgets to count herself and in counting to four learns to count herself (as nothing).

The oscillation between Stan Jr. and Ollie Jr. highlights what should already be obvious in the relationship between Laurel and Hardy: the second does not make the first whole, nor does the second overcome the first as the work of the negative, which only takes off in the redoubling. Instead, the two opposites are somehow always already wrapped up in the other because both are constituted by the crack that binds and separates them. There is no Laurel without Hardy, nor Hardy without Laurel. The tension between the two sustains both sides. It is precisely because each is bound to his distinct role that the severity and seriousness of the one has already crossed over into the lightness of the other. In turn, the frivolity of the second has already been sucked into the gravity of the first, where the second finds his lightness. What may be already obvious to us must become obvious to the double itself. As Stan says in one of his famous nonsensical proverbs, "You can lead a horse to water, but a pencil must be lead." Ollie—the spirit of gravity—must get hit on the head with a block by the second set of doubles to realize Stan's second accidental insight when he confuses himself and Ollie with their mini-mes. Stan scolds the boys, "If *you* don't quiet down, we'll have to send *us* to bed." To which Ollie replies, "Not *we*! *Them*!" But Stan's misspoken words are always closer to the truth.

Between the double and the redouble, *nothing* changes, and for this very reason, both the tension and the possibility of a comic eruption are heightened twice-two. Comedy is not in the second repetition but in the crack that makes Being and Nothing a game of "It" ("Not It!"). The comedy of spirit emerges when nothing itself changes, when the crack is split open by yet another crack in the doubling of the double: the transformation of negativity itself.

Chapter 2

✦

Comic Abortions and the Birth of Self

Does the revelation of the ontological primacy of the crack in Being inspire tragic despair or comic relief? This depends on who is counting. Being begins in a moment of radical skepticism. Like a cartoon character suspended for a split second over a chasm, Being passes a mirror and, to its terror, finds its missing reflection. This foundational moment of self-doubt is imprinted on Being, whose lingering insecurity manifests itself as a stutter in existence. Nothing's account of the same moment is not exactly symmetrical. The abyss blushes with vanity as it sees itself being seen. The chasm glances up toward the heavens and embraces the subject, who comes plummeting toward it. The missing reflection gasps at the glorious Being who stands before it. Being's self-doubt is mirrored in Nothing's self-certainty. Nothing's certainty, however, is not simply secured in the figure of Being but rather in the mirror image of Being's nothingness. Nothing can be more certain than the crack in Being. Nothing can be more certain of nothing more than its own nothingness. Becoming is thus the constant process of trying to reconcile Nothing's calm faith in nothing and Being's desperate insistence on its being.

The self-revelation of Nothing reveals thick layers of different expressions of negativities. Nothing follows Being around performing a constant determinate negation, which Being internalizes in the form of a crack or stutter, (Being | Being). There is also a crack between Being and Nothing that stitches the two together for eternity while simultaneously protecting each side from being swallowed up by its partner (Being | Nothing) (Nothing | Being). Then there is negativity in the form of the second pair of identical twins (Nothing | Nothing). One Nothing follows her sister around as a kind of constant echo that simultaneously amplifies her nothingness while calling her integrity into question. The second Nothing shadows the first, a determinate negation of Nothing that does not result in anything positive. Finally, there is the crack between the negative twins, indicating a kind of restless negativity that stirs within the stillness of pure Nothingness itself.

Nothing touches herself in her own nothingness and finds joy and release. The self-relation of Nothing may simply be called self-relation, which may simply be called self. From yet another perspective this self may simply be called relation. Dialectical negativity nearly always expresses itself through the determinate negation of this or that being. The rare moments in which Nothing grasps itself in the nakedness of its negativity are startling. Chapter 1 offers a comic reading of Hegel's *Science of Logic*, emphasizing the impossibility of resolution despite the persistence of the protagonist. In the beginning, the comic odd couple immediately questions who is the real main character of the ontological drama. To put this differently, staging Nothing as the protagonist of the drama turns a logic of noncontradiction itself into a laughing matter. I now move from a comic reading of the *Science of Logic* to Hegel's formal philosophy of comedy. The scene that I animate in the beginning of the *Science of Logic* is repeated in the *Phenomenology of Spirit*, when Hegel interrupts the dialectical flow of his stage play with an intermission between Greek "Art-Religion" and "Revealed Religion." The stage darkens, and we witness Nothing sink into the blissful certainty of its own nothingness. Hegel calls this dialectical suspension in darkness "Self."

In the *Phenomenology of Spirit*'s penultimate section on "Religion" paving the way to "Absolute Knowledge," Hegel arrives at Self by beginning with the question, "What is the object of art and religion?" He traces the shifting object of art through various ancient Greek artistic practices before arriving at comedy, which he identifies as the last stage of art-religion. He finally asks, "What is the object of comedy?" Unlike other artistic practices that are positively defined by their created object or creative activity, ancient comedy appears purely destructive, terminating anything traditionally recognizable as art. Hegel points to Aristophanes and Socrates as representing two sides of the defacement of the object of art-religion. We can easily identify this negative force in Aristophanes's plays in which the gods—the object of other forms of Greek art—evaporate into a puff of air. Negativity in comedy manifests itself in the determinate negation of this or that object of art, objects once revered as divine. Comic negativity expresses itself most powerfully, however, when comedy turns on itself. The comic poet directs his protagonist to set fire to the stage to the horror of his audience. But is this aesthetic stage, which destroys its own object/objective, wholly negative? Can negativity be creative without rendering any positive remainder or emergence?

A shadowy figure can *almost* be detected lurking in the negative space left by the comic destruction of Greek art-religion. The object of art-religion is aborted. Art-religion aborts itself. A subject is born. This wholly negative shadow, more similar to a phantom than a defined ego or actor, does not resemble anything that will become traditionally recognizable as the modern subject. And yet, for Hegel, the birth of this phantom figure, which emerges from the crack between two stages of negativity, represents the first abstract conception of self.

Hegel casts Socrates and Aristophanes in the roles of midwives with the vital task of delivering the Self into existence. Is this odd couple a competent candidate to be entrusted with such a weighty task? The familiar image of Socrates as a midwife presents the philosopher as the one who aids in the birth of truth in the presence of the Good and the Beautiful. In contrast to the figure of the philosopher-midwife, Aristophanes's *Clouds* depicts Socrates as the abortionist.[1] In a moment of comic-horror, a knock at the door disrupts the concentration of the philosopher-midwife who accidentally performs an abortion on the verge of delivering a new concept.[2] The comic poet is often seen as mocking the philosopher with the dark, comic image of the clumsy midwife. However, Plato himself oscillates between presenting the philosopher as the midwife who delivers living truth into the world (the *Symposium*) and the image of the abortionist who induces labor only to snuff out the life of the newly born concept (the *Theaetetus*).[3] With the image of the midwife-abortionist, an alliance is drawn between the comic poet and the philosopher, who self-consciously mirror one another in the act of aborting the very object/objective of aesthetic and philosophical reflection.

Although Socrates and Aristophanes are sometimes staged in opposition, Hegel saw Platonic skepticism and ancient comedy as a mirror double that reflects the internal erosion of an entire way of life. And yet, aesthetic negativity and philosophical negativity usher in the most essential expression of negativity, Nothing's self-consciousness. Rather than taking Hegel's word for it, I offer my own analysis of the birth of the Self through an ancient alliance between Platonic skepticism and comedy. Following Hegel, I explore the structural similarity between Aristophanes's comedies and Platonic skepticism, which have a destructive impulse that is simultaneously creative. On a performative level, I offer a comic delivery of Aristophanes's comedy and Plato's *Theaetetus*, which explicitly defends both Aristophanes and comedy while employing humor.

In the performative destruction of the object of aesthetic production and the concept of philosophical reflection, something slips into being that may be identified as the phantom form of the self. Throughout the Platonic dialogues there are suggestions of theories of subjectivity, not yet fully realized, but rather phantoms that are later taken up by modern philosophers to be raised into something concrete. In this sense, Socrates, in his role as a midwife, leaves behind orphans that he neither adopts nor rejects. One of these orphans is an unrealized conception of self, who Hegel adopts and raises in his own spiritual drama.

The phantom shadow of the subject lurks in places where Socrates takes on the contrary duties of the midwife-abortionist. As one strange metaphor leads to another, I continue to attend to the motif of twins and odd couples. Plato's repeated metaphor of twin birth offers an image of a subject that is split in two, or the self as the split between two. Plato's myths and metaphors allow the double to be rendered differently. For example, the *Symposium*'s myth of the birth of the human being as a consequence of the split circle people allows us to grasp the subject as a composite of two positive halves joined and separated by a split (Being | Being).[4] However, the severed circle people may also be conceived as a composite of a positive half and a negative half. What appears as subject is defined by a missing or fantastical double (Being | Nothing). The extended metaphor of midwifery and twin birth in the *Theaetetus* repeats and inverts the structure of the subject in the form of a negativity conjoined with a positive appearance (Nothing | Being). The inversion, in which negativity hovers over positivity, leans into a fourth formulation of the self as a double negativity (Nothing | Nothing). The subject may be understood as a composite of what appears and what disappears. Yet, what appears as subject is itself nothing more than a composite of a determinate negativity (the aborted concept that never sees the light of day) and an indeterminate negativity that slips into existence (a phantom birth).

The Socratic figure of the midwife-abortionist points to a double-movement of coming-into-being and coming-out-of-being. However, what comes into being is also another expression of negativity. In this movement between Aristophanes and Socrates (and between the ancient duo and Hegel), I adopt a concept of self in the shape of the "monstrous compound" of the aborted object and its phantom double.[5] Self is a compound of two kinds of self-relating negativities: the determinate negativity of Being's nothing, the terror of radical doubt, and the indeterminate negativity of Nothing's nothing, the tranquility of undisturbed confidence.

Hegel on the Terminated Object of Art-Religion

In the final paragraphs on the "Art-Religion" of the Greeks in the *Phenomenology of Spirit*,[6] Hegel reflects on the mirroring of ancient comedy and Platonic skepticism. Hegel, at last, arrives at the conception of subject by pursuing the question, "What is the object of art?" To answer this question, he asks, "What is the object of religion?" since art and religion in ancient Greek society are intertwined. Hegel traces the shifting object of art in Greek aesthetic and religious practice, beginning with the marble statue that depicts the idealized human form as a deity. The statue reflects none of the sculptor's passions or angst. It is a product that conceals its maker and the creative process that engendered it.[7] Hegel contrasts the marble statue to art in the form of spoken or sung words. Unlike sculpture, which presents the object of art as a thing to be passively admired or worshipped, performed speech makes artistic practice itself the object of art. In singing a hymn, for example, a group of worshippers is at one with their art-object (and with the divine). In contrast to the statue, which outlasts and erases its origin, the hymn vanishes when its own production comes to an end.[8] The shift from the object of art as a product to the object of art as creative production is also expressed in the festivals of Dionysus and Demeter. At the festivals devoted to the gods, the festivalgoers also reflect on their own activity since each god represents a different aspect of human life.[9] The various activities and customs that comprise human life are each upheld as sacred in themselves. The aesthetic representation of the activity of the gods and the activity of human beings becomes indistinguishable, as reflected in the epic, in which the gods and human heroes mimic each other's actions.[10]

On the theatrical stage of tragedy, however, gods and human beings do not often intermingle. The object of tragedy is the individual human being who boldly steps forward before the audience. However, the object of tragedy is not only the human individual who is one with the immediacy of her action. The tragic object is also the reflective account of that action, which the tragic hero must provide in defense of her deed before the chorus. In the process of defending her action, the tragic subject fully identifies with her action, defending the absolute rightness of that action even at the cost of her own life. Art in the form of individual human activity becomes indifferent to the human agent. In this sense, tragic performance resembles the inanimate sculpture more than the performed hymn. The art-object—even in the form of action—becomes an impersonal maxim as individual creative expression vanishes.

Art-religion begins with an art-object that is separate from the artist. The object of art is given to the audience as something to be passively admired; the art-object shifts to the immediacy of human activity, something transient that comes in and out of existence with the immediate expression of its maker; and finally, the art-object takes the form of a self-reflective account of human activity. And yet, in this moment of aesthetic self-reflection, the individual is most alienated from the production of her art (that is, the action that she mistakenly identifies as most essentially her own). Indeed, the art-object, for which she sacrifices herself, will continue to be reproduced by new actors with the same "self-reflective" conviction. This irony is not lost on comedy, which breaks with the progression by aborting the object of art-religion altogether.[11] Hegel's pursuit of the question, "What is the object of art?" leads him to ancient comedy, which answers, "Nothing."

Hegel identifies the art-religion of the Greeks as ending in comedy and connects what occurs on the theatrical stage to the philosophical stage of Platonic skepticism. In tragedy, the character who first steps forward before the audience is terminated, leaving the defense of her action as a placeholder for her missing individuality. Comedy looks with irony upon the tragic hero who sacrifices herself for the sake of an action that was given to her as an absolute imperative. But rather than opposing this self-destructive character of tragedy, comedy elevates it, bringing tragedy's vanishing act to completion. Aesthetic production turns on itself, destroying even its final remaining object, its own reflective account of its activity. On the comic stage, the gods—each of which enforces a different aspect of social activities and customs—now dissolve into laughter.

Hegel sees this destructive spirit of the comic toward the gods and the ethical ideals that they enforce as paralleled in philosophy by the forms of the Good and the Beautiful, which ultimately show themselves to be comic spectacles.[12] Plato's forms may seem like a strange place to locate comic destruction within philosophy. However, Hegel suggests that even a dogmatic reading of Plato—one that identifies a positive metaphysics in the theory of the forms—results in a kind of cultural or ethical skepticism. The forms, which are without determinate content, challenge the ethical maxims and customs of an earlier cultural stage. Because the forms are without determinate content, they may be continually reinterpreted to various ends without offering certain instructions concerning our daily ethical life.[13] We can thus say of the gods and the societal maxims that they enforce: "They are clouds."[14] As comedy may be viewed as an aesthetic stage that betrays itself—destroying its own object—so might skepticism be viewed as a philosophical stage that betrays itself, extending its critical spirit to its own determinate contents.

Despite the fully negative character of these movements, Hegel sees comedy and skepticism as producing a pathos that expresses absolute certainty. In overturning the values of a former stage, nothing could be more certain than negativity itself. The sun sets and darkness covers over all that we once knew to be true. But this is not yet the midnight of consciousness.[15] Darkness, *for the moment*, is met by the skeptic's tranquility and the comic poet's detached laughter. As our vision adjusts to the darkness, we begin to sense with certainty "the coming-to-be of a shape whose existence does not go outside of the Self, but is purely a vanishing object."[16]

At the end of "Art-Religion," moving into "Revealed Religion," Hegel passes over what he sees as the embryo of the subject conceived between comedy and skepticism, only making indirect allusions to the specific crossings of Aristophanes and Socrates in his discussion of the forms as clouds. In the following, I leave Hegel to the side and turn to Aristophanes's *Clouds* and Plato's *Theaetetus* to attend to the subject that emerges from the consummation of ancient comedy and Platonic skepticism. My first proposal is that the comic poet and philosopher come together in the figure of the midwife-abortionist. My second proposal is that the midwife-abortionist, who straddles the twin stages of comedy and skepticism, delivers the unrealized concept of a phantom subject, which is necessarily conjoined with an aborted object of aesthetic and philosophical reflection.

Aristophanes's Intentional Flop in Honor of Socrates

Aristophanes's *Clouds* is by far his most celebrated play because of its connection to the historical life and death of Socrates. *Clouds* is often taught as a satire of Socrates that contributes to the negative public image of the philosopher, leading to his execution twenty-three years later. Although the relationship between the two may be interpreted as antagonistic, leading to the tragic negation of one side of the double, their relationship may also be

Comic Abortions and the Birth of Self

understood as an alliance made through comedy. The first irony of *Clouds*' legacy is that it is quite possibly built on mischaracterizations of both Aristophanes's framing of Socrates and of Socrates's framing of Aristophanes.[17] In my reading, *Clouds* does not drag the great philosopher down from his high seat in the sky but pays him homage. The second irony of *Clouds*' historical legacy is that its first performance in 422 at Dionysia was a flop—possibly Aristophanes's only flop. What is more, it appears to be an intended flop. Following four consecutive wins for the category "best comedy" at the festivals, *Clouds* was likewise anticipated to be a great success. Aristophanes dashes his audience's expectations for the comedy on a number of levels. I see these two ironies as closely connected. Aristophanes pays tribute to Socrates, whom he portrays as an abortionist, by purposefully aborting his own comedy to the horror of his audience.

Clouds employs none of the usual comic conventions that Aristophanes's audience had come to expect of his drama. It is his only play, for example, that does not end with resolution for the protagonist, or if not for the protagonist, then for the communal whole. Instead, the play ends as it begins. It begins with an uneducated countryman, Strepsiades, who has accrued a great deal of debt due to his arrogance and foolishness. He pretends to be a pious man so that the gods might come to his aid. When the gods fail to come to his aid, he redirects his desperate plea to the philosophers, whom he naively imagines to have special powers to bend the will of the gods and men alike. Of course, this image of the philosopher has nothing to do with the philosopher but is instead a product of Strepsiades's greedy fantasy of employing philosophy to cheat his way out of debt. The play's characterization of the philosopher highlights the paradox of Stepsiades's expectation for the philosopher, whom he imagines to be both lofty and removed while at the same time ready and able to serve the ambitions of corrupt men. The absurd depiction of the philosopher does not mock Socrates's view of himself or reflect Aristophanes's critical view of Socrates. The perspective belongs to Strepsiades, who might be seen as representing the average Athenian (although Aristophanes counts on the fact that his audience won't recognize themselves as the object of laughter).

Strepsiades bangs on the door of what he childishly calls "The Thinking Institute" and demands that Socrates take him on as a student.[18] Although Socrates is mildly amused by the man's astonishing shallowness, he has no interest in coming to the aid of this despicable protagonist. Socrates, in his usual way, plays along with his new interlocutor's assumptions, guiding them to their contradictory dead ends. Socrates responds to Strepsiades's feigned piety with a series of fart jokes that make up the majority of the dialogue. *Don't wait on the old gods to deliver you from your troubles. You'll have just as much luck praying to the thundering clouds, those billows of farts from the great anus in the sky.*[19] This overt mockery is not intended to be clever. It might have provoked a more reflective man to blush, coming to terms with his hypocrisy. But the joke is lost on Strepsiades, who, to Socrates's astonishment, immediately redirects his prayers to the Clouds. When the Clouds do not come to his rescue, Strepsiades becomes like Alcibiades. His childish admiration for Socrates turns to bitterness. In one last pathetic attempt to overcome his impotency, Strepsiades sets fire to the Thinking Institute. Not only does the play end as it begins but there is no comic inversion of power dynamics. In *Frogs*, for example, Dionysus is dragged through the underworld and treated like a slave, while his human slave Xanthius is worshipped as a god.[20] In *Clouds*, however, the poor, uneducated fool remains just that while Socrates and his students walk off the stage unharmed by the flames.

Twentieth-century comedy, taking place on the bleak historical stage of world wars, has made us accustomed to dark comedies that offer no relief from misfortune, that make us suffer the company of protagonists for whom we have little sympathy and tedious plots that lead to nowhere. But Aristophanes's audience was not at all prepared for a play that had no payoff. They hated *Clouds*. And what is more, it seems that Aristophanes intended for them to hate it. At the parabasis—the monologue in which the chorus leader steps forward to explain the forthcoming moral of the comedy—the head Cloud steps forward. In a shocking moment, he leans in toward the audience and speaks in the voice of the playwright himself. Allow me to summarize the tone and main points of the long-winded attack on the audience:

> Listen here. I'm going to give this to you straight. Your love for my comedies has made me famous, it's true. But you praise my work for all the wrong reasons. My cleverness is completely lost on you, and I'm losing my mind. Each time one of my plays is performed, it's like I'm a virgin about to deliver a firstborn. But you greedy bastards pluck the baby from between the mother's legs and raise the child to be as stupid as you. Well this time, you're not going to do that. This comedy is not for you but for the virgin midwife herself, Artemis, goddess of childbirth, goddess of the hunt.[21]

Amid a comedy of fart jokes, Aristophanes goes really dark on his audience, essentially promising to sacrifice his comedy before allowing his audience to appropriate it. He confesses that it is his most successful work, although he knows it will be misunderstood. He begins by sarcastically mocking the intelligence of this audience, blaming the "*sophisticated* spectators" for its initial failure at its first performance in 423 (leading us to believe that this version was revised).[22] He then compares himself to a young mother forced to give up her newborn infant: "And I, like an unmarried girl not yet allowed to give birth, had to expose my baby and another girl took it for herself, and *you* were the ones who reared and trained it so proudly." The speech then lists all of the commonly loved comic devices that the play *refuses* to employ. Aristophanes closes the speech, claiming that Artemis directly told him she is angry with the audience. As if the parabasis wasn't already the ultimate mic drop, the stage itself goes up in flames in the final act. The way the comic poet viciously turns on his fans would surely get him canceled today.

Does *Clouds* attack Socrates for being overly intellectual or the Athenians for being dangerously basic? The comedy pokes fun at Socrates by portraying him as mishandling fragile objects (in the form of thoughts), which he inevitably terminates, for example, when a gnat farts or a gecko shits.[23] We learn about these episodes through one of Socrates's students, who answers the door when Strepsiades first arrives.[24] "You idiot," the student shouts, "You kicked the door so hard and without any trace of self-reflection. You *aborted* a thought my mind had just discovered!" He continues to narrate a similar mishap with Socrates, "Two days ago Socrates lost a big idea because of a lizard . . . He was puzzling over the curving paths of the moon across the heavens and gawping up at the sky when down from the roof in the dark came—a gecko's shit."[25] The accidental abortions are often interpreted as Socrates's failure to deliver his own positive concepts. But given the emphasis of the parabasis, we might conclude instead that Aristophanes admires the way Socrates refuses to give his followers what they want. If Socrates delivers anything at all—and is not simply full of gas—it is a hideous child resembling himself that no one would want to claim as his own (in truth, not even Plato is willing to directly claim Socrates's concepts as his own).

Clouds makes an alliance between comedy and Socratic philosophy, mocking the Athenian attitude toward both. Aristophanes stresses the contradictory framing of the philosopher as one who is both too removed and too involved, too frivolous and too cunning. Such expectations will lead to bitter disillusionment when the philosopher, who claims to be neither a cosmologist nor a rhetorician, fails to offer solutions. The comedy is a prophecy. When the philosopher fails to deliver you from your misfortune, you will in turn identify him as the source of that misfortune. The farce that the Athenians have created for themselves will surely end in horror: the termination of one of Athens's greatest offspring by her own hand.

Theaetetus's Sextuplets

Just as *Clouds* may be read as paying homage to Socrates, Plato's *Theaetetus* might be read as paying homage to *Clouds*. Or at the very least the two works suggest that Aristophanes and Plato were aligned in their view of Socrates as the midwife-abortionist with one foot on the comic stage and one foot in horror. While *Clouds*, in my reading, defends philosophy against Athenian public opinion, the *Theaetetus* defends comedy, even when its laughter is at the expense of the philosopher. Plato's most explicit defense of Aristophanes is in the *Apology*, in which Socrates at his trial carefully distinguishes between those who attack him "with animus and malice" from the comic poet's harmless "nonsense."[26] The *Theaetetus* echoes this defense of comedy, offering a lengthy digression about self-deprecation and the virtue of being able to take a joke.[27] These passages about critical laughter (*katagelōs*) might seem out of place in a dialogue dedicated to epistemology rather than poetics.[28] Beyond the explicit discussions of humor, the *Theaetetus* takes the form of a joke book. Although Plato's humor is expressed throughout the Socratic dialogues, he chooses this work on the nature of true knowledge to be an explicit exercise in comic writing.[29] The *Theaetetus* mirrors *Clouds* in a number of ways: (1) in the tone of the dialogue, which borders on comic-horror—after all, the book of fart jokes is dedicated to Theaetetus, who is dying of dysentery,[30] (2) in the explicit defense of joking and mockery, (3) in Socrates's portrayal of himself as the midwife whose primary function is to perform abortions, and (4) in presenting itself as a work of epistemology but failing to deliver a single successful theory of truth or knowledge. Like *Clouds*, it strings the reader along, and if it delivers anything at all in the end—and is not simply full of gas—it is something unrecognizable from what the reader had expected.

The *Theaetetus* extends upon *Clouds*' motif of the philosopher-abortionist by adding a twist to several concepts introduced in the *Symposium*, which is traditionally marked as an earlier dialogue. In the *Symposium*, Diotima presents the young Socrates with the inspirational vision of the philosopher-midwife who aids in the birth of new living concepts.[31] In the *Theaetetus*, the older Socrates likewise presents himself as a midwife to his new young friend, whom he declares to be pregnant with fledgling concepts of knowledge.[32] "I suspect you're suffering birth-pains from something you're carrying inside you," he tells his young friend, "so treat me as the son of a midwife who has some midwife's skills of his own . . . If at any point I think, on examination, that something you've said really is a phantom, not a true child of yours, and I take it from you and dispose it, don't go wild like a mother over her first baby."[33] Through this extended passage in which Socrates steps into the role of the midwife, he emphasizes that the midwife's responsibilities include dealing with failed births.[34]

Like *Clouds*, the dialogue opens with an evocation of Artemis. *Isn't it strange*, Socrates notes, *that the skilled huntress, a virgin herself, is given the task of overseeing childbirth? But then again, the farmer who plants a crop also tends to the harvest; he, too, oversees the process of coming into being as much as the process of coming out of being, as in the case of miscarriages.*[35] The peculiar tasks belonging to the midwife of concepts involve overseeing the fruitful birth of living concepts and phantom births. Socrates admits that it is often difficult to identify the phantom birth. In the case of the birth of living concepts, the midwife must help the mother decide whether the object of thought is worth raising into a mature theory or whether it should be disposed of immediately. Thus, there are four diagnoses that the midwife of concepts might arrive at: (1) the individual is not spiritually pregnant at all but full of gas, (2) the individual is pregnant, but the conception should be terminated before coming to full term, (3) the concept is deserving of being raised into a developed theory, taking the risk that others will steal it and raise it as their own, or (4) the individual is pregnant but with a phantom, a sort of orphan concept that slips through the midwife's hands so that it can neither be nurtured nor terminated.

The dialogue takes off as Socrates prods the young Theaetetus into labor, provoking him into conceiving a definition of true knowledge. As it turns out, Theaetetus is not suffering from gas but is pregnant with triplets. After much intellectual labor, he gives birth to three unique concepts of knowledge: knowledge as perception, knowledge as belief, and knowledge as a rational account. In a perverse joke—which is explicitly delivered as a joke—Socrates snuffs out the life of each of Theaetetus's newborn concepts: *Okay, my boy, now that you're ready to give birth, let's see if it's worthy of seeing the light of day.*[36]

Although Socrates ultimately judges each newborn as an unfit concept of knowledge, he never fully rejects the corresponding concepts of perception, belief, and account. With each concept that is terminated as a concept of knowledge, something slips by which Socrates neither affirms nor denies. We might further speculate that Theaetetus is not pregnant with triplets but rather sextuplets, in the form of three sets of twins.[37] One twin is terminated at birth. The other survives. What, then, is conceived in the failed concept of knowledge? The conception is a monstrous compound of a terminated birth and a phantom birth. The surviving twin that escapes the judgment of the midwife-abortionist is shadowed by the negative outline of the terminated twin that attaches itself to its sibling.

The configuration of the twins, in which one is terminated and one survives by slipping past the midwife, structures the delivery of each of the three sections of the dialogue. The model of the twins is also explicitly taken up in the content of each of the three failed theories of knowledge: the theory of perception as a twin birth, the metaphor of belief as a combination of two birds, one that takes flight as true judgment and one that is flightless and false, and the analysis of an account as a compound, which Socrates illustrates with the example of syllable (such as, "Ba") that is composed of an unvoiced consonant (B) and vowel (A).[38] In each case, one side represents the continual process of slipping out of being, retreating into the background. But the passive or failed side of the compound proves to be a necessary condition for the expression of the second twin's visibility (in the example of perception as twins), motion (in the example of belief as two birds), and voice (in the example of the rational account as a compound of consonant and vowel).

In the first of these three iterations, Socrates reveals that the "humble" position of the relativist—who only claims that *x* appears as *F for me*—houses stronger ontological claims that the relativist attempts to avoid.

Protagoras's weak epistemology leads us to Heraclitus's metaphysics. It is not only the case that you and I perceive x differently, but it is also the case that I will experience x differently from one moment to the next: x appears to me as F at T1 but as Y at T2. The only thing that may be said to be true of the perceiver and perceived is F, where the two both touch and fail to touch. But F itself is inconsistent from one moment to the next. Thus, every phenomenological observation involves a hidden implication about time and change. The framing of (lowercase-t) "truth" in the claim—it is true that you perceive x one way and I perceive x another way—relies on a stronger truth claim about being in time as always in flux: Being as Becoming.

It only takes a tiny push for phenomenological description to yield its latent metaphysical contents. With this tiny push, Socrates shows the impossibility of remaining both epistemologically and metaphysically neutral. The tiny push furthermore results in a provocative suggestion about the nature of the subject itself, as Socrates shifts the metaphor of the twins, introduced initially as a description of perception, to a metaphysical register.

At the beginning of his discussion of how Protagoras's measure doctrine immediately slips into Heraclitus's metaphysics, Socrates presents perception as the twin offspring of two kinds of change. Change itself takes the form of twins: in each instance, change in the form of some kind of activity is accompanied by change in the form of what is acted upon. Change is a kind of ontological double, opposite forces that always occur together. We might think of change as an odd couple that takes the appearance of identical twins. As Socrates later argues, in every instance, it is impossible to show which twin acts upon which.[39] As we experience through the exercise of meditating on our own hands folded in prayer, we can focus on the right hand grasping the left or the left grasping the right. But it is difficult to experience both sides simultaneously grasping and being grasped at once.[40] Change or Becoming as an ontological double gives birth to another double in the form of perception. A perception strikes us as such when something shifts in our horizon (what Socrates calls fast change). Perception is thus the twin experience of something that is perceived, coming into being as it shifts into the foreground, and something coming out of being as it slips into background: "From the coming together of these two motions [belonging to change], and the friction of one against the other, offspring come into being—unlimited numbers of them, but twins in every case, one twin being what is perceived, the other a perception, emerging simultaneously with what is perceived and being generated along with it . . . as for the kind of thing that is perceived, it shares its birth with the perception."[41] When Socrates discusses the "unlimited number" of perceptions within a relativist framework, he does not describe perception as infinite difference in flux. Instead, the perception of change, of something new in my horizon or acting on my body, is the product of the tension between two (a proposition that seems to lean into Heraclitus's theory of opposites over his theory of flux). The ontology that Socrates identifies as attached to Theaetetus's firstborn does not flow organically like a river but rather mechanically in the process of doubles redoubling themselves without resolving the original tension between two: "kindred births in every case."[42]

Relativism identifies conflict as arising between at least two inconsistent positions: either between two people who perceive "the same thing" differently at the same time; or between the contrasting perceptions of the same person concerning "the same thing" experienced at two different times. To avoid conflict, we agree only to make descriptive claims about our perception rather than truth claims about the world or ourselves. But as Socrates follows relativism to what he sees as its own conclusions, we find that avoiding conflict is not so easy. Conflict also exists in what is traditionally identified as one: one perception, one stance, one belief, one body, one identity. As the skeptic shows us, if we dwell with any one (perception, stance, belief, body, identity) long enough, we will run into a paradox that was present in the one from the beginning. One is already divided into two. In shifting from a weak epistemology to an ontology grounded in equipollence, Socrates extends the theory of perception as "co-generated" to all identities:[43]

> The consequence of all of this, according to the theory, is that nothing—as we were saying at the beginning—is just one thing, itself by itself, but instead is always coming to be in relation to something. The verb "is" must be removed from every context ... we shouldn't consent to using "something," or "somebody's," or "mine," or "this," or "that," or any other name that brings things to a standstill. Instead our utterances should conform to nature and have things "coming to be" ... [and] "passing away" ... the rule applies to talk both about the individual case and about many collected together—the sort of collection for which people posit entities like human being.[44]

The argument about the nonidentity of things over time becomes an argument for the nonidentity of things in a given moment. And this rule applies not only to objects but to the human subject, both in the form of the *individual* and *community*.[45] For each subject that comes into being, there is also a disappearing objective side: something that comes out of being, the ghost of an aborted twin who attaches itself to its sibling.

The *Theaetetus*'s specific configuration of the twins—one of which appears as subject against the background of its terminated double—is an inverted mirror image of the subject in the *Symposium*'s myth. Both images serve as models for contemporary theories of subjectivity that resurface in German idealism and psychoanalysis. In the *Symposium*, Plato's Aristophanes offers the model of each individual as separated from their mirrored half.[46] This passage about the flayed circle people inspires Lacan's lamella myth in *Seminar XI*.[47] Earlier in this same lecture, Lacan makes the strange claim that the analyst performs the dangerous work of the abortionist, who attempts to bring something unrealized up from limbo to the surface: "It is the abortionist's relation to limbo . . . It is always dangerous to disturb anything in that zone of shades, without always being able to bring them up to the light of day."[48] The danger lies in the analyst's inability to either terminate or give life to what is brought to consciousness. And yet, the risk for the subject of analysis is also the shape of subjectivity, represented by the lamella: a phantom fetus or placenta shed at birth that continues to haunt what appears as subject. Although Lacan refers to the sliced circle people, the lamella also resonates with the *Theaetetus*'s twin birth in which something unrealized slips by the midwife-abortionist.

Aristophanes's myth in the *Symposium* rests on the fantasy of recovering an original wholeness that perhaps never was. The subject grasps herself as something incomplete and is erotically driven by the sustained fantasy of achieving wholeness. Being chases after nothing (B | N), hoping to achieve unity and self-sameness by reattaching itself to its missing half (B | B). This erotic drive fuels all creative endeavors belonging to becoming. The inversion of the structure in the *Theaetetus* retells the same fantasy as a nightmare that resembles Lacan's lamella. The twin fetus, which was neither given life nor terminated, threatens to reattach itself to what appears as subject. Nothing haunts Being (N | B), threatening to expose what appears as subject as nothing more than a mirror image of its phantom double (N | N). The fantasy of achieving pure being and the nightmare of being exposed as nothingness are two different ways of grasping the same split subject. What is more, the double negativity that threatens to bring an end to the subject as such—even before the subject is fully conceived—is found also in the beginning as the very condition of self.

The Orphan Subject of Comedy

Socrates asks Theaetetus for his thoughts on the proposal that all perceptions and entities are expressions of twin births. Theaetetus responds for all of us: "Actually, I can't make out where you stand on this. Do you agree with what you are saying or are you saying it to challenge me?"[49] Socrates carefully dodges the question, avoiding taking his own stance on the matter: "You're forgetting, my friend, that I myself neither know anything of such things nor claim to know anything of them; none of them is my offspring. I'm acting as a midwife to you."[50] As a result of Socrates's concealment of his own position (if he has one), the passage about Protagoras and Heraclitus has become one of the most influential and disputed passages in the history of philosophy. On the one hand, Socrates, in his role as the midwife, clearly terminates the concept of knowledge as perception since the claim "everything is as it seems for me" leads us to the conclusion that "nothing is as it seems for anybody."[51] There is always something that fails to appear, which conditions an appearance. On the other hand, in aborting the concept of knowledge, a concept of perception, which entails an ontology of the subject, slips by the midwife's judgment. The subject herself cannot be defined by a single identity or set of fixed properties, but is rather the expression of twins brushing shoulders.

Some scholars argue that Socrates himself embraces aspects of the ontology that unfolds from his framing of Protagoras. Others insist that Socrates himself thinks all aspects of the argument about perception are absurd, leading to the impossibility of language.[52] As I see it, each definite termination of Theaetetus's three theories of knowledge leaves behind a philosophical orphan as the result of a secondary phantom twin birth. On one level, Socrates's role as the midwife in the *Theaetetus* is purely destructive, since he doesn't allow a single one of Theaetetus's theories of knowledge to survive. Like the comic stage that turns on itself, this skeptical method induces a line of thinking only to bring it to its own destruction, the germ of which is in the beginning. And yet, this destruction leaves behind strays that may be adopted by future philosophers who will raise the orphan into their own developed theory or school of thought, which was indeed the destiny of several of Theaetetus's abandoned strays.

Philosophical orphans sometimes take the form of philosophical fragments, underdeveloped concepts still in their infancy. But philosophical orphans also take a negative form, phantom concepts. Hegel, for one, adopts a phantom self that he locates in the negative space left by comedy and skepticism. The comic hero, including both the actor and spectator, leans into the space of the stage's aborted contents and experiences tranquility in the negativity of its terminated essence. And yet the space of determinate negation should not be conflated with a second indeterminate negativity found in this very same space. Through its doubling, negativity relates to itself, not as an undifferentiated unity, but by grasping itself in the crack that divides pure Nothingness. The divided structure of self-relating negativity, which is not itself self-identical, gives rise to the "pure certainty of self."[53]

In Hegel's historical drama, ancient comedy and skepticism are two kinds of negative movements that give birth to a second negative double. Ancient comedy and skepticism abort their own contents, leaving nothing positive in their place. What appears to be an act of self-termination sets Spirit on fire, giving birth to a movement that cannot yet be identified. The negative space of art-religion is a clearing with which one (the artist, the philosopher, the audience) fully identifies. From another (non)perspective, the negative space fully identifies with the actuality of its own nothingness. Negativity stirs within negativity: "The individual self is the negative power through which and in which the gods [and all that they represent] . . . vanish. At the same time, the individual self is not the emptiness of this disappearance but, on the contrary, preserves itself in this very nothingness, abides with itself and is the sole actuality. In it the religion of Art is consummated and has completely returned into itself."⁵⁴ The skeptic's path of doubt, which belongs to Being, "leads" to Nothing's certainty in itself. This foundational self, a certainty born in doubt, cannot be counted as a thinking ego. The emergence of the subject is a double negativity that does not take the form of a negation of negation that results in a new positive position, but rather the form of negative twins: the aborted object and the phantom subject.

In Hegel's narration of art-religion, the birth of the subject comes at the price of the termination of the entire form of life, since the gods are not separate from us but representations of different aspects of human experience. Thus, a certain shape of self is formed in the shadow of the aborted gods, a shadow which the shadow herself cannot shake. The phantom is haunted by her aborted twin. Nothing haunts nothing. The negative space of the aborted gods will not be completely filled by the new gods and new values and customs of the next stage of history. Instead, what appears as subject is necessarily constituted by a kind of double negativity represented at the end of the ancient world by the comic abortion of art-religion. Each new appearance of Self will be sustained by the negativity of an aborted object and its phantom double.

As we see in chapter 3, the newly formed Self, who emerges in this brief but critical passage at the end of "Art-Religion" steps into the leading role of "Revealed Religion." At the end of art-religion, the lights go down, and after a brief intermission, the drama resumes with Christianity, which opens with a repetition of comic negativity. On this new stage, God himself takes over the midwife's duties from the comic poet and skeptic philosopher. In ushering in the birth of his own son, God aborts the object of revealed religion before it has begun by terminating himself as One. Thus, the scene of the nativity causes even the skeptic to gasp, "Oh my God, what has God done?"⁵⁵ At the incarnation, what has already occurred on the comic stage sinks in deeper. The morning after the Bacchic revels, the sun rises, and Agave's laughter turns to sickly horror as she sees that the severed head of her enemy is her own flesh and blood.

In act 2, "Revealed Religion," the subject of comedy and skepticism takes the form of the "compound" of Christ.⁵⁶ From one perspective, Christ is a compound of a new appearance of the divine-human subject and the determinate negation of God-as-Absolute (B | N). From another perspective, the life and death of Christ are a double negativity (N | N) that reveals what was already true of God the Absolute (B | B). The object of revealed religion may be counted as three-in-one but equally as four-in-one when negativity is counted twice. With one tetradic turn, the crack in Christ exposes the originary crack in the Absolute.

In the beginning was the Stutter, and the Stutter was with God, and the Stutter was God. In a moment of heightened drama in the Hebrew scriptures, God reveals himself to Moses, who leads the Hebrew people despite being marked by a tragic stutter.⁵⁷ Moses calls himself into question, "Who *am I* that . . . I should bring the people out of Egypt?" And yet, it is God who stutters on Mount Sinai when he insists on his Being, pure Being: *Ehyeh asher Ehyeh*.[58] Is it the frailty of the human embodied subject, represented by the question "Am I?" that introduces uncertainty into Being? Or does the "Am I?" repeat something that was already true of the Great I am? The repetition of "I am. I am!" points to an insecurity in divine Being. Why must God repeat himself? Was the first "I am" lacking? Why must he speak at all? On Mount Sinai, God exposes his crack by accidentally counting himself twice. As I explore in chapter 3, the great "I am, I am" plays out its internal drama through the mantra: nothing, nothing, nothing, nothing. Through the dramatic repetition of nothing, Self grasps her own negativity as both sacred and profane, human and divine. The dramatic coming-of-age story about Self's search for a body is simultaneously shadowed by the question of how to put an old age to the grave.

Chapter 3

The Birth of Community at the Comedy of the Cross

When read as a stage play, Hegel's *Science of Logic* begins with two protagonists in the form of the odd couple: Being and Nothing. The comic double is immediately redoubled in its mirror image: Nothing and Being. The redoubling offers a kind of dramatic resolution. But resolution does not take the form of a synthesis that releases the tension between the first two as we move forward to act three. Instead, Being and Nothing remain eternally suspended (*aufgehoben*) in an oscillating movement named Becoming. Although suspension, in my interpretation of dialectic, does not give way to synthesis, the doubling of the double reveals something new that was already true from the beginning. The crack between Being and Nothing was already present in Being and is mirrored in Nothing.

In order to begin, the immediate conflict between Being and Nothing must be overcome, but the conflict is revealed to belong to Being itself, which leaves little hope for reconciliation. How can two be unified when One is not unified with itself? What kind of dramatic resolution can be found in the revelation of the crack within Being? Far from being left behind in the beginning, Being and Nothing—and the crack between two and within each—reemerge under the guise of new names.[1] Being and Nothing make cameos in Hegel's writings on aesthetics and religion under the thinly veiled disguise of *it is* and *it is not*. Universal indeterminate affirmation and negation take on the form of the particular although still impersonal. In staging *it is* and *it is not*, ancient tragedy and comedy play out the social significance of the abstract oscillation between Being and Nothing. As spectators we hold our breath as we watch Being and Nothing step onto the stage and attempt to grasp their particular historical existence.

This chapter circles back to ancient tragedy and comedy to locate their dramatic redoubling in the incarnation and crucifixion of Christ. Hegel's analysis of Christianity follows directly on the heels of Greek drama. There are multiple renditions of this dramatic double in the *Phenomenology of Spirit*,[2] *Lectures on Aesthetics*,[3] and *Lectures on the Philosophy of Religion*.[4]

The sequence is strange from a purely historical perspective. Christ appears to rise like a phoenix from the rubble of Greek polytheism. But when viewed through a theatrical lens, Hegel's staging of Greek drama and Christianity form one dialectical tetrad in the reiteration of the dramatic proclamations "it is" and "it is not." In a helpful comment in his lecture notes, Hegel encourages this theatrical interpretation, referring to Christianity as a "divine drama," following Greek drama.[5] The curtain of Greek art-religion sets on the spectacular emergence of Self in darkness. Self is nothing more than a hissing from the crack between comedy and skepticism, two negative stages standing side by side. Self also hisses between two successive historical acts in Hegel's spiritual drama, Greek ethical life and the ethical community of revealed religion. Despite Self's confidence, our comic hero at the end of Greek ethical life appears to be nothing more than hot gas.

Revealed religion opens with a plot twist as the infantile phantom twins (the disembodied split Self from chapter 2) procure a human body, which is named Christ. In the shape of a human body, the negative double takes the shape of a monster rather than a ghost. Like Frankenstein's monster, the "monstrous compound" of "God-man" must be put to death by the rabble.[6] Self loses her body almost as quickly as she obtains it, a conclusion that reveals yet another plot twist.

As a shadow of a shadow, self-relating negativity poses little threat. The appearance of nothing against the backdrop of a burning stage is met with the skeptic's tranquility and the comic poet's detached laughter. From ashes to flesh, Self takes the shape of a human body. At the sight of the monstrous compound in the flesh, the philosopher and comic poet can no longer keep their cool. New affects erupt from the players, the gods, the audience, and from the crack that constitutes self and stage. Hegel tells the story with a melodramatic flair inspired by Lutheranism: Horror! Joy! Anguish! Although the structure of Self does not change from one stage to the next, the emergence of new affects indicates a shift in negativity's self-relation. From ancient comedy to the comedy of the cross, the shadow grasps herself first as self, then as *this* human body, then as a communal body, and only then concretely as self.

In his *Lectures on the Philosophy of Religion*, Hegel explicitly frames the life and death of Christ as drama in direct comparison with Greek drama. Although he doesn't specify the genre of divine drama, he discusses its capacity for profound sorrow. As mentioned above, there are different perspectives through which Christianity may be grasped as a drama that parallels ancient drama: the perspective of the human actors, divinity, the audience, and the constituting crack. The different perspectives on the same story influence whether the drama is experienced as tragedy, comedy, or horror.

When ancient drama and Christianity are placed side by side, Christ initially falls neatly into the paradigm of the tragic hero. In his incarnation, Christ mirrors Antigone, the hero who is suspended between what appears to be two external orders: the divine and the human. And yet the life of Christ verges on comedy because the shape of the double is revealed to belong to this one body, a truth that tragedy concealed. The subjectivity of Christ is nothing more than a crack: a crack between divine being and human being (B | B), between the affirmation of divine-in-man and the negation of God-as-One (B | N), and finally, the crack between two self-relating negativities, represented by the double death of God first in the incarnation, then in the crucifixion (N | N).

Moving from tragedy to comedy, Hegel's interest in ancient drama shifts from the repressed pathos of the tragic hero to the emergent affects of the audience of comedy. Reading Christianity as drama, he likewise shifts his focus from the pathos of Christ to the affective experience of the audience of the cross. The audience extends to the reader who, when reflecting on the image of the cross, steps into the position of a spectator of the drama. The attention to the audience of the cross is particularly strong in the lectures on religion where Hegel imagines the reader's experience of the cross: "Here any merely historical view [of Christ] comes to an end . . . the subject itself is drawn into the process."[7] In the *Phenomenology of Spirit*, the cross is itself a stage character who pops up at unexpected moments, both in "Revealed Religion" and, in the last instance, stealing the show at the finale of Spirit.[8] For the Old Hegelians, the "Calvary of Absolute Spirit" is not only the last stanza of the *Phenomenology of Spirit* but also the last stage of history as such. But from another perspective on the same ending, the cross does not bring closure to a grand historical narrative. Its reappearance indicates an itch that cannot be scratched. The repetition of the cross questions why "we" (Hegel's readers, contemporaries, and perhaps readers today) remain fixated on the cross. At the very least, the image still has the power to arouse new emotions, pulling its spectators into its drama. What does the image of the cross allow both believers and nonbelievers to experience on the level of affect that perhaps has yet to be realized as concept? The pairing of Greek drama with the drama of Christianity raises more questions. What kinds of communal affects arise in response to the dramatic repetition of the death of the gods? What changes through the transformative power of dramatic repetition and destruction?

Ancient tragedy draws a clear division between the conflict on the stage and the audience members perched safely in their seats. The tragic hero cannot fully comprehend the great mess she finds herself in. She swallows an initial wave of despair to convince the chorus that everything is exactly as it should be. *Everything is fine. It really is.* The audience, however, clearly sees that despite her insistence, the hero is damned. The audience, however, cannot see how the destruction of the hero has anything to do with their own lives.

Comedy delights in exposing the tragic blindness of the audience through the revelation that the conflict between the characters on stage belongs to society.[9] Comic release allows for an outburst of emotions both from the stage and from the audience, which is no longer safely separated from the stage.

A portal opens between the theatrical stage and the historical stage. Release does not offer resolution, but unleashes the drama within the audience.

Ancient tragedy deceives the audience by blinding it to the truth of its own contradiction, initially presented as belonging to another (the guilty hero). Ancient comedy exposes this farce, inviting the audience members to transfer their humiliation onto the divine, by laughing down the gods. Yet, as Hegel emphasizes in his lectures, the liberated laughter of the audience at the comic demystification of the gods conceals yet another layer of repression. What is destroyed cannot be so easily dismissed. The aborted form of an old way of life returns to haunt the midwife. The destruction of what we declare to be *no more* is at once the destruction of everything, life as we know it. The comic celebration of a society's break with a tragic stage cannot be separated from the sting of the necessary destruction of a former way of life.

Ancient comedy reproduces and conceals the "unhealed sorrow" of tragedy.[10] Although Hegel anachronistically stages ancient comedy as dialectically following tragedy, comedy does not overcome tragic contradiction. Nor does Christianity overcome the contradiction that shaped ancient ethical life. By repeating tragedy and comedy in the life and death of Christ, divine drama exposes the two opposed stages as mirror images in suspension. At the cross, ancient tragedy sees itself comically as comedy grasps itself tragically, each seizing itself by the contradiction that constitutes its stage.

Hegel's drama of revealed religion highlights the repressed pathos of the tragic hero, who must choke back his tears as he leaves the garden and soberly utters, "Thy will be done."[11] While Christ's life mirrors the tragic hero, his death mirrors the death of the gods in comedy. As with the audience of ancient comedy, the spectator of the cross is also taken up into the drama. The drama of Good Friday spills out into everyday life. The crucifixion of Christ follows the ancient ritual of celebrating the execution of the criminal as a public comedy. Yet, the detached laughter of the comic audience at the cross is interrupted by an unexpected swell of anguish.

The anguish that arises out of Good Friday laughter represents the deepening of self-relation in the surfacing of a crack within the communal body and each of its members. With the death of Christ, one particular substantiation of the embodied negative double breathes its last breath. The veil of the temple splits in two as the crack in pure Being surfaces in one and all.[12] The crucifixion is a mere repetition of what has already occurred in the beginning: of the beginning of the drama, of Genesis before the beginning begins. However, the contradiction that once appeared to belong to this one exceptional being is revealed in each individual and the collective. Comedy's greatest insight tickles Spirit to the bone. In a moment of comic-anguish, the monstrous compound that slips through the clumsy grasps of philosopher and comic poet is revealed to belong equally to all.[13]

Hegel pairs the Greek dramatic reconciliation achieved through a flight from anguish (i.e., abstract freedom) with the dramatic reconciliation represented by the picture of Christ's suffering (i.e., concrete freedom). He writes in his notes on the lectures, "In contrast [to the Greek representation of reconciliation], there is in the higher forms of religion the consolation that the absolutely final end will be attained despite misfortune so that the negative changes around into affirmation. 'The sufferings of this present time are a path to blessedness.'"[14] Drama utilizes repetition to heighten our sense of what has been lost in the necessary destruction of what we once believed was our essence. The repetition of the death of God is a stubborn echo of an aborted way of life that we thought we happily left behind. It forces us to pause to allow the moment of destruction to sink in, pointing to something that is left unresolved even where there is nothing left to destroy.

Drawing on two accounts of ancient and divine drama in the *Lectures on the Philosophy of Religion* and *Phenomenology of Spirit*, I read Greek tragedy and comedy and the incarnation and crucifixion as one tetradic dialectical turn composed of two theatrical doubles: (1) the tragedy of tragedy | the tragedy of comedy, and (2) the comedy of tragedy | the comedy of comedy. The repetition of the stages of tragedy and comedy in the life and death of Christ allows Spirit to grasp itself by the materiality of its crack. Negativity on the Greek comic stage is expressed through detached laughter directed toward the destruction of a conflict viewed as belonging to another and another time. At the comic stage of the cross, the response to negativity is comic-anguish: the realization that the audience is not separate from what is destroyed for their own liberation. The death of the laughing gods in Greek comedy and the serious figure of Christ in the comedy of the crucifixion reveal an unhealed sorrow even in the happy separation from a former oppressive way of life. For even in recognizing the gods, and more importantly, the broken societal structures that they represent, as the source of our suffering, something profoundly personal is experienced in what must be destroyed for the emancipation of an entire society. What is this anguish experienced in the freedom of bringing the old gods to the grave once and for all?

It Is | It Is Not

The process of bringing a conflicted social and political order to the grave is represented in ancient drama by the death of the gods. As Marx famously claims, the old gods must die twice, once tragically and once again comically.[15] Yet, where Marx sees double, Hegel has four eyes, seeing double, twice-two. The old gods must die twice and then twice again.

The first tragic death of the gods occurs with a surrogate sacrifice. A human being is killed in place of the clashing gods when the societal order that they uphold is shown to be contradictory. For Hegel, this tragic sacrifice of the human individual for the sake of something identified as external and absolute is exemplified on the Greek stage by Sophocles's *Antigone*.[16] While the conflict between Antigone and Creon is presented as a conflict between divine law and human law, each tragic hero acts in defense of a particular social role which he or she sees as absolute. Antigone understands her disobedience to Creon's order to be justified by divine law, which demands the act of burial out of respect for the dead. She tells Creon: "I [did not] think your proclamation so strong / That you, a mortal man, could overrule the laws / Of the gods, that are unwritten and unfailing. / For these live not now or yesterday / But always."[17] Antigone understands her obedience to a divine order as pitting her against the political order. She cannot see that the divine order that she perceives as positioning her against human law is also a product of human law. In the *Phenomenology of Spirit*, Hegel argues that Antigone does not act out of a personal love for her brother as a unique individual but out of devotion to the impersonal role of Sister, which reflects a specific Greek conception of woman and her role in society.[18] Her dutiful enactment of this role belonging to the private sphere of the household, which Antigone sees as governed by divine order, drives her action and the account she gives of it. Likewise, Creon's commitment to the law of the public sphere, which he sees as unalterable, reflects his treatment of a political order as absolute. As Hegel points out in his *Lectures on the Philosophy of Religion*, each aspect of Greek life (natural life, interior life, political life) is represented by a different god. Zeus, the god of the state, is represented as ruling over the *polis*, demanding that Man keep peace over his community by punishing those who cause disorder.[19]

Hegel argues that the Greeks saw many of the gods as personifications of the aspect of finite life that they represented. Yet, the representational figure of the divinities suggests something absolute or unalterable about the way society enacted that sphere.[20] "The gods of the Greeks [were] products of human imagination . . . formed by human hand" to affirm a certain kind of human activity or experience.[21] The tragic perspective mistakes these representational images for an actual power that dictates what is essential to that area of human life. Thus, the conflict that Sophocles highlights between two human individuals, who see themselves as representing two conflicting absolute orders, points to a contradiction intrinsic to Greek life.[22] As Terry Pinkard argues, "The conflict between Antigone and Creon is . . . an expression of a kind of essentially institutionalized clash between men and women in Greek life, which is itself an expression of a conflict between equally essential principles of Greek life."[23] In this respect, both Antigone and Creon act rightly according to the ethical law of the social sphere to which each is assigned according to the binary construction of their gender. These roles are reinforced as essential to Greek life through the figures of the gods that rule over each sphere. In treating his or her role with serious reverence, each is found guilty according to the law of the other: "both are in the wrong," Hegel writes, "because they are one-sided, but both are also in the right."[24]

True reconciliation requires the destruction of the social and political system that holds man and woman, politics and family, public life and private life in contradiction. But both of Sophocles's tragic heroes in *Antigone* would rather die for their role than deny its absolute rightness according to the established order. A superficial reconciliation is achieved through the destruction of a *human* representative of one of the absolute, yet conflicting, maxims embedded in the social and political structures of the community. Antigone's physical death at the end of the play is a reiteration of her social death, implicit at the beginning of the drama and preexisting her birth. In this sense, Creon can be seen as equally tragic because of his submission to an order that he sees as unalterable. Both individuals sacrifice themselves for the sake of maxims they accept as absolute.

In the oscillation between Antigone and Creon—two figures formally opposed who mirror each other's contradictory contents—we find yet another tetradic dialectical turn. To illustrate this tetradic structure, I return to the ancient skeptic slogan "nothing more" or "no more" (short for X is no more Y than Z). The statement "nothing more" initially suggests a double affirmation (both | and) but with repetition it becomes a double negation (neither | nor). The statement "Antigone is no more a sister than a citizen" initially implies that Antigone's role within the household and the state are of equal value. She is split between two beings. But the repetition of this phrase, "Antigone is no more a sister than a citizen" reveals that since Antigone is both a sister and a citizen, and these roles demand opposing ethical actions in Greek society, Antigone can neither exist as a subject within the *oikos* nor within the *polis*. Likewise, Creon is no more sovereign than man, no more symbolic than embodied. The negative subjectivities of both characters are no more a (both | and) than a (neither | nor). They are the crack between double affirmation and double negation. The doubling of the split subject magnifies the fact that both subjects are nothing more than the enactment of the nothing more. The opposed sides of the double are already doubles of themselves, split by the comma that holds together and separates each (Antigone | Antigone) and (Creon | Creon).

Two sides mirror each other, reproducing a conflict belonging to all, without being symmetrical or held equally accountable for the blame. Antigone's public punishment is intended to provide a sense of resolution for the whole of society through the destruction of the representative of one side of a conflict that plagues the community. In partial reconciliation, as Marx explains, a representative "must stand for the notorious crime of the whole society so that liberation from the sphere appears universal."[25] The hero in ancient tragedy is sacrificed for a crime belonging to all since the contradiction is not personal but embedded in a way of life that is upheld as absolute.

Hegel reflects in his lectures on the superficial reconciliation of tragedy: "there remains an unhealed sorrow . . . because an individual perishes."[26] Yet, even in the face of the senseless death of the individual, tragic experience paradoxically has little to do with suffering and anguish. There remains an "unhealed sorrow" in tragic reconciliation precisely because of tragedy's blindness to suffering and anguish. The tragic figure's attitude of seriousness and reverence toward the action demanded of her prevents her from experiencing anguish at her own loss. She remains stoic even when she is sentenced to die in the place of the god or the ethical maxim she defends as absolute. When her conflicting social duties demand her destruction, she does not long for a world in which her possibilities might have been otherwise. Instead the tragic hero soberly affirms the absolute rightness of her deed. As Hegel writes in the *Phenomenology of Spirit*, tragic characters "are artists, who . . . give utterance to the inner essence, they prove the rightness of their action, and the 'pathos' which moves them is soberly asserted."[27]

In moments when Antigone does sense the absurdity of her situation, her affective response is misdirected. Although Antigone does experience remorse late in the play, she never turns on the gods themselves or the Greek conventions that the figures of the gods reinforce. Antigone responds to opposition not with despair but with laughter. Creon emphasizes that Antigone's unredeemable crime is that she has laughed defiantly at the law and, thus, the king himself: "She laughed at having done it. I must be / No man at all, in fact, and she must be / The man."[28] And yet despite this appearance of comic rebellion, Antigone cannot direct her irreverent laughter toward the contradictory customs that ultimately lead to her execution. Her laughter itself is one-sided. And so the joke is on Antigone, whose derisive laughter is directed at another who mirrors her own position. She does not see that she is equally the object of her own derisive laughter. Laughter that properly belongs to Spirit sees that "the ethical powers themselves appear as severed and as coming into collision."[29] Yet, any flashes of spirited laughter or anguish—vague detections of a contradiction within the very core of Greek life—are ultimately silenced by the tragic hero's solemn belief in the rightness of her deed.

As Hegel sees it, the tragic acceptance of one's societal role as unalterable offers one a deep sense of peace, a deceptive sense of purpose, and a superficial sense of freedom. In his *Lectures on the Philosophy of Religion*, he writes:

> Inner peace [is achieved] in saying: It is this way and there is nothing to be done about it; I must be content with it. This conviction implies that I am content with it and thus that freedom is present after all, in that it is my own state . . . In adopting this standpoint and saying, "It is this way," one has set aside everything particular, one has renounced it . . . Human beings have withdrawn into this pure rest, this pure being, this "it is." In that abstract freedom there is . . . in fact no solace for human beings. One needs solace only insofar as one demands a compensation for a loss, but here no compensation is needed, for one has given up the inner root of what one lost. One has wholly surrendered what has been given up.[30]

The tragic proclamation "it is" testifies to the deep yet unacknowledged anguish of a subject who cannot recognize what was deprived of her from the beginning. Robert Williams characterizes Hegelian tragic reconciliation as a combination of the affects of grief and satisfaction: we grieve the death of the individual, but are satisfied at the resilience of the ethical maxims that remain intact in their rightness.[31] Williams explains, "The point of tragedy lies not simply in catastrophe or suffering but in the satisfaction of the spirit. And what satisfies spirit is not suffering for its own sake, but rather a final recognition that there is right and justification on both sides of a tragic conflict."[32] Tragic reconciliation offers a strong sense of satisfaction. However, I would argue that this sense of inner peace prevents tragic resolution from achieving concrete freedom.

Benjamin's analysis of the logic of consolation in modern melodrama helps elucidate Hegel's analysis of consolation as inoperable in ancient drama, which denies the need for solace. Benjamin defines the logic of consolation as the theatrics of superficial resolution, which justifies or glorifies the suffering and death of individuals in the name of a higher purpose.[33] In Benjamin's view, resistance to consolation is impossible for the melancholic consciousness of early modernity, represented by the German *Trauerspiel*.[34] In Hegel's reading of ancient tragedy, however, both the acceptance and resistance of consolation are also impossible for the ancient tragic hero—not because her grief is inconsolable—but because she sees no need for consolation. Even in her own death, she has no sense of loss. In order to accept consolation (or refuse consolation and demand compensation, as Marx and Benjamin would have it), we must first experience the anguish of our own senseless suffering. But in the case of tragedy, the logic of consolation, which falsely elevates the senseless death of individuals to a meaningful sacrifice, is already at work in the first instance of the hero's action. She has accepted her role and its consequences before she is found guilty, before she must give an account of herself to the chorus.

Although the death of an individual is never properly mourned in tragedy, comedy has its revenge on what blinded the hero to her own suffering. The gods are dragged out on stage and made to step forward and speak for themselves before the audience. In tragedy, the gods hide behind a human subject, who is sacrificed to protect the status of an order given as absolute. This human representation of the divine is inverted in comedy when the gods enter the drama and are exposed as mere representatives of a contradictory ethical order belonging to society. In comedy, the deities can no longer hide behind their fierce devotees who, without questioning the gods, die in their place.

Aeschylus's *Eumenides*, Hegel's primary example of Greek tragedy in the *Phenomenology of Spirit*, verges on comedy when the gods and the Furies appear on the stage.[35] What appears to be a conflict between the human and divine order in Sophocles's tragedies is exposed as a contradiction within the divine itself by Aeschylus, who depicts the gods quarreling among themselves.

As Hegel explains in his lectures, the warring old gods and new gods in Aeschylus's play illustrate that "the gods are scattered . . . [their unity] is without content, is empty necessity, an empty, unintelligible power."[36] In presenting the gods themselves as divided, Aeschylus frames tragic opposition as a conflict that is internal to a single order. We see the impossibility of self-sameness even within the divine.

The staged tension between the old and the new exposes divinity as historical while exposing the particular historical stage reflected in the drama as tragically divided. The comic insight of this double exposure invites the audience to grasp itself by its own contradictions. What does the audience do with this insight? Aristophanes achieves comic resolution by setting fire to his stage. The comic stage turns on itself, spilling out onto the historical stage. The audience laughs in the face of the gods for whom they once stoically laid down their lives. Does the audience's outburst reflect its members' own impulse to burn it all down?

In the *Phenomenology of Spirit*'s "Art-Religion," the hymn represents a kind of activity in which a collective of artists and worshippers are not separate from their creation or from the divine. Comic destruction on the stage sparks a vision of a kind of collectivity formed in the gleeful destruction of its own creation. The shadow of self that confidently emerges in the collapse of an entire way of life foreshadows the emergence of a community that grasps itself as such in its own comic destruction, in which agent and object are one.

Comedy appears to shatter the tragic perspective when divine contradiction mirrors societal contradiction back to the audience. Hegel, however, remains suspicious of comic resolution that comes too easily. The festivals where the dramas were performed celebrated the human content displayed in the glorified form of the gods on stage. At the festivals for Dionysus and Demeter, where the gods are made the object of laughter on the comic stage, exposed as all too human, the participants and audience members "let the divine be seen in themselves, in their joyfulness and cheerfulness."[37] And yet, as Hegel argues, even in the exposure of the content of the divinities as belonging to humanity, "freedom . . . is still an abstract freedom. To this extent it is a flight."[38] Comic laughter and cheerfulness serve as a flight from a deeper recognition that is repressed in witnessing the destruction of the gods. Even when the divine itself is exposed as belonging to the human order, the conventions and beliefs that must be destroyed for the reconciliation of the community are nevertheless treated in ancient comedy with a spirit of detachment.

On one hand, the gods are exposed as indistinguishable from the human characters on the stage. The collapse of the distinction between humanity and divinity represents the understanding that values once taken as absolute are products of a historically constituted way of life. The gods do not dictate human life, but are the expression of a particular society. On the other hand, the figures of the gods, who belong to society, may be destroyed without bringing further harm to the resilient human subject. The suffering of the gods does not appear to cause the human beings to suffer. The destruction of the roles and values that the human subject once claimed as her essence does not seem to shake her.

Comedy inverts the human representation of the absolute with the divine representation of humanity. However, ancient comedy continues to mirror tragedy because it represses a deeper sense of anguish in witnessing comic destruction. The tragic hero could not mourn the loss of her own life in Greek drama. Neither are the gods, who are no longer viewed as separate from human life, able to grieve when it is their turn to be put to death. In Aristophanes's *Frogs*,[39] for example, Dionysus and his human slave Xanthias make an excursion to the underworld. When Dionysus is convicted of robbery, Xanthias must determine his master's proper punishment: "Oh, give him the whole works. Rack, thumbscrew, gallows, cat-o'-nine-tails: pour vinegar up his nostrils, pile bricks on his chest—anything you like."[40] At this point in the play, the audience can determine no substantial difference between the authority of the god and his mortal slave. In fact, the human slave who is portrayed as the stronger, braver, and shrewder of the two often appears at moments to be more godlike than the god. The citizens of the underworld are likewise unable to distinguish between the mortal and immortal. To put divinity to the test, they inflict violence on both figures to see which one can withstand physical torture. To prove their own divinity, Dionysus and Xanthius each respond to the violence with wisecracks and laughter. To every blow each responds, "Ha! I feel nothing!" "It is nothing!"

On the theatrical and historical stage of comedy, the human subject comes to see her role as determined by society, but also comes to see herself as a member of society who is equally marked by conflict. In understanding her mask as such, she does not drop the mask but reclaims it as something that society as a whole has the power to destroy in this particular form. When the content of an established way of life is exposed as farce, the creative agency of the artist can be replenished, as a society turns on what it no longer takes seriously. In comedy, the artist reclaims her creative agency by laughing in the face of a creation that she formerly exalted as a god.

Hegel himself locates the birth of community at the foot of the cross, representing humanity's most shameful act. However, his reading of ancient comedy fuels the revolutionary fantasies of the Young Hegelians, who envision a comic community formed in their own self-destruction. As I discuss in the following chapters, comedy demands compensation for what the human being has been denied—life, dignity, creativity, solidarity. The gods of the old order must be made to suffer the horror of the historical stage of comedy. The tragic assertion "it is" shatters as a community looks upon the rubble of a disinherited past and claims instead, "Ha, it is nothing!" The comic community does not pause to lament the failure of their creations but rather looks upon the destruction of the past as the freedom to re-create itself from the rubble.

Yet, for Hegel, the freedom claimed by the spirit of ancient comedy remains abstract because of this dismissal of loss in comic destruction. The unhealed sorrow of the tragic subject is preserved in the collective denial of the experience of loss, even in the necessary destruction of structures that caused us to suffer. Comic destruction, like the tragic figure, "has given up the inner root of what has been lost" and "has wholly surrendered what has been given up."[41] The conversion of tragic seriousness into comic levity—the displacement of "it is" with "it is nothing"—equally neglects the experience of anguish at the exposed absurdity of an old stage. The tragic form is preserved in its comic double that appears to negate it. Comedy demands compensation for a historical stage that denies life to those born within its cracks. But does it alter tragic consciousness? In reconciling the community in the present, does comedy achieve reconciliation of the present with the memory of the past?

The Tragedy of the Incarnation | The Comedy of the Cross

As I explore in the following chapter, the Young Hegelians draw on ancient laughter in Hegel's aesthetics to battle the attitude of Christian seriousness that they identify as characteristic of modern Prussia. Hegel himself ironically locates comic release precisely in the attitude of Christian seriousness. Ancient laughter initially echoes the hero's seriousness in comedy's simple opposition to tragedy. To find release from tragic seriousness, Hegel turns to the expression of seriousness on yet another dramatic stage. In contrast to Spinoza, who argues that a societal affect can only be overcome by a stronger opposing affect, in a Hegelian framework, an affect undergoes transformation through the repetition of that very same affect.[42] In ancient drama, seriousness and laughter are held apart, appearing as dispositions belonging to separate dramatic stages. For this reason, both tragic affirmation and comic negation fail to grasp the negativity of an originary loss: the ontological and political impossibility of unity with oneself and society. The weight of loss is concealed on one stage by the spirit of gravity and on the other by the spirit of frivolity.

In my reading of Hegel's drama, the coupling of tragedy and comedy is itself repeated, once tragically in Greek life and then comically in Christianity. Greek comedy remains tragic, because the stages of tragedy and comedy remain in formal opposition. We recall that both Agathon and Aristophanes drift off to sleep before Socrates is able to convince them that the tragic dramatist and comic poet must be embodied by the same individual.[43] In order for Greek tragedy and comedy—both tragic in their one-sidedness—to be repeated comically, both stages must be grasped as inherently involved in the other without collapsing the distinction. As Dolar puts it, "Perhaps this is what comedy does, it sees double in what ought to be clearly separated . . .

and precisely by seeing them as a couple, as the double of each other, as twins, it produces the comic effect . . . There is an object x that emerges between the two."[44] The comic redoubling of tragedy and comedy themselves results in the transformation of the comic consciousness as something that no longer simply opposes while simultaneously mirroring tragic blindness to loss and suffering. In the redoubling of tragedy and comedy in the life and death of Christ, seriousness and laughter come to their full expression on the same stage. Comic-anguish emerges when seriousness and laughter each respond to the other, reflecting a protagonist who is both the tragic hero and comic relief. In the doubling of the dramatic double, history unfolds in four stages: the tragedy of tragedy, the tragedy of comedy, the comedy of tragedy, the comedy of comedy.

The incarnation and crucifixion of Christ dialectically redouble the death of the gods on the Greek stage. While the incarnation, the comedy of tragedy, is a story of the absurdity of an individual caught between two coexisting and irreconcilable orders, the cross is a story of the birth of a community who no longer sees this contradiction as between two independent orders. Nor does this comic community view the conflict situated within the divine as a separate entity that determines human life. At Good Friday, drama is elevated to the comedy of comedy, because the conflicting orders identified within the singular figure of Christ are witnessed at the event of the crucifixion as something inherent to one and all. At the death of Christ, one who is both divine and the despised criminal is seen as equally belonging to every aspect of life.

The incarnation is the story of the first death (third in my tetrad) of the divine absolute. At this event God does not dissolve into laughter like the ancient gods in comedy, but into "the finitude, the weakness, the frailty of human nature."[45] At the end of "Art-Religion," Self simultaneously steps into this very same feeble body. The Christian representation of "God as man" resembles the festivals dedicated to the gods but celebrating the ingenuity of the playwrights, the skills of the performers, while acknowledging every aspect of human experience as sacred.[46] The victorious double of ancient comedy (Subject | Substance) is celebrated once again in the incarnation with a slight twist: (Substance | Subject).[47] In the vital inversion of the *tragedy of comedy* as *the comedy of tragedy*, the two terms of the odd couple are preserved. The image of the Christ child inspires jubilation as the content once attributed to a higher order is celebrated as belonging to this human being. With the elevation of the human being comes the sensation that all that was absolute and certain is not. The incarnation repeats the cry of ancient comedy: *the gods are dead, God himself is dead*.[48]

Repetition and inversion offer a new grasp on the same contents. With the reiteration of the comic utterance there is a shift in affective registers. In the transition from "Art-Religion" to "Revealed Religion," the experience of anguish occurs for the first time in both the *Phenomenology* and *Lectures on the Philosophy of Religion*.[49] As Findlay notes in his commentary, "What is to the comic consciousness a vast joke is to the Unhappy Consciousness a vast misery."[50] The Lutheran hymn cries out "God himself is dead" at the incarnation rather than the crucifixion. "This is the most frightful of all thoughts, that everything eternal and true *is not*," Hegel explains, "the deepest anguish, the feeling of complete irretrievability, the annulling of everything that is elevated, are bound up with this thought."[51] The audience of the incarnation is struck by the implication of the divine manifesting itself in this one feeble body. Far from achieving resolution, the incarnation of God as man points to the dissolution of the monotheistic absolute, magnifying what appears as a rift within the divine as well as a rift between the human and divine.

Although the proclamation of the incarnation is the same as that belonging to ancient comedy, Christ is a tragic hero in two ways. As in Aeschylus's play, the conflict appears within the absolute itself, revealing the universality and oneness of the divine as scattered. As Hegel explains in his lectures, the incarnation is represented through the divine figures of "God the Father" and "God the Son" because, according to reason and the senses, it is inconceivable that two could exist in one.[52] "Two cannot be one," he writes, "each is a rigid unyielding, independent being-for-self. Logic shows that this category of 'the one' is a poor category, the wholly abstract unit."[53] However, the conflict of the incarnation is not only in the representation of one God divided into two divine independent figures. The tragic conflict is also situated within Christ himself. The illogical notion of two-in-one is represented by the picture of incarnation through the "monstrous compound" of "God-man," Christ as representing both God and man.[54] In this way, tragic conflict appears similar to that of Sophocles's *Antigone* in which the irreconcilable conflict between divine law and human law is represented by one who must answer to both. Christ is *no more* God than man: the crack between both God and man and neither God nor man.

The incarnation further parallels *Antigone* since the conflict that both tragic heroes represent is not only between the divine and human but also between what is identified as more-than-human (both | and) and less-than-human (neither | nor) within this concrete human life. Like Antigone, Christ embodies unwavering devotion to a more-than-human order. Christ is not merely a man but represents the perfect human being. Despite the divine virtue of Antigone and Christ, both are simultaneously marked as less-than-human: the criminal who represents society's inability to achieve unity, both with itself and with the divine. Both Christ and Antigone are sentenced to be sacrificed for the sins of all.[55] Yet the two heroes are not completely parallel. Antigone must "choose" to represent one side of the conflict that determines her, forsaking her role as citizen under human law for her role as sister under divine law. The tragic stage makes the hero accountable for a contradiction belonging to society by offering her a superficial sense of agency. She must make a choice, although both choices lead to death. Christ, in contrast, as the illogical enactment of God-man, is bound to both sides of the conflict that are intrinsic to his existence, while making his existence impossible. This human individual is not a unity or oneness but a body that speaks to the crack that constitutes his existence.

The incarnation verges on comedy because it exposes the forced false choice between two sides that constitute one. One does not really have a choice in the matter. The tension between what is identified as more-than and less-than is understood as belonging to a human being. However, the life of Christ remains tragic because this conflict, which belongs to humanity as a whole, is presented as belonging to this one individual alone. The isolation of the divine as belonging to this man alone is reflected in the way the two sides of Christ, his divinity and his humanity, are opposed and separate.

To understand why the story of Christ as a figure that is both God and man is not yet comedy, we may turn to Zupančič's analysis of why the common understanding of comedy does not alter the tragic framework it repeats. In *The Odd One In*, Zupančič argues that the point of comedy is not, as it is often understood, to bring an aggrandized figure down to earth, exposing his weakness to reveal a side of the character that is as human as the rest of us. Such formulas function by making a character sympathetic and familiar while leaving their sovereignty unaltered. "Convincing as this fusion-in-representation might be, it still remains exactly that: a fusion of two," she writes, "we are still dealing with the classical mode of representation, a constellation of two elements in which one represents the other."[56] Her critique of the common formula of comedy, which fails to subvert what it appears to oppose, applies to the incarnation. The representation of the two heterogeneous sides of the monstrous compound of God-man does not truly disrupt or transform our understanding of either order. God the absolute is brought down to earth, so we can relate to the all too human side of Christ: his temptation, his desire, his tears and suffering. Yet his divine side exemplified in his perfect obedience to an order which reigns above all longing, fear, and sorrow ultimately remains untouched by his human struggles. The representation of Christ as both human and divine preserves the two orders in a relationship of opposition without allowing either side to undergo transformation and without allowing for our own transformed understanding of either side. Following Zupančič's logic, we may say that the point of the comedy of Christ is not the recognition of the miraculous manifestation of both the more-than-human and also less-than-human in one human body. Rather, "the point is precisely that the two cannot in fact be dissociated."[57] The comic insight that can be gained through the compound of God and man is the recognition of the sacred as intrinsic to every instance of human life, even what is marked less-than-human, such as the criminal. In Hegel's staging of the divine drama, the final death of God represents a transformed consciousness, which grasps the sacred and profane within its communal body.

Although the life of Christ may be read as a tragedy, the tragic hero of Christian mythology meets his final end, like the Greek gods, in comedy. The crucifixion—the comedy of comedy—is the second and final death of the Christian God who has already died once in the incarnation. The Roman custom of dressing a madman or criminal as a king or god to be paraded through the streets before his execution allowed a community to passionately denounce a figure that represented what was deeply perverse or contradictory within its society.[58] This joyful destruction of human corruption took the form of a ritualized comedy involving public participation. For an ancient audience, the story of the crucifixion is not striking because horrific violence has been done to God by humanity. The Greek gods were already tortured on the ancient comic stage. Instead, it is striking because the crucifixion of God-man is treated with such gravity. As Stephen Halliwell claims in *Greek Laughter*, although the public torture and execution of a criminal in the form of communal comedy was not an unusual event for the ancients, the story of the crucifixion would have been unsettling in the depiction of a god that does not participate in the audience's laughter as he is put to death. Halliwell writes, "To a pagan mind accustomed to the idea of cruel laughter as an appropriate behavior for the gods themselves, Jesus's meek submission to jeering humiliation was bound to seem utterly unintelligible: to some, indeed, a refutation of claims to divinity."[59] The serious tone of the comedy of the crucifixion emphasized in Christ's refusal to laugh contrasts vividly with Aristophanes's representation of Dionysus, who provokes his torturers in the underworld. In *Frogs*, the human slave and the god are tortured side by side in comedy. Both characters counter the jeering laughter of the audience with their own jeers and laughter, which only augments the laughter of the audience. In the story of Good Friday, the god and the two criminals are also tortured side by side while the audience laughs and jeers. The criminals next to Christ join in the audience's mockery, as would be expected. Christ's seriousness interrupts the laughter of the first criminal, who not only sees divinity in Christ but also recognizes himself as one who might dwell with divinity.[60] Ancient comedy permits us to laugh at the dissolution of the divine by depicting the gods as laughing along with us in their own destruction. The comic gravity of the crucifixion does not offer the audience the same sense of ease and detachment in bringing an old order to the grave.

The repetition of the double-death of the gods in the drama of Christianity allows for two realizations. One realization is that the less-than-human and more-than-human are not simply opposed. Instead, each is active in the other. The divine is within the criminal, and divinity itself is not above and opposed to the crimes of humanity. The second realization is that the illogical form (less than | more than), appearing to belong to this one who is destroyed for all, also belongs to one and all. The experience of excess in standing in awe of what is sacred and the horror of perversion is inherent to human life. The source of both anguish and joy at the image of the cross is the recognition that the representative who is executed for the sake of the reconciliation of society is not in fact other.

On the one hand, the response to the death of Christ made available to the audience of the comedy of the crucifixion is one of joy, since the criminal represents the corruption within society that inhibits harmonious social and political life. But on the other hand, the response is one of anguish. Comic laughter is disrupted by anguish, for in the face of the criminal-god at his execution is the reflection of every member of society. In his lectures, Hegel imagines the emotional experience of the audience being drawn up into the drama: "On the one hand, the death of Christ is still the death of a human being, a friend, who has been killed by violent means; but . . . this very death becomes the means of salvation, the focal point of reconciliation."[61] While the second death of the Christian God represents the possibility of concrete freedom, it also represents the loss of a friend, the death of something deeply familiar that disrupts the comic audience's ability to view the crucifixion as the death of one who is fully other. The identification is not with one side of Christ, his relatable humanity. The identification with the more-than and less-than in this man, now seen as in humanity, disrupts the categories of both oneness and otherness altogether.

The death of the God-criminal represents the death of a former image of the human being as in relationship to a higher order from which she received her essence. In this sense, what is sacrificed in the comic death of God—in both Greek comedy and its doubling in the death of Christ—is a particular imperfect representation through which the human being could grasp herself as sacred. However, as Louis Dupré argues in his article "The Despair of Religion," the difference between the death of the gods on the Greek comic stage and the death of Christ is that the latter forces its audience to grapple with the full weight of their own loss:

> The Greeks envisaged death as a mere cessation of activity, an abstract passage to the unknown without terror. But once subjectivity adopts the primary significance which it did in Christianity, death's negativity becomes the negation of subjectivity itself . . . In its theology of Christ's passion and death faith has succeeded in giving its fullest expression to the pain it brought into the world—the death of God, which is also the death of the soul. . . . The despair of the unhappy consciousness is, in fact, a sacred sadness unknown to the ancients. The mind unacquainted with it has never sounded the full depth of existence.[62]

The destruction of this singular enactment of the divine in man in Christianity gives rise to the fear that humanity is forever cut off from any relation to the absolute. The anguish experienced in the death of the divine criminal recognizes that destruction is not simply the positive restoration of creative agency. The destruction of an already failed, broken social and ethical system must itself be experienced as a second death. A new form of reconciliation and freedom comes only with the understanding that the joyous act of communal destruction of our own failed creations can be the experience of personal anguish at the loss of what was sacred according to a former social and ethical framework because it was through this framework that the individual understood herself and her place in society. In the idea that "Christ died for all . . . in Christ all have died,"[63] the individual experiences her own death in the death of the divine criminal.

It is not. It is not. It is not. It is not.

The negation of negation is the second/fourth death that pauses to dwell with death. Death pauses to reflect on itself. This time, negativity grasps itself not only abstractly as Self but in its historical existence as Community. Negation experiences itself not only in the death of this singular tragic hero but in the audience who identifies with the criminal-god. In this drama, Self is born in simple bliss when Greek ethical life comically collapses under its own contradiction. Community is born in Christianity's comic self-destruction. The shadow secures a material body in the form of a Community that grasps its Self by its historical contradiction. The second birth-abortion, represented by the cross, disrupts tranquility with an eruption of emergent communal affects. Skepticism itself deepens, allowing itself to feel the impact of what it cannot possibly understand. Layers of negativity reflect on themselves in their historical materiality: (1) the ontological negativity of an originary crack in Being or the Divine, (2) the impossibility of individual and communal unity, (3) the unjust death of individuals who were never permitted life by their society, and (4) the necessary destruction required to procure life for future generations. The outburst of communal affects, which are themselves in contradiction, are a response to what cannot be conceptualized: the experience of awe in grasping the sacred in the body of the community, the horror of humanity's most heinous acts of senseless violence, the grief of one's own loss and the suffering of those who remain out of touch, anguish at the necessary destruction of an entire way of life, and joy in the vision of emancipation and concrete freedom for all.

In my tetradic reading of Hegel's staging of art-religion and revealed religion, the tragic and comic call and response (it is | it is not) is repeated in the incarnation and crucifixion (it is | it is not). From another perspective, nothing is repeated. Nothing is dramatically repeated four times:

> *The tragedy of tragedy*: In ancient tragedy the sober utterance "It is" contains the implicit acceptance "I am not." The affirmation of divinity and the absoluteness of divine and human law entails the

immediate denial of the individual's relationship to her self, community, and world.

The tragedy of comedy: Ancient comedy gives voice to the victorious "I am" through the reversal "The gods are not," "It is nothing!" Or to put this differently, Nothing touches herself in her negativity and joyously affirms her own existence: "I am (nothing)!" The comic "I am (nothing)," which steps into the place of the tragic "It is/I am not," is initially as abstract as the gods it displaces. The newborn is abstract in her one-sidedness. The shadow of the shadow cannot yet grasp the historical Being of her Nothingness.

The comedy of tragedy: The mirror image of the end of art-religion and the beginning of revealed religion is an inversion that allows each side to reflect on its identical contents. The incarnation repeats the comic utterance "God is dead," "It is nothing." In the same breath it experiences the thrill of the divine manifested in this particular human body. Repetition offers a moment of retrospective anguish and joy. What have we done! What has God done! When we take the death of the divine more seriously than the gods take their own death, God can begin to wrestle with God's own death. Human society can begin to grieve loss and long for life.

The comedy of comedy: Comedy makes death dance to its own tune when it forces tragedy to take itself seriously and thus seize itself by the historicity of its contradiction. At Good Friday, God himself confesses, "It is finished," God's own anguish at the realization that "God is not." Self grasps the full weight of its own negativity by grasping itself by the flesh of its communal body. Comic release allows for joy, horror, and sorrow at the affirmation of the crack within one and all.

Nothing changes in the dramatic repetition of nothing, which is to say, *everything changes*. Negativity itself undergoes transformation by grasping its historical existence and material body. There is a shift in registers that allows something new to be experienced in the same confession. The divine drama of Christianity attempts to heal a wound that is unacknowledged in Greek comic resolution: the crack between the past and present, between tragedy and comedy, between divinity and humanity, the sacred and profane. As we will explore further, the Old Hegelians saw the cross as successfully mending the split in Being and in the world. But from another view, the affective potency of the cross is in its magnificent failure. Christianity's failure to overcome the split that it dramatically exposes in the figure of Christ allows its audience to experience a moment of anguish over our own failures to reconcile ourselves with our past failure. The dramatic failure of the divine to overcome the split is also the condition that allows divinity to be affirmed within the comic community at Good Friday. The cross offers the experience of comic-anguish—a mixture of relief and horror—with the realization that the conflict that we thought we crucified with the criminal belongs to all. The split that we identified in the tragic hero—first in Antigone, then in Christ—is revealed to be constitutive of all.

As William Desmond states, "One can say 'it is nothing' in many ways."[64] "It is nothing" is repeated four times in the tetradic dialectic from the tragedy of tragedy to the comedy of comedy: first in sober acceptance of an unjust order on the ancient tragic stage, then in tranquility and detached laughter on the comic stage, then in the anguish of the unhappy consciousness at the end of Greek life and the beginning of Christianity (delivered anachronistically through the voice of Luther), and finally with equal parts comic-anguish and relief at the cross. The newly born community looks at the incomprehensible manifestation of the sacred and profane in one single body and gasps, "It is not (other)."

The collective declaration "it is nothing" unto itself is revealed as limited, for while it allows for the concrete reconfiguration of political and social structures, vengeful laughter in the face of absurdity does not acknowledge the experience of personal identification with what must be destroyed. Hegel identifies Greek comedy as marking the end of art as representation, because the object of art grasps itself in the creative/destructive capacity of a commune of artists both on the stage and in the audience. However, he also emphasizes that the Greek affect of cheerfulness in the destruction of a past way of life reflects abstract freedom because the community and its past art/activity are still experienced as separate. For a community to destroy and re-create itself without feeling the seriousness of its loss, it must imagine itself as standing over and above its creation, that is, its social existence.

The fourth death of the gods (the second death of the Christian God) represents the possibility of parting ways with the failures of our past while still maintaining an attitude of seriousness toward that from which we seek to sever ourselves. In the representation of the execution of God-man, divinity is recognized as active in otherness/weakness/perversity/contradiction itself. With the demystification of a higher order belonging to the gods, the self-grounding acts of creation, destruction, and re-creation belonging to a self-conscious community are seen as sacred. To repeat Hegel's words, "There remains an unhealed sorrow in tragedy because an individual has perished."[65] The sorrow is unhealed in tragedy specifically because the representational sacrifice, whether human or divine, was seen as properly outside of the community. What is destroyed may be destroyed and forgotten happily because it does not belong and has no real connection with the members of the community who survive its death.

While the eruption of communal laughter is a response to contradictory symbolic and institutional structures that we can no longer take seriously, comic destruction must take loss and suffering more seriously than tragedy takes itself. If societal revolution is to offer not only compensation but also deep reconciliation, it must acknowledge that when we destroy the source of our suffering—those gods for whom we once laid down our lives—each of us also undergoes a kind of second death.

Chapter 4

Censoring Laughter

In Hegel's drama of art and religion, the abortion of ancient comedy, by its own hand, gives birth to Self, who confidently grasps itself by a crack in nothingness. The abortion of revealed religion, by its own hand, gives birth to Community when society grasps itself by its own contradictory contents, which are not separate from its Self. Negativity grasps itself by its materiality at a historical stage that reflects on its own destruction. Hegel's dramatization of tragedy, both on the ancient stage and at the incarnation, focuses on the tragic hero within the play. His dramatization of comedy, both on the ancient stage and at the cross, focuses on the comic audience. The audience's emergent communal affects—laughter, tranquility, anguish, sorrow, joy—indicate its own transformed self-relation as it grasps itself first in its abstract individuality, then concretely as a social body.

The richness of Hegel's historical scholarship is often in its infidelity to history, captured by his imaginative flourishes. Hegel extends upon Aristophanes's comedies and the Christian gospels by retelling well-known stories from the perspective of the audience, whom he restages as the protagonists of the dramas. The communal interiority of the audience, of course, remains an extension of his own fiction. This powerful narrative device breaks two fourth walls at once: the imagined fourth wall between ancient drama-religion and its audience; and the fourth wall between Hegel's dramatization of ancient drama-religion and his readers. The concept of the fourth wall is immediately a double, conceived simultaneously with the concept of breaking the fourth wall. Like an appliance designed with a defect, the fourth wall is designed with the possibility of being broken. This invisible wall, conjoined with its negation, were conventions of nineteenth-century theater and theory attributed to Denis Diderot, whom Hegel highlights as the quintessential dramaturge of modernity.[1] We have already seen Aristophanes address his audience through the voice of his lead chorus member speaking as a cloud in a somewhat provocative manner. But with the conceptualization of the fourth wall, the modern audience could fully feel the shock of its retroactive violation. The fourth wall comes into existence through its immediate termination. As a result, ancient and modern comedy provokes the modern audience in a way that Hegel could only imagine in his vision of the audience of ancient drama.

The violation of the fourth wall not only challenged the conventions of modern realistic theater but incited responses from the audience that were explicitly condemned by the Prussian censorship laws of 1842. The earlier 1819 Carlsbad Decrees placed heavy restrictions on the press, requiring a government license to publish, and ousted university professors and students whose political and apolitical views were perceived as a potential threat to a state backed by orthodox Lutheranism. These original censorship laws not only silenced political critique but any notion seen as potentially leading to political or religious critique of the reigning order. The 1842 censorship revisions, however, targeted "undemocratic" emotional tones and "tendencies" (*Tendenzen*) of public speech, scholarship, media, and artistic expression. The new censorship made all speech suspicious by questioning the inner mood of the author and the *potential* mood of its audiences. The warnings against emotional speech and inner feeling only fueled widespread interest in emotional displays of irreverent expression. When a parent scolds a child for inappropriate laughter, the child only laughs harder, even under the threat of punishment. Comedic theater in Berlin flourished under suppression and attracted the attention of philosophers, who had been expelled from the university under the same censorship. A new alliance was drawn between critical philosophy and comedy. The first alliance between ancient skepticism and comedy was also formed against Athenian censorship, which similarly advised against public displays of "undemocratic emotions," highlighting laughter in particular as having destructive tendencies. Nineteenth-century critical philosophers drew on ancient laughter in response to the censorship of their own times.

Hegel's drama tells a story about how the spirit of ancient comedy spills over into the historical drama of its modern and contemporary audiences, who recognize themselves as part of a tragic structure enacted by their society. In the context of Hegel's drama, the historical stage remains an aesthetic representation belonging to his historical fiction. However, this representation of the ancient comic community, in turn, spills out into Hegel's audience, who identify with his fictional audiences of another historical stage. Hegel's staging of ancient comedy and the cross especially caused public drama during his own lifetime—first in the university, then in the streets.

The concrete enactment of Hegel's historical drama occurs through a double split in the first generation of Hegelian scholarship. The first split surfaces within debates between competing interpretations of Hegel's audience of the cross, resulting in a rift between what becomes known as the Left and Right Hegelians. The crack at first may appear abstract, expressing itself as a theoretical debate within a specialized academic discourse. But the crack almost immediately grasps the drama of its concrete existence when it becomes a target of Prussian censorship. In response to the antagonistic double, Church and State, the dramatic action of the Left Hegelians unfolds outside of the university in the form of underground political writings and protests.[2] The political movement, which became known as the Young Hegelians, gained momentum by self-consciously modeling itself on Hegel's conception of the audience of ancient comedy. Despite their common portrayal as antireligious, the Young Hegelians didn't abandon the audience of the cross in their turn toward ancient comedy.[3] Instead, the question of the relationship between the two audiences gives rise to the second split within the Young Hegelian vision of *revolution as a historical comedy*. Will the modern Prussian audience of the cross be the object or agent of historical laughter in the anticipated comic destruction of an entire way of life?

The spirit of comedy had the strongest grip on Karl Marx, one of the youngest and most celebrated members of the Young Hegelians. Friedrich Engels had been trying his hand at comedy writing for some time before Marx entered the scene. We know of Engels's "aspirations" through the charming comedy sketches he included in letters to his sister.[4] To my knowledge, however, Marx was the first to introduce comedy and laughter into Young Hegelian revolutionary politics. Marx's engagement with comedy begins with his very first journal writings against Prussian censorship (1842),[5] in which he explicitly defends the critical value of laughter over and against Prussian seriousness. A year later he further developed a two-part model of critique in relation to comedy in his introduction to "Contribution to the Critique of Hegel's Philosophy of Law" (1843).[6] We see humor across his corpus in the comic performance of his texts: in his sarcasm, in his self-conscious contradictions and animated style. Marx's humor, of course, is not merely stylistic, since Marx directly argues in his own defense of humor that style is never merely style.[7] Engels finally had some success as a dramatist when he and Marx wrote their own philosophical comedy, *The Holy Family* (1845),[8] which was both an obituary for and a satire of the Young Hegelians themselves: the moment when the Young Hegelians grasp themselves comically in their own destruction. The theme of comedy continues to run through Marx's later works, even into volume 1 of *Capital* (1867),[9] where he develops a notion of the capitalist's laughter, complicating his earlier notion of the critical theorist's laughter.[10] Marx's most developed theory of historical comedy is, of course, in his *Eighteenth Brumaire of Louis Bonaparte* (1852), which begins with his engagement with Hegel's dramatization of history, introducing the well-worn slogan that I've already played with in excess, "first as tragedy, then as farce."[11]

Comedy plays a central role in shifting first-generation Hegelian scholarship from a theological academic debate to the enactment of revolutionary politics. This shift from theology to politics via comedy remains the foundation of Marxism and its concrete enactments in the twentieth- and twenty-first century. The following chapters explore the philosophical, aesthetic, and political life of historical comedy, extending from the revolutions of nineteenth-century Europe to the antifascist resistance of the twentieth- and twenty-first centuries. This chapter first explores the historical conditions that give rise to historical comedy in the formation of Young Hegelian and Marxist politics through (1) the theological split between the Left and Right Hegelians, (2) the political split within the Young Hegelians, producing a redoubling of comedy and religion, (3) the conflict between Prussian censorship and communal affects, and (4) the redoubling of ancient censorship and comedy within nineteenth-century Germany.

I begin with the double split within first-generation Hegelian scholarship that centers around debates about the contemporary significance of Hegel's philosophy of art-religion and revealed religion. I then take a brief intermission in Young Hegelian drama to return to the ancient stage to touch upon the relationship between Athenian censorship of laughter and comedy. Does ancient comedy challenge censorship? Or do these two opposing sides of Athenian life sustain each other in their opposition? A glimpse of Athenian censorship and its relationship to comedy raises questions central to the modern stage where the Young Hegelian drama begins. In what ways can an affect be censored? Can a specific affect be inherently political, conservative, or (un)democratic? What is the role of affect for critique and revolution? Do affects belong to Self or Community? Does a historical stage erupt in its own affects? After exploring the peculiar censorship laws targeting public and private affect, especially humor and laughter, in ancient Greece and modern Germany, the following chapter presents a Young Hegelian comedy set to a tetradic dialectic in four acts.

The First Split: Left | Right

The initial division in the first generation of Hegelians between the Right and Left Hegelians can be formulated as the crack between *the defenders of the seriousness of religion* and what becomes *the defenders of the comedy of religion*. The distinctions "Left" and "Right" first emerged within the context of a theological debate, when David Friedrich Strauss adopted the political terms from the French *ancien régime*, applying "Right" to orthodox interpretations of Hegel's philosophy of revealed religion. Right Hegelians defended biblical miracles as literal events, testifying their faith in the absolute unity between history and the supernatural. He applied the term "Left" to his own alternative account of revealed religion, emphasizing the mythical value of Christ for Hegel, the ancient world, and contemporary society. The Young Hegelians as a political movement was formed when one side of a theological debate was pushed out of the university by the dangerous duo, Church and State. The Young Hegelian comedy of religion was born when it became clear that a purely theological debate was necessarily political.

Carl Friedrich Göschel was the first and foremost defender of the religious seriousness of Hegel's work. At the end of Hegel's life, Göschel set the terms for a theological debate that would last about a decade before shifting to a social and political register. In his 1829 work *Aphorismen über Nichtwissen und absolutes Wissen*,[12] Göschel framed Hegel's philosophy as the highest form of speculative thought, which for him meant the highest expression of the truth of Christianity. As Lawrence Stepelevich explains, for Göschel "Christianity and Hegelianism were related as premise to conclusion, and to be a true Christian was to be a Hegelian."[13] Göschel argued that becoming a Hegelian also involved a religious conversion. A proper intellectual pursuit of Hegel's thought necessarily led to the spiritual (religious) transformation of the individual. As Göschel claims, "Without a re-birth no one can rise from the sphere of natural understanding to the speculative height of the living notion."[14]

The division that gave rise to the Right and the Left Hegelians came out of two different theological understandings of spiritual conversion in the dialectical relationship between Christianity and Hegelian philosophy. Both sides saw the potential for modern Lutheranism itself to undergo a transformation through the actualization of Hegel's thought. How did Hegel's philosophy represent Lutheranism's new self-relation in modernity? How might Lutheranism grasp itself differently on the modern stage? Both sides also equally identified a moment in Hegel's thought in which Christianity comes to its end and beginning at the same point. Göschel framed Hegelian philosophy as the conversion of the individual to Christian truth but also as a kind of conversion of Christianity from a theoretical truth to the incarnation of truth realized in praxis. Christianity could grasp its Self concretely by grasping its mirror image in Hegel's Community. The telos of Christianity reached its fulfillment in Hegel's philosophy as its final earthly realization.

In 1835 Strauss presented a compelling alternative Hegelian account of Christian conversion in his work *Das Leben Jesu*. Whereas Göschel identified the beginning of Christianity in its end (Hegel), Strauss identified the end of Christianity in its own beginning. The death of the Christian God as Absolute was in the birth of Christ: the thought that caused Luther's despair, according to Hegel, as I explore in the previous chapter. The telos of Christianity was not only to come into existence to immediately destroy itself but to destroy all religion as such. As Strauss saw it, the significance of the image of the cross is in the way it transforms the mythical consciousness of its contemporary audience. The image of the cross allows the sacred to be identified as belonging to all individuals as a collective, Hegel's vision of the ethical community, rather than this one individual alone. Conversion is double: as the audience of the cross comes to recognize themselves as sacred, God also experiences a conversion, recognizing himself as *nothing more* than the profane human community.

In his final years, Hegel endorsed Göschel's reading, which promised to protect the future of Hegelianism in academia as censorship increased its grip on the university. Yet Strauss's reading, published several years after Hegel's death, quickly became accepted by many as Hegel's own position. Some deemed Strauss to be truer to Hegel than the aging Hegel was to his own corpus. As a result, Hegel's philosophy, which was tolerated with some suspicion by mainstream politicians and religious clergy during his lifetime, suddenly became threatening to orthodox Lutherans, who used their political sway to suppress varieties of Left Hegelianism within the university. Strauss's reading of Hegel's philosophy of religion not only shook the unchallenged authority of the Right Hegelians, who saw themselves as Hegel's faithful disciples, who neither added nor took away from the master's truth. Strauss's success also caused him and nearly all other Hegelian philosophers to lose their positions in the university. Adding insult to injury, Schelling was awarded Hegel's chair in Berlin. What began as a theological debate took on a radical political character when Lutheran orthodoxy, in collaboration with state censorship, exiled Hegelianism from the university. As a result, Young Hegelianism grew out of the Left as a political movement that developed outside of academia and in fierce opposition to academic philosophy, which they saw as a submissive handmaiden to religious dogmatism and a reactionary state.

The Second Split: The Comedy of Religion | The Comedy of Religion

The debate about the role of religion in Hegel's philosophy experienced its own comic conversion when it was forced underground in the early 1840s and continued in the medium of journals that took the form of "pop-up" pamphlet series, which were terminated by Prussian censorship almost as soon as they emerged. Arnold Ruge spearheaded several of the journals that served as the leading platform for the Young Hegelians, notably the *Deutsche Jahrbücher*, which he ran in Dresden from 1841 to 1843 after the *Hallische Jahrbücher* was shut down. Drawing on Hegel's philosophy of ancient drama, the Young Hegelians developed the concept of comedy alongside the concept of critique, often using the terms interchangeably. The main object of this comic critique was the double, Church and State.

Yet, as dialectics would have it, the Young Hegelian *comedy of religion* was itself immediately divided: a tetradic split born from a split. The structure of the genitive is a full tetradic turn in one breath. One little signifier acts as a split conjoining two terms while simultaneously redoubling the terms in both a relationship of belonging and one of opposition. The Young Hegelian *comedy of religion* simultaneously points to the critical act of making a comedy out of religion and religion's own immanent critique of the historical stage that forms it. In the first sense of the comedy of religion, comedy is opposed to religion. The joke is on religion when the critical philosopher lifts the veil of religious ideology, exposing its empty contents. In the second sense of the comedy of religion, comedy belongs to religion itself. Religion is the exhibitionist who lifts her own skirt. Religion makes the joke, exposing its own contradiction. This self-exposure sabotages the political stage that sought to appropriate religion to secure its power. The first model posits critique as a destructive power that is applied to the object of laughter. The second model suggests that to be transformative, critique must take the form of self-destruction/transformation. Laughter must arise from the crack of the contradiction that grasps itself as such.

These two sides of the comedy of religion within Young Hegelianism are played out in a concentrated debate that takes place primarily between Marx, Ruge, and Max Stirner across 1842–44 at the height of the *Jahrbücher* and *Rheinische Zeitung*:[15]

> Marx, "Bemerkungen über die neueste preußische Zensurinstruktion," *Rheinische Zeitung*, written in January and February 1842;
> Stirner, "Kunst und Religion," *Rheinische Zeitung*, June 1842;
> Ruge, "Hegels Rechtsphilosophie und die Politik unserer Zeit," *Deutsche Jahrbücher* 189–90, August 1842 (Dresden); and
> Marx, "Zur Kritik der Hegelschen Rechtsphilosophie. Einleitung" (written December 1843–January 1844), *Deutsch-Französische Jahrbücher* 7 and 10, February 1844 (Paris).

Ruge and Marx first discussed the relationship between comedy and politics in a series of private letters. Their official collaboration began in 1842, when Marx joined the *Deutsche Jahrbücher* as a contributor and a year later as the coeditor of the *Deutsch-Französische Jahrbücher* in Paris. Ruge and Marx immediately used the platform of the *Jahrbücher* to stage the uprisings across Europe as a historical comedy. Ruge announced that the rising spirit of comedy—a Spiritual comedy—indicates the political spirit of the times.[16] One might indeed say that comedy was in the air in Germany during this time both in terms of its popularity in the arts and in the backlash against the Prussian censorship of humor and its "tendency" to cause civil disorder, as the censorship claimed. Kierkegaard, for one, attributes the theme of laughter in his own work to the comedies that he attended in Berlin in 1842, during the time that he (along with the aspiring comic playwright Engels) attended Schelling's lectures.[17] This same year a second wave of censorship laws were published, which Marx saw as directly attacking Germany's growing political spirit of comedy. In response to the new censorship, the Young Hegelians looked to the ancient audience of comedy and the cross to form their own response to Prussian censorship.

Censorship and Laughter: From Ancient Athens to Modern Prussia

I take a brief intermission from my dramatization of the Young Hegelians to revisit ancient laughter. The revised 1842 Prussian censorship instructions echo ancient Athenian censorship in several distinct ways. Both censorships claimed to protect free speech and identified specific affects or emotional tones as destructive for civil discourse. In Marx's perspective, comic affects were one of the central targets of the new censorship. Censorship, above all else, would not allow itself to be laughed at (of course any attempt to make oneself exempt from laughter is the surest way to become the butt of a joke). The Athenian attempt to regulate public laughter, in particular, sheds light on the Young Hegelian appropriation of Greek comedy in response to the new Prussian censorship.

Leaving Hegel's narration of ancient comedy momentarily to the side, I again engage Halliwell's account of ancient attitudes toward laughter expressed in law, ritual, and drama. By contrasting Spartan and Athenian relationships toward laughter, Halliwell highlights the ancient politics of laughter. In contrast to the Athenians, who restricted certain forms of public laughter in the name of democracy, the Spartans institutionalized laughter to enforce class division, slavery, and a militant spirit.[18] The Athenian festivals, where comedy was performed, appear to free laughter from both democratic censorship and tyrannical weaponization. On the stage and in the crowds, festival laughter could reflect on itself, grasping its Self in the crack between its capacity to divide and unify a community. Dramatic laughter challenged both the censorship of laughter and the violence of laughter: battling democratic seriousness with laughter as well as battling tyrannical laughter with laughter. Whoever gets the last laugh wins. Yet, as drama and history warn, the last laugh often comes at the expense of one's own self-destruction (mirrored in the self-destruction of one's opponent). We may question along with Hegel whether festival laughter, a third institutionalization of laughter toward which the censorship looked the other way, was really free. Could ancient laughter be instrumentalized for a modern revolution which fought for concrete freedom?

At first it may seem ironic that the Spartans, who prided themselves on their severity, placed laughter at the center of their ideology and practice while the Athenians, who hosted the Dionysian festivals, discouraged certain kinds of public laughter. According to Plutarch, the Spartans erected monuments representing the fundamental forces that shape human experience. Of these deities, Death, Fear, and Laughter are the only ones mentioned by name and appear to be upheld above the rest with a sanctuary devoted to each.[19] Aristotle famously claims that laughter is an activity proper to human beings.[20] Yet Greek literature more commonly characterizes laughter as a violent force of nature and the gods, which could be directed against humanity. In the *Homeric Hymn to Demeter*, for example, Gaia makes a joke by creating the narcissus, an irresistible flower. Persephone, an innocent human child, falls victim to the joke. When she plucks the flower, she is sent to the underworld, and all of nature shakes with laughter at her damnation.[21] The members of the Spartan religious cult carried tiny figurines of the deity

Gelos as a constant reminder of this destructive primordial force within their bellies.[22] They did not submit with reverence to Gelos but instead harnessed his power by institutionalizing laughter within their educational system and military training. In a coming-of-age test, a clan of teenage girls was directed to single out a boy of the same age whom they would ridicule in front of an older male audience. The boy's task was to take the jokes while the old men laughed heartily at his humiliation. For another edifying use of laughter, a Spartan boy and a slave boy were brought side by side in front of an audience. Each was brutally beaten (a ritual that perhaps inspired the satirical torture scene in Aristophanes's *Frogs*). The audience anticipated that the Spartan boy would take his beating without flinching. When the untrained slave boy would cry, the crowd would erupt in laughter.[23] The institutionalization of communal laughter was used by the Spartans to enforce a hierarchical class structure and train their citizens to face their own death and the death of their enemy without fear.

The Athenians also saw Laughter in connection with the forces of Fear and Death, but in acknowledgment of its violent tendencies, they approached laughter with more caution than the Spartans. Aristotle writes in his *Rhetoric* that although an important part of maturation involves learning how to take a joke, as the Spartans taught, one must also learn how to make a joke with moderation.[24] Athenian culture defended the freedom of speech. However, certain affective tones of speech were identified as capable of inciting violence and were prohibited by laws dating back to Solon.[25] To protect the freedom of the content of speech, Athenian law concerned itself with the spirit in which this content was delivered. These laws on affect, tone, and style specifically targeted public speech that took on a mocking tone and could induce *katagelos*: the sort of laughter that, as Hobbes noted,[26] fills one with glory through the experience of the defeat of another. Athenian law specifically restricted mockery that could induce ridiculing laughter in public places such as the temples, the courts, official buildings, the games, and agora. The concern about the violent tendency of mockery was so great that censorship extended to the dead, who were protected by law from the laughter of the living.[27] These laws, presented as cultivating a democratic environment for free speech, directed each citizen to treat laughter with seriousness, applying it to the appropriate context and always with a degree of modesty.

We don't know whether theater was officially exempt from the censorship laws regarding ridicule, but there are plenty of accounts in ancient drama of mocking laughter directed at both the living and the dead. Festivalgoers could indulge in the kinds of laughter that were discouraged in public life. Both tragedy and comedy experiment with illicit laughter, reflecting on its destructive and liberating potency. The role of the audience in tragedy, like that of the chorus, is to cast judgment on the tragic hero, who will ultimately be ruined by the violence that is presented as a natural consequence of hubristic affects (e.g., Antigone). In comedy, however, when the protagonist mocks worn-out customs, corrupt political leaders, and contradictory laws, including those regarding censorship, the audience openly shares in illicit laughter. The censorship reflected political and societal anxiety toward laughter. When liberated festival laughter reflects on itself, it also expresses some self-doubt.

The ancient fear of being publicly mocked is evident in the anxiety expressed by the heroes of Greek drama. Even (especially) kings, queens, and gods cower at the idea of being ridiculed by their foes. In the *Bacchae*, Pentheus, not considering the physical violence that awaits him, begs Dionysus not to make a joke out of him in front of the women whom the king himself has recently ridiculed with laughter. It often appears that, for the Greeks, to be laughed at by one's enemies is directly connected to the fear of physical violence and death. The same laughter that could be used to enforce the structure of power equally threatened to disrupt it.

The *Bacchae* stresses the unifying and antagonistic sides of laughter by tracing the degeneration of laughter from its most noble form to its most debased expressions. The opening of the play highlights the profoundly unifying quality of festival laughter. The chorus describes laughter as a gift from Dionysus to the gods and humans alike, "These are his powers, / to blend us, by dance, with the worshipful band, / to laugh to the sound of piping, / and to vanquish care."[28] At the beginning of the play, Thebes is divided between the women who have gone to worship Dionysus in the forest and the men who have sided with King Pentheus against the new gods. Yet despite this hostile atmosphere, Teiresias and the former King Cadmus meet in a joyful reunion. The two old friends hold hands and agree to commit to a night of dancing and laughter in honor of Dionysus.

The unifying laughter of Teiresias and Cadmus is opposed to the antagonistic laughter embodied by the relationship between Dionysus and his cousin Pentheus. When Pentheus encounters his father and Teiresias wearing deerskin garments like that of the Bacchae, he mocks them, stating that the foolish sight of the two old men is laughable. Teiresias responds by accusing Pentheus three times of the impious act of "laughing down" (*katagelan*) his elders. Dionysus's unmerciful response to Pentheus's mockery reflects how the gods, like mortal sovereigns, hate to be laughed at. Pentheus ridicules Dionysus's claim to divinity, but as the play unfolds, Dionysus retaliates by making Pentheus the object of laughter. Pentheus is put under a spell and paraded into the forest dressed in female Bacchic garments that he mocked. The perversely satirical *komos* brings Pentheus to his death as a frenzied pack of worshippers led by his own mother attacks him. The messenger later reports that the women laughed all the while as they ripped him apart.

Dionysus gets the last laugh at his enemy who had antagonistically laughed at the laughter and dance of the Bacchae. However, this frenzy of battling laughter, which escalates into the gruesome murder of one of the opponents, ends in a moment of sudden anguish. It's a motif that is repeated throughout Greek drama, as we recall in the story of Electra. As Electra holds the head of her stepfather and stands victoriously over her mother's corpse, Agave holds the severed head of her son.[29] The one who seeks vengeance on behalf of her own people does not initially recognize the body of the one she has killed as her kin. Both dramas suggest that *katagelan* turns one's opponent into one who is fully Other, beyond human recognition. In the last instance, laughter ceases and the dead is recognized not as Other, but as one's own flesh and blood.

The brutal use of institutionalized laughter in Spartan society, which used laughter to silence opposition, seems to justify the Athenian anxiety toward laughter expressed in theater and in law. As we might come to expect, the opposed attitudes toward laughter in Athenian and Spartan cultures also mirror each other, as each society attempts to regulate laughter to maintain a specific political order and power. In one context, laughter is seen as courageous (and destructive), and, in another, as undemocratic (and destructive). Both political stages play out their own self-defeating comedy, raising the questions: Can communal affect be regulated? Can laughter be forced? For how long can laughter be suppressed?

The Spartans and Athenians attempt to regulate laughter to enforce a certain way of life. The ritualization of Dionysian laughter, in contrast, allowed the festivalgoers to break character by violating their daily reverence toward Athenian law and custom. Festival laughter did not simply oppose the censorship of laughter by stepping forward before the chorus to defend its rightness. Instead, without the interruption of censorship, laughter could fully play out its contradictions, grasping itself in the thrill and terror of its own comic self-destruction. We might frame theater as a radical space for social and political critique.

We might also frame theater as a space that preserves the status quo by providing a sanctioned space for critique, granted by the very object of critique (the State). The contradiction is found in a single grasp. The festivalgoers could temporarily "feel freely" for the length of the festival. In response to the Prussian censorship of affect, Marx and the Young Hegelians find inspiration in Greek comedy. However, they envision a contemporary comedy not as occurring in a festive space that is an exception to the law but instead as emerging in the final destruction of the law itself. Festival laughter swells into revolutionary laughter transforming the world stage.

And so begins the Young Hegelian historical comedy.

Chapter 5

A Young Hegelian Comedy

Act One. Marx's First Laugh

Marx's first publication as a new member of the Young Hegelians was a fiery essay published in the *Rheinische Zeitung* entitled "Comments on the Latest Prussian Censorship Instruction." His essay attacks the 1842 Laws on the Freedom of the Press, an amendment to the state censorship laws established in 1819. The original censorship named a series of subjects that could not be criticized by the papers, academic research, religious publications, and political writings. The new amendment claimed to release critique from these "temporary" measures, originally instated for five years but stretched to twenty-two in the name of "state security." The amendment claimed to "free the press from improper restrictions" and expressed disapproval of "any undue constraint on the activity of writers."[1] In a single stroke, the new censorship denounced censorship while instating itself indefinitely: a censorship to remedy censorship. As the 1842 instruction lifted the former restrictions on the content of speech, it simultaneously adopted the ambiguous task of monitoring the "affective tendencies" of different kinds of speech. Addressing itself to each press individually, the revision recommended emotional tones conducive to "frank and decent public speech" while discouraging tones that it identified as having destructive tendencies. Staging a battle of affect against affect, it coupled positive affective doubles against negative affective doubles.

	both	and	neither	nor
public speech	frank	decent	humorous	immodest
academic press	serious	modest	frivolous	hostile
religious press	respectable	conventional	fanatic	confused
political press	well-intentioned	goodwilled	spiteful	malevolent
publicity	decorous	candid	offensive	defamatory

Marx narrates the performative contradiction within each instruction:

To the general press (on truth): censorship cannot prevent an investigation of the truth, which is both serious and modest.[2] Marx points out that for seriousness and modesty to take their roles seriously, they must sometimes break character. Otherwise, they betray themselves. An academic who takes themself and their research too seriously cannot be taken seriously at all and perhaps does not take the content of their investigation seriously enough. And there is nothing more arrogant than a researcher who sees their work as nothing more than a modest presentation of the facts at hand. "Serious and modest!" Marx declares, "What fluctuating, relative concepts! Where does seriousness cease and jocularity begin? Where does modesty cease and immodesty begin . . . If you want to be consistent . . . forbid also a *too serious* and *too modest* investigation of the truth, for too great seriousness is the most ludicrous thing of all, and too great modesty is the bitterest irony."[3] Seriousness and modesty present investigation as objective but expose their own subjective and emotional character by mirroring their opposites: humor and immodesty. As Marx claims, the object of investigation, the truth of the matter, is as emotional as the subjective process of investigation. When affect denies its affective character—declaring itself "not affect!"—it cannot approach truth at all, for truth is an emotional matter.

To the philosophical press (on religion): censorship cannot silence critiques of the Christian religion as long as they are neither frivolous nor hostile.[4] As Marx notes, critique is considered frivolous when it focuses on a minor feature in a light manner and hostile when it targets its object as a whole in its essence: "Religion can only be attacked in *a hostile or a frivolous way*, there is no third way . . . Religion must not be attacked, whether in a hostile or a frivolous way, whether in general or in particular, *therefore not at all.*"[5] In an age in which the state declares religion to be the air one breathes, the critique of religion is self-critique. Critique is a mode of grasping the contradiction in which we find ourselves. Frivolity responds to the absolute absurdity of one's situation. Hostility turns on the conditions that make one's existence a farce. To deny critique emotions is to prevent critique altogether.

To the religious press (on politics): censorship cannot impose itself on religion as long as religious speech is neither fanatical nor confuses itself with politics.[6] Marx shoots back, the Prussian state adopts the *general* spirit of Christianity as its *particular* national identity while insisting on the separation of church and state: "Either forbid religion to be introduced at all into politics . . . or allow also the *fanatical* introduction of religion into politics. Let religion concern itself with politics in *its own way.*"[7] The state justifies its positions in the name of Christianity, without allowing Protestant or Catholic theologians or bodies to critique the political appropriation of religion. Only a fanatical defense of Christian belief can produce an immanent critique of the corrupt political misappropriation of religious doctrine as the general spirit of Prussia.

A Young Hegelian Comedy

To the political press (on the state). Censorship must permit any perspective on the state as long as it is well-intentioned and goodwilled and neither spiteful nor malevolent.[8] The public is asked to trust the intention of the censorship. Yet the censorship is permitted to be suspicious of the affective disposition of every citizen, even toward those feelings that have not yet been felt. Censorship is permitted to feel freely but individual feeling—and thus Public Spirit—is aborted before it is born!

To the general press (on publicity): censorship affords publicity that is both decorous and candid; however, it must be neither offensive nor defamatory, whether of individuals or of a whole class of individuals represented by a party name.[9] As Marx emphasizes through his scrutiny of each instruction, the censorship of affect makes us fall out of touch with ourselves. We become bored with ourselves and fail to grasp ourselves as political actors who are the thrilling protagonists of our own historical drama. The ideal of moderation deadens our emotions toward Self and Community. Yet, it simultaneously treats the state as a dramatic hero, protecting *it* from *personal* attacks. It openly announces its purpose: to heighten each citizen's arousal toward the Fatherland, replacing Public Spirit with National Feeling.

At first glance, one may tend to agree with the sentiments of the 1842 amendment. Who can object to the call for philosophical discourse open to diverse perspectives, the call for tolerant religious discourse, and the call for the media to have basic decency? Yet, as Marx sees it, the appearance of fostering an atmosphere conducive to "serious critical inquiry" is more deceptive than the old laws that directly inhibit what can be said. When we believe we are free, ideology has its strongest hold. Marx writes: "You may write freely, but at the same time every word must be a curtsey to the liberal censorship, which allows you to express your equally serious and modest opinions. Indeed, do not lose your feeling of reverence!"[10]

Marx mirrors Hegel, focusing on the audience of the censorship. The censorship comically acts out the contradictions of the Prussian state while explicitly forbidding its citizens from laughing at the farce that frames their existence. The audience of the censorship is given the impossible task of maintaining a straight face while being ordered not to laugh. "I am humorous," Marx declares, "but the law bids me to write seriously. I am audacious, but the law commands that my style be modest. *Grey, all grey*, is the sole, the rightful color of freedom."[11] Marx continues, the censorship of individual feeling is at once the censorship of Public Spirit, "which glistens with an inexhaustible play of colours."[12] "Free" critical thought grows bored with itself and forgets its power to destroy the contradictions that play out around it and within it. For critique to overcome its own self-alienation, it must have the audacity to laugh in the face of what was once treated with moderation and reverence, including moderation and reverence: "I treat the ludicrous seriously when I treat it ludicrously . . . should not the manner of investigation alter according to the object? If the object is a matter for laughter, the manner has to seem serious . . . You conceive truth abstractly and turn Spirit into an examining *magistrate*, who draws up a dry *protocol* of it."[13] The suppression of emotion alienates us from our social-historical existence. Spirit seizes itself by the specific contradictions that constitute its material body. Yet, National Feeling forbids Spirit from laughing at its own absurdity. *Laughter is a matter of Spirit*—laughter belongs to Spirit—when the contradictions of its historical material existence are a *laughing matter*.

Act Two. Stirner on Self's Comic Destruction

Stirner and Ruge enthusiastically responded to Marx's first essay the following summer, offering their own renditions of critical laughter in dialogue with the themes of censorship, politics, art, and religion. It's no surprise that each of their responses captures opposing senses of what they both formulate as the comedy of religion. Ruge was a diehard Hegelian who remained devoted to the Young Hegelian political cause long after their devastating defeat. Stirner, who also studied under Hegel, was a loud critic of Hegel and an even louder critic of the Young Hegelians, who tolerated his internal antagonism. In their responses to Marx, Stirner imagines the destruction of modern art-religion by philosophy's "pulverizing hand," which may be interpreted as a playful middle finger to Ruge, who passionately defended the comic double;[14] Ruge, in contrast, imagines modern art-religion as a potential force for the comic destruction of an entire historical moment. Both Stirner and Ruge characterize religion in its contemporary expression as a hollow corpse, which lacks political spirit, becoming both a private matter of the individual and an ideological mask adorned by the state. However, while Stirner sought to destroy the ghostly corpse of religion, Ruge sought to resuscitate religion to revive its affective potency. As he puts it, "Those who now cry out so much for religion have nothing to fear but the reawakening of religion."[15]

Despite representing opposite sides of a split within Young Hegelianism, Stirner and Ruge form another odd couple, sharing as much in common as in difference. The split between them arises out of a single paragraph in Hegel's corpus that they both highlight at the center of their philosophy: the emergence of Self in comic destruction. Ruge notes that although critique is missing from Hegel's system, its aesthetic double lurks in the Shadow at the end of art-religion: "In relation to comedy [the other side of critique], the position of Aristophanes in relation to the Greek Spirit brings the most profound and most beautiful discussions of this great philosophy."[16] While Marx first identifies defiant laughter as belonging to Spirit, Stirner and Ruge identify historical comedy as the destruction of a tragic stage of Spirit. Their mutual attention to Hegel's ancient comedy in response to Prussian censorship becomes one of the most profound influences on Marx and Marxism, both in theory and in revolutionary politics.

Stirner's "Art and Religion" follows the narrative of Hegel's "Art-Religion," offering an early account of his "Egoism" through Hegel's account of the comic emergence of Self. Familiar questions drive the essay. When deciding what counts, does one remember to count herself? How exactly does one count oneself as self? Stirner's answer is also familiar. The counter has double-vision, counting herself twice-two: "No force is great enough to overthrow [the thought], two times two is four . . . 'Here I stand, I can do naught else!'"[17]

Stirner universalizes Hegel's narrative about ancient art-religion playing out the drama on a modern Christian stage. Religion cannot exist without Art: "Art is the beginning, the *Alpha* of religion, but also its end, its *Omega*. Even more its—companion . . . when the artist takes back his art unto himself, so religion vanishes."[18] Art and Religion are midwives that foster the birth of Self, who appears in the form of a conjoined double. The artist, who represents every human being, redoubles herself in her art or artistic act, the concrete embodiment of her deepest emotions and desires. The artist counts herself as nothing without her art, which is not separate from herself. She realizes herself through her creation (B | B). Yet when she tries to grasp herself in her mirror image, her timid reflection withdraws from her reach:

> [People] would rather be doubled than be alone . . . they seek out a spiritual man for their second self . . . this Other is he himself and yet it is not he: it is *his otherside* [*Gegenüber*] to which all thoughts and feelings flow but without actually reaching it, for it is his otherside, encapsulated and inseparably conjoined with his present actuality . . . His arms reach outward, but the Other is never reached; for would he reach it how could the "Other remain"? Where would this disunion with all of its pains and pleasures be?[19]

Self, in the form of the conjoined twins, longs for unity. But she equally desires disunion, for the split within self makes her self-reflection possible. The impossible task of satisfying—while simultaneously not satisfying—two opposing desires requires a delicate dance: the redoubling and inversion of "I am" and "I am not." To make her art something more than a mere art-object, the artist makes art something less: a something-more in the form of negativity, a mystery that remains beyond even her own reach (B | N). The creative self falls to her knees before her double, whom she longs to bring back into herself. She empties herself so that she may be filled up by her Other who is All. She cries out in the spirit of the worshipper, "Not I, but Christ lives in me" (N | B).

The drama of the twins continues with a plot twist. Self prostates herself before her mystified double. She sees her aesthetic double as spiritual and reduces herself to nothing. Now the *otherside* has all the power, and the creator is a mere representation of what she created. Then suddenly from deep within the belly of her nothingness something stirs. To be exact, nothing stirs within nothing. In fully acting out her negative role, the artist unearths a new kind of creative power. With chilling composure, she turns on her (other) self in an act of horrific destruction. The imposter must die so that Self may reclaim her freedom. But how does one kill one's own mirror image without destroying oneself? In this last act of (self) destruction, the self and her double once again mirror each other. Self finally grasps her true nature as the perspective of each side fades into darkness (N | N).

At the surface, it may seem that Christianity is the primary object of Stirner's scorn. But as with most Young Hegelian commentary on religion, the real object of critique is a reactionary state that prescribes traditional Christian affects—reverence and modesty, moderation and seriousness—as the general mood for all of its citizens. In *Ego and Its Own*, Stirner analyzes the way Prussian censorship recodes specific affects as undesirable: "So *Schimpf* (contumely) is in its old sense equivalent to jest, but for Christian seriousness pastime became a dishonor, for that seriousness cannot take a joke."[20] The censorship only exposes what is already implicitly at work in Prussian society, reflected in all aspects of social life, from education to work to leisure. Stirner develops Marx's position, arguing that the normative ideal of "serious inquiry" mirrors religious worship. The worshipper seeks to know the will of God with a spirit of humility and reverence. The ways of the Lord, she must admit, are beyond her comprehension. And yet, it's the believer's duty to chase after the unattainable mysteries of the divine. The state maintains itself through this paradoxical imperative: chase after the truth of the matter, but do not catch up to it! Guided by moderation, wise citizens recognize that they cannot challenge what they cannot possibly comprehend: the political staging of their own existence. The mystified object of inquiry is one's self as a political subject.

Self-alienation is preserved through the learned dispositions of moderation and seriousness, which appear to be neutral modes of reasoning without affective content. Thus, the destructive power of critique must be born out of the spirit of irreverent laughter. "Art and Religion" repeats the same story twice, oscillating between the split subjective perspective of the twins and the objective perspective of the world stage at the end of an epoch. Stirner brings the tale to a close by retelling Hegel's finale of art-religion in his own words:

> But, at the last, art will stand at the close of religion. Serene and confident, art will claim its own once again . . . Here art no longer will enrich its Object, but totally destroy it. In reclaiming its creature, art rediscovers itself and renews its creative power as well. It appears, at the decline of religion, as trifling with the full seriousness of the old belief, a seriousness of content which religion has now lost, and which must be returned to the joyful poet. Hence, religion is presented as a ridiculous *comedy*. Now, however terrible this comedic destruction

A Young Hegelian Comedy

might be, it will nevertheless restore to actuality that which it thinks but to destroy. And so, we do not elect to condemn its horror!"[21]

A historical stage that exposes its own contradictory contents by terminating itself is a comic-horror, the tone of which is only heightened by the skeptic's uncanny serenity. Art, at last, destroys its mystified double through an act of self-destruction. And yet, it simultaneously grasps itself in this very same act. As Stirner admits, comic destruction only clears a negative space for a new appearance of the double. Religion needs Art, but Art also needs Religion. The indestructible structure of the double itself emerges in the destruction of this particular form of the double. In the destruction of both sides, Self finally grasps itself by the crack between two (negativities). Self cries out, "*Nothing is more* to me than myself!"[22] Almost as if adding an afterthought, Stirner alludes to a philosophy-to-come that would come down from nowhere to pulverize the tetradic dialectical redoubling of art-religion once and for all. However, his primary comic conclusion is almost an exact repetition of Hegel's art-religion with one significant difference. Hegel stages comic destruction at the conclusion of ancient history, while Stirner restages the same historical comedy on the horizon.

Act Three. Ruge's Historical Comedy

Ruge, the unsung founder of the coupling of aesthetics and critical theory, tirelessly stressed the role of art for revolutionary politics. Once imprisoned for his radical Hegelianism in the form of political activism with student organizations (in his eyes, the only true form of Hegelianism), Ruge happily passed his five-year sentence reading Hegel and ancient Greek verse. Needless to say, Ruge was one of the most nuanced readers of Hegel among the Young Hegelians in his focus on lived politics, art, and religion. Unlike the Old Hegelians, who saw themselves as the faithful messengers of *the word*, Ruge expressed his devotion through his rigorous infidelity, forcing Hegel from the grave to engage in a political conflict that Hegel himself narrowly avoided.

In "Hegel's 'Philosophy of Right' and the Politics of Our Times," Ruge criticizes academic philosophy for carefully tiptoeing around the censorship in the name of "self-preservation." As Kant directly advises, "keeping silent in a situation such as the present is the *duty of a subject*."[23] If religion had become a walking corpse, academic philosophy, in a desperate effort to save itself from the death sentence of censorship, buried itself alive. In Ruge's words, "Humans caught for years of indolence forget that their theory is dead when they bury themselves in it instead of reshaping the world from it."[24] The university echoed the censorship, by demanding reverence toward its own suffocating normative order while identifying itself as the defender of free thought. In Ruge's view, philosophy suffered the death of the tragic hero, who declares her own slow execution to be *the good life*.

Hegel's philosophy arguably coaxes hidden contradictions to the surface of each social-political stage that it attends to, but Hegel personally avoided coming into conflict with the political contradictions of his own times. Ruge argues that in this way German philosophy follows the "good old Protestant custom, to avoid conflict and to let the contradictions die out rather than to let them live out their lives in battle."[25] Hegel, like Kant, feigned ignorance of the contemporary political implications within his own thought. "Well then, even Hegel was a diplomat!" Ruge declares; "We Germans are not as awkward as we seem; even Kant, this *anima candida*, was a diplomat. Neither of these men *came out* in opposition . . . they did not wish to *represent* the opposition that they really *were*."[26] In attempting to avoid conflict, Kant and Hegel magnified their own positionality as nothing more than the crack between conflicting roles. On one side, the duty of the subject is to remain silent in the face of "circumstances beyond one's control" (i.e., censorship). On the other, as Ruge insists, "philosophy is outspokenness."[27] Lady Philosophy, adorned in her cap and gown, rekindles her romance with Lady Tragedy: "the conflict between the duty of a subject and the duty of the philosopher . . . is the same as the conflict between the written and unwritten laws in *Antigone*. . . . The *subject* in Wöllner's state was not permitted to be a *philosopher*. The 'subject' is a diplomat; he does nothing absolutely, but only what is to be done under 'circumstances beyond one's control.' "[28] Hegel is both a philosopher and a political subject, which is to say, Hegel is neither a philosopher nor a political subject.

The subject is the living embodiment of the contradiction that the philosopher exposes in the concept of the subject but fails to locate in his own historical subjective position. In counting history in stages, the counter forgets to count himself. For this reason, Hegelian contradiction appears to be a theatrical production that never leaves theory. As Ruge claims, Hegel highlights the twin structure of the subject without exposing the otherside of the modern German subject: "the political nothingness of the states," which are without values or conviction and stand for nothing other than the preservation of their own power.[29] The dutiful philosopher, in doing nothing absolutely, mirrors the nothingness of the state that reduces the subject (N | N). But rather than comically exposing the empty content of a corrupt political regime by displaying one's own nothingness for all to see, both sides tragically insist on the substance of their thinking and being (B | B). Philosophy conceals the empty contents of the state, which stands for nothing more than preserving its power, when philosophy stands for nothing more than its own preservation.

Yet even Hegel cannot restrain contradiction from breaking the fourth wall between philosophical theory and revolutionary praxis. When theory grasps itself by its body—and when history grasps itself through theory that arises out of its own tensions—living critique is incarnated as a new public art. Ruge writes, "Art is *joyful* praxis, 'the play (*Schein*) of the idea in its opposite.' . . . *It liberates the entire contemporary Spirit from its old form because it gives it a new form* and shows it this new form in this mirror. However, the highest form of art is that which also breaks out expressly into self-critique of Spirit; it is *comedy*."[30] Spirit reflects on itself through its comic double that takes the form of self-critique. Critical philosophy is the voice of Spirit who does not step forward before the chorus to defend the rightness of its current tragic shape. Critical Spirit instead testifies to the material conditions that make its existence a farce. Academic philosophy censors Spirit when it avoids conflict in the name of self-preservation. True philosophy is the very voice of Spirit who grasps itself by its own institutional contradictions. Philosophy as the voice of Spirit cannot avoid conflict, for "the minute philosophy comes forward critically . . . the conflict is here."[31]

Ruge casts critical philosophy as the voice of Spirit and religion as a potential source of Spirit's reignited pathos. Together critical philosophy and religion—the articulation of communal affect—allow a collective body to reflect on its current historical form. When religion revives its own passion for itself, its content is nothing more than "the *historic*, i.e., the political movement of feeling, the life of human Spirit."[32] Self-reflection's inward grasp at once acts on the world (Self's content) as communal pathos spills over into praxis. When self-reflection encounters inner conflict, its praxis takes the form of political struggle since this inner conflict was always a matter of politics: "Practical pathos breaks off contemplation at some stage and then throws the subject, as it then exists, into battle."[33]

Ruge exchanges ancient theater for the Christian church in his contemporary German rendition of art-religion. Modern religion, like ancient drama, is without its own proper aesthetic object. Its dramatic content is only the communal affects and activity of its (historical) actors: "True religion concentrates in itself all the content of the Spirit of the times—the content is the essence—and, as subjective power or movement of feeling, aims to establish it in the world." Because the content of religion is its historical existence, religion, like the Greek stage, mirrors society. In contrast to Stirner, who laughs in the face of religious seriousness to break the spell of worship, Ruge aspires to take religion more seriously than it presently appears to take itself. As Ruge put, "The practical pathos of religion is much more powerful than the defenders of religion think."[34] What would it mean for religion to take itself seriously? As Marx argues, sometimes "taking oneself seriously" involves playing out one's comic role. Ruge retells Stirner's narrative about art and religion from the perspective of the otherside: the spiritual subject's relationship to her aesthetic double. The church gave birth to the spirit of the worshipper, which the state appropriates to maintain its power. However, the state, which censorship protects as a person, is never compelled to explicitly explain how its "private inner conviction" reflects the Christian values it claims to uphold.

Like a Spartan boy trained to take a beating, religion sits by quietly, doing nothing absolutely, and reverently watches itself dissipate into nothing (nothing more than National Feeling). Does the true believer begin to feel the tickle of indignation stir within her belly? If religion gave birth to worship so too could religion birth blasphemy when its worship had been made blasphemous. If it allowed itself to really feel itself in its current bastardized form, its righteous indignation would spill over into political conflict. As Ruge puts it, "If the heart is really filled, it immediately spills over, and it cannot fail that any religious reality existing in every heart must become a great world celebration, a last judgement, and a 'destruction of something determinate.'"[35] The tragic stage on which the individual is sacrificed for an abstract and impersonal power is the very site for the comic destruction of the same power that turned its convictions into a farce. For the spiritual self to reclaim itself, religion must set fire to its own stage.

What's stopping philosophy and religion from becoming the dynamic duo that passionately speaks out against corruption and fights to reclaim the dignity of the subject and its own creative praxis? Ruge concedes that the temptation to cling to the preservation of one's own present form (as an individual; as an institution) prevents one from achieving new life. It's no wonder the Germans, according to the Young Hegelians, could not locate their own political subjectivity to stimulate themselves. They bored themselves to death without properly achieving the sensation of dying. The double of self-preservation and self-termination takes two forms: *self-preservation* as living death and *self-termination* as a means of reincarnation; the latter can only be achieved through the destruction of the former by the hands of the former, the negation of negation found in the relationship between two kinds of negativity. And yet as rebellion spread across Europe, Ruge detected a "heightened political feeling of life" in Germany, too, hinting at the spirit of "the Greeks, those utterly political humans."[36] In his vision, Spirit's self-critique would take the form of "the emergence of *historical comedy* in our times."[37] From whose perspective will Spirit at last comically grasp itself? Ruge is the first to stage the proletariat as the protagonist of a revolutionary historical comedy:

> This feeling of indignation at being a proletariat, as it is exposed in our history and literature in such harsh colors, is engendered by our awakened interest in the state and our sense for politics, and it everywhere produces new life; we will now be able to detect among ourselves a new virtue, the *public*, a new form of art, the *historical* (the *historical lyric* and the *historical* comedy); we will now be able to detect among ourselves the comedy that, as opposed to the *genre* comedy . . . destroys Spirit's actual historical stages.[38]

Those who know they have nothing to preserve have nothing to lose but a political system that determines their lives to be nothing. Nothing recognizes its own nothingness, sending a jolt into the nation's political consciousness. The material body of Spirit's inner critique is the self-termination of a historical stage, which takes the form of revolution.

Act Four. Marx's Revolutionary Tetrads

Marx's early ambition to establish a journal for theater criticism, as noted in a letter to his father, took an unexpected twist when he later helped Ruge found journals for political critique.[39] In the failed delivery of theater criticism, a new form of political criticism through the lens of historical theater slipped into existence. In his second contribution to the Young Hegelian debate about censorship and critique, Marx adopts Ruge's formulation of a revolution as a historical comedy with the proletariat center stage. Ten years before his proclamation, "first as tragedy, then as farce," Marx plays with the motif of historical repetition as theatrical stages through the Hegelian image of the double death of the gods, encapsulated by Marx's well-known passage: "History is thorough and goes through many phases when carrying an old form to the grave. The last phase . . . is its *comedy*. The gods of Greece, already tragically wounded to death . . . had to re-die a comic death . . . Why this course of history? So that humanity should part with its past *cheerfully*."[40] Although I earlier accused Marx of seeing double where Hegel has four eyes, it's possible to recount Marx's couples as tetrads. "Comments on the Latest Prussian Censorship Instruction" highlights affective twins paired with their negative doubles and shows how each side can only fully realize themselves in their counter-affects. Resistance only sharpens one's mirror image in what it suppresses, while self-relation occurs through the perversion of leaning into what one believes she is not. The introduction to "Contribution to the Critique of Hegel's Philosophy of Law" returns to a tetradic dialectic on the register of both politics and social affect, offering a second framing of Spirit's comic self-critique, this time in direct dialogue with Hegel. Marx's two stages of history, on which the gods are terminated twice, correspond with two sides of critique, which are themselves split by dueling affects.

"Contribution to the Critique of Hegel's Philosophy of Law" is dripping with doubles, beginning with theology and politics, heaven and earth, the gods and the state. The opening metaphor of religion as the opium of the people is commonly mistaken as a critique of religion.[41] However, Marx wastes no time unmasking one object of critique to reveal another mask. Beneath the mask of religion is a "government system which, living on the preservation of all wretchedness, is itself nothing but *wretchedness in office*" felt in "the dull reciprocal pressure of all the social spheres on one another."[42] In order to flesh out the materiality of critique, Marx questions its object. We've already followed Hegel's pursuit of the object of art-religion, which led us to comedy, which reveals nothing. As you might guess, Marx's pursuit of the object of critique similarly leads to comedy, which reveals nothing. While Hegel's pursuit of the missing object unfolds as a linear progression of historical fiction, Marx's pursuit peels back layers of a partially fictional present, arriving at the same conclusion. The vanishing object of critique is nothing more than a moment of self-relating negativity in suspension (*Aufhebung*). The subject victoriously emerges from a political drama in which nothing seems to happen, when she finally grasps herself by her own political nothingness.

Marx's historical tragedy corresponds with his first stage of critique. On one side of the stage stands the tragic hero who insists on the substance of her historical inheritance and her present satisfaction. In Marx's account, the German subject locates herself in the borrowed history of other European nations, which was itself tragic "as long as this regime believed and had to believe in its own justification."[43] Germany plays the part of a modern society that has happily parted with its past without sharing in the revolutionary struggles of France and its partial emancipation. Germany's ghostly historical double consists of a borrowed present shadowed by a borrowed past. The past, represented by the image of the old gods, is impossible to terminate because it was never living to begin with. The historical phantom slips into existence without ever really being born. Although Marx juxtaposes the dead and the living, he simultaneously calls into question the status of the latter. As he double-checks their pulse, the living begins to appear more similar to their phantom shadows, who, in comparison, seem more lifelike. The one who declares herself living is rightfully afraid of the ghost she might see if she were to look in the mirror.

Marx follows up his initial description of the intoxicated masses with a punchline, as he goes on to describe a communal experience entirely unlike the heightened bodily sensation of opium-induced euphoria. The joke plays into one of the Young Hegelians' central irritations expressed in their complaint that arousal does not come easily to the German people. Even their "opium high" is nothing more than a carefully rehearsed sobriety that calls itself happiness. The constant performance of moderation is itself the addiction that numbs the masses to their needs and desires. The metaphor of religion as opium expresses a wish as much as a critique. *If only* religion, like opium, had the power to make a (communal) body buzz with pleasure or itch with discomfort. Marx's insight applies to both history and affect: Emancipation is illusory without the destruction of the material conditions that cause self-alienation; happiness is likewise illusory without grasping suffering or the joy that comes through risk. The cool-headed sobriety of the tragic "I am" (I am happy; I am satisfied; I am my past and present; I am my own) insists on a historical and subjective substance that never was.

On the tragic stage of history, the abstract "I am" is met by an equally abstract "not." Across from the tragic subject is the critical philosopher, the ghost hunter with night vision, who sees things as they really are, which is to say, as they really are not. The critical philosopher commits himself to refuting the historical farce, picking away at the beliefs of the other with a surgeon's scalpel. Critique makes itself perfectly clear to itself. And yet it somehow fails to make itself felt by its otherside. To put this differently, it has yet to grasp itself from its otherside. It does not yet fully feel its own body and forgets to count itself in its refutation.

Marx's second stage of historical comedy opens with twins rather than opposites: "Not" is amplified by another "not." On a social-affective register, happiness and indignation repeat themselves through a transformed relation. Critique also repeats its negative proclamation, but its negation undergoes transformation, as its object shifts to a subjective register. The object of critique is no longer a religious otherside, as it was in Stirner's comedy. In the space of its vanishing object, critique encounters the alienated subjectivity of its own standpoint. Its misdirected indignation toward the other now shifts toward the conditions that have made even the critic's existence a living contradiction, encountered in the impossibility of escaping the grip of the ideology that is exposed as such.

Marx's initial pursuit of the object of critique gives way to a new question: Who is the subject of critique? From which subjective position can negativity fully feel itself? As long as the critical philosopher still believes he has something to protect and preserve—the furious production of his critique as an object and end in itself—critique cannot grasp itself from its subjective position. The critical theorist gives birth to theoretical critique, a puff of hot wind. As Marx states, "Only a revolution of radical needs can be a radical revolution and it seems that for this the preconditions and birthplaces are lacking."[44] Once again Marx's statement contains a hidden twist. The birthing conditions of living critique (revolution) are lacking precisely because the masses are out of touch with their lack, which is necessary to give birth. Marx searches for a midwife to induce labor, who can perform the double duty of bringing both destruction and new life: "No class of civil society can play this role without arousing a moment of enthusiasm in itself and in the masses, a moment in which it associates, fuses, and identifies itself with society in general, and is felt and recognized to be society's *general representative*; a moment in which its demands and rights are truly the demands and rights of society itself; a moment in which it is truly the social head and the social heart."[45] Self-arousal does not come easily to people who are not permitted to touch themselves. For if people were to feel themselves, they might experience the heightened sensation of their own nothingness: the itching indignation of coming to sense what has been denied to them from the beginning; the buzzing sensation of finally grasping themselves for what they really are (not); the reckless thrill of having nothing to lose. Self-arousal is the desire to give birth to a subjectivity that does not yet exist, through the termination of another negativity that insists on its substance. Self-arousal is necessarily contagious, for self can only be born when the communal body desires its own death and reincarnation. Living critique, as opposed to theoretical critique, arises from the cracking open of one's own illusory subjectivity. Negativity (living critique; revolution) is born from negativity (self-alienation; need; oppression) that feels itself. Only radical lack, which feels itself as such, gives birth to life through the destruction of the conditions that long prevented the true birth of the political subject.

Beneath another of Marx's catchy slogans lies another layered riddle that he slowly peels back to reveal nothing: "To be radical is to grasp the root of the matter. But for man the root is man himself."[46] What then is the human being? The world, society, the state. And what, then, is the present condition of the state? Contradiction, corruption, illusion. What is perfectly clear to critique must become perfectly clear to the conditions themselves that press upon the bodies that cannot touch themselves. Human beings can only grasp themselves by the root of the matter by grasping themselves. But the root of the human being, in a society that denies self-relation, is negativity, a crack between Self and Self. To grasp the root of the matter, one must grasp one's self by the nothing. After auditioning other potential candidates, it comes as no surprise that Marx, following Ruge, locates his comic hero in the proletariat, a communal body that is reduced to nothing more than a shadowy outline of society:

> The *complete loss* of humanity can only redeem itself through the total *redemption of humanity*. This dissolution of society existing as a particular class is the *proletariat* . . . When the proletariat announces *the dissolution of the existing world order* it merely states *the secret of its own existence,* for it *is in fact* the dissolution of that world order. When the proletariat demands the *negation of private property* it merely elevates into a principle of society what society has advanced as the principle of the proletariat, and what the proletariat already involuntarily embodies as the negative result of society.[47]

The embodied negative representation of society exposes itself by exposing the conditions of the state. From another angle, by exposing its own social negativity, the proletariat mirrors society back to itself (N | N). Whatever is truly grasped from a subjective standpoint of the proletariat must be simultaneously grasped from another side: Spirit's relationship to its body (the conditions of society) and the conditions' self-conscious relationship to itself (Spirit). Rather than refuting the contradictory logic of the conditions, the logic must be played out so that the conditions feel their own cracks: "The actual pressure must be made more pressing by adding to it consciousness of pressure . . . these petrified relations must be forced to dance by singing their own tune to them! The people must be taught to be *terrified* of themselves in order to give them *courage*."[48] In historical tragedy, a sociopolitical stage soberly defends its Nothingness as Being. In historical comedy, the same stage is struck by a terrifying moment of radical self-doubt. Spirit grasps itself by its material roots and radically questions its own state of Being. The terror of Spirit's "I am not" is echoed in the reckless thrill of the proletariat's affirmation of its nothingness.

The double unmasking reveals the alienated Self. On a stage that denies her subjectivity, she can only come into self-relation by recognizing the impossibility of self-relation in the society that forms her. Self-alienation understands itself for what it is not; however, this moment of negative self-relation does not overcome alienation. Critique is self-revelation when Self and Spirit, the stage constituting Self, finally grasp their self by the impossibility of grasping their self. Overcoming self-alienation requires a birth of a new Self, in the destruction of the state and society that is Self's contents. In historical comedy, an entire sociopolitical stage feels the terror of radical self-doubt as its negativity is mirrored back to it by the proletariat, who experience Nothing's thrill of affirming its nothingness: "revolutionary audacity which flings at the adversary the defiant words: *I am nothing and I should be everything.*"[49] Now, illusory happiness is threatened by an indignation that aims at true happiness through the final destruction of past and present. Spirit seizes itself by its material roots and turns on its own structures. Only universal negativity that grasps itself as such births universal emancipation. Self-affirmation can only be achieved when it is realized universally, when Spirit's body reflects the wholeness that tragedy shallowly enacts (in theory).

Chapter 6

Benjamin's Comedy of the Damned

The narrator of the *Phenomenology of Spirit* looks back upon ancient historical comedy, reflecting on the ruins of an old way of life. A faint outline of an indiscernible figure appears hunched over in the rubble. The narrator feels a slight chill or thrill when the phantom-like figure straightens and looks in his direction. The figure is no more human than monster. No more something than nothing. And yet the narrator senses that the shadowy figure is no more a stranger than someone more similar to himself than anything he has known. He squints into the bleak landscape. Do his eyes deceive him? Is this blank "face" that peers across history into him his own?

When the Young Hegelians step into Hegel's surreal landscape, they do not see themselves lurking in the shadows of the past. The phantom appears to them too, but they interpret the figure as a visitor from the future. The blank face of the shadow is a prophecy of a new self who has not yet been born. The phantom will rise from the rubble in its full form when the dramatic archetypes of history have been destroyed once and for all by a great and terrible historical comedy to come.

The phantom returns ten years later, although without a glorious uprising. The narrator of *The Eighteenth Brumaire* walks down familiar streets. Despite the lives lost in the counterrevolution, there are no mountains of rubble to indicate the total collapse of an old way of life. Instead, grand monuments have been erected to commemorate the nonevent of 1848: the separation with a past that was never properly lived out or put to rest, the inauguration of a new day that does not dawn. With his hands in his pockets, as he kicks pebbles, he begins to sense the old phantom following timidly behind him at a distance. What does it want from him? Now lacking its former mystical aura, the clingy shadow is an annoyance, if not an embarrassment. The great historical comedy that never arrives mocks Marx and his shadow. The dream of a new self, born either in the past or future, is exposed as nothing more than farce.

The Eighteenth Brumaire opens with tragedy and farce but goes on to perform something closer to a light-hearted comic-horror with a cast composed of ghosts, zombies, and little evil elves. Tragedy and farce are overshadowed

113

by negative twins as historical comedy takes on the form of two kinds of ghostly nonevents, two kinds of failed proletarian revolutions, opposed in form, but impossible to entangle. One is the affective buildup of political and social tension, which can only find release in the explosion of a stage of history turning against itself. And yet, the great revolution on the horizon never arrives. Another is the repetition of small rebellions, adding up to nothing more than a stutter in all that has been articulated: the comic slapstick of history. The tension of the buildup is slowly released in a hiss of hot air that leaks through the tiny cracks left by the soft impact of failed revolts. In this battle of laughter against laughter, the narrator has the uncomfortable sensation of not being in on the joke.

Is Hegel's shadow, cast by the setting sun, and the Young Hegelian shadow, cast by the rising sun, the same phantom seen in a different light? Or does each phantom exist in separate historical timelines? The shifting narrators of historical comedy throughout history oscillate between the perspectives of the old owl and flightless cock, first reflecting back on historical destruction with a mixture of admiration and sorrow, then looking forward in fearless anticipation of destruction to come, then looking backward in defeat at the repeated failure of revolution to break free from the genre of historical fantasy.

When Benjamin inherits the director's chair, he retells Marx's dramatization of failed revolution at a moment when the partisan resistance seemed to have been defeated at the height of Hitler's power. A nightmare descends upon Europe more terrible than any vision of destruction in the Young Hegelian's darkest fantasies. Benjamin draws on Young Hegelian historical drama to narrate his own experience. Despite often being typecast as the Melancholic, Benjamin grasps himself as the Comic against a hellish landscape realized on earth. A dramatic narrative about the apparent defeat of the resistance is repeated until it plays out a form of resistance that takes place in the realization of defeat. In a battle of laughter against laughter, the phantom returns to get the last laugh.

Two dark suns, slowing revolving in opposite directions around the same arch, cross paths over Benjamin's comic stage. The narrator stands in the middle of the stage between his flickering shadows. In split moments, the phantom of the past and the phantom of the future appear together. The narrator of historical comedy stands back to back with the first phantom, who stretches out its wide owl wings as it surveys the past. The first phantom weeps over rubble as the narrator confronts a second phantom. A demonic cock with sharp talons sporadically struts backward into the horizon with its eyes locked on the narrator. Its shrill crow, composed of tiny punctuated explosions, is a warning cry.

The two phantoms, which Benjamin sometimes calls angels, initially take the form of the odd couple. The inconsolable melancholic angel is seemingly born from the pages of a mourning play, with the demonic angel borrowed from Baudelaire's nightmarish verse. Upon closer look, however, Benjamin's reader notices that the phantom-angels only appear in the context of comedy. According to a letter from Benjamin to Gretel Adorno, his 1940 "On the Concept of History," which contains the most famous reference to the angel of history, was intended as a theoretical preface to a planned book on Baudelaire and nineteenth-century Paris. Benjamin worked on the manuscript from 1937 to 1940 alongside the *Arcades Project* (whose working title was *Passagenarbeit*), where Benjamin collected quotations on Baudelaire's laughter.[1] Other references to the angels occur in essays on comedians, such as Karl Kraus and Charlie Chaplin.[2] In a 1933 autobiographical essay, Benjamin gives the second phantom a name, the angel of Santander, which Gershom Scholem later unscrambles as an anagram for "Satan."[3] The phantom appears to Benjamin as he reflects on the beginning of his life from a place of exile. He recalls that his parents gave him two additional German names: "When I was born, it occurred to my parents that I might perhaps become a writer. If that happened, it would be a good idea if people did not immediately notice I was a Jew."[4] The two additional names were intended to offer Benjamin visibility in the eyes of the public by concealing his identity. However, while offering the appearance of visibility, the names simultaneously highlight the impossibility of really appearing. To accept the names, he explains, would require him to reject "the gift of appearing as a human being."[5] But by rejecting the names, Benjamin acknowledges that the gift of appearing was denied to him from the beginning. He chooses to play out his negative role as the phantom who haunts the space that denies him life.

As Benjamin contemplates the people and possessions he left behind in his exile, his thoughts turn to the Klee painting above his former mantel. The creature in the painting he left behind now appears to him as a demonic phantom rather than a divine angel. As Benjamin locks eyes with the phantom, he simultaneously sees himself through its eyes as it looks backward from the future to witness Benjamin in his naked negativity. His empty hands mirrored by the phantom's outstretched arms do not indicate items lost, but what he never possessed: the gift of appearing as a human being. This time, the spirit of the angel, which is not separate from himself, does not appear to be an attitude of mourning or melancholy but of determination and vengeance.

The angel-phantoms highlight two sides of Benjamin's relationship to the world stage. But the odd couple is no more opposed than conjoined twins. They speak in one voice: in mourning we recognize that what has been lost was never ours; in laughter, we seize ourselves by our negativity, turning on the stage that damns us. The one who weeps for the loss of what was never born and the one who seeks vengeance in the name of life belong to the same comic stage. Whether the mourning angel and vengeful angel are two or one is a matter of perspective (as we see in the accounts of Scholem and Giorgio Agamben, who count the same figures differently).[6] From whose perspective is Benjamin's comic-horror told?

Hegel's and Marx's dramas reach their climax when the comic protagonist (the narrator, the audience, the proletariat) encounters themselves in a negative double. But Benjamin's historical drama is narrated from the start from the otherside: the negative standpoint of one who is at the center of the drama but is prevented from appearing as an actor. At last, historical comedy is narrated from the perspective of Nothing, who grasps herself by her negativity. Or, from another perspective within the same perspective, comedy is narrated from the split between the negative double: a crack that casts two shadows. Scholem interprets the birdlike phantoms as Talmudic angels representing a Jewish person's secret name.[7] Benjamin, caught between two phantoms, is split between not only two, but four, secret names: two German names that overwrite him at birth and two sacred names hidden in the shadows. It's no wonder that Benjamin is drawn to the scoundrel in Charlie Chaplin's 1928 film *The Circus*, who escapes the authorities by slipping into a maze of mirrors. Benjamin's mirror image is immediately redoubled in inversions of inversions.[8] In this play of negative reflections, grasping one's self is like grasping at straws. Benjamin steps forward to name himself, accepting his predetermined role, not of the Melancholic, but of the Damned.

In Marx's drama, Nothing grasps herself by her social negativity in the Proletariat's negative self-relation, represented by the cry "I am nothing!" Benjamin extends social negativity to encompass his own positionality in the context of Nazi-occupied Europe. Unlike Marx, he doesn't define the comic protagonist by a contradiction embodied by another. The narrator of historical comic-horror plays out his role as the damned, who is cast into social negativity before the drama has even begun. In playing out his negativity, the narrator brings visibility to the impossibility of appearing as subject. Benjamin's comedy of the damned is the comedy of the ghosts of revolutions, resistances, and subjects that were never given life—but now return for revenge.

The Mother Tongue and the Stutter

In *The Eighteenth Brumaire of Louis Bonaparte*, Marx famously compares the dream of the revolution-to-come to the imagined experience of forgetting one's mother tongue: "A beginner who has learnt a new language always translates it back into his mother tongue, but he has assimilated the spirit of the new language and can freely express himself in it only when he finds his way in it without recalling the old and forgets his native tongue in the use of the new."[9] The revolts of the 1830s and 1840s seemed to be generating a force that would culminate in a final shattering of all former political articulations. Without clearly knowing what new political articulation would take the place of the old, each small revolt attempted to begin a new sentence. Although the Young Hegelians anticipated the emergence of a Hegelian self-articulated comic community, 1848 failed to generate a new language. As Marx would later assess the period, what appeared to be a revolutionary breaking point only took the form of newness while reproducing the content of what each revolt rebelled against.

The proletarian attempts to achieve new political expression failed to rip themselves free from repetition's inertia. Despite being slightly older and perhaps slightly disillusioned, Marx returns to the Young Hegelian dream of a new common language in the erasure of the mother tongue: a historical comedy that would shatter tragic speech, which defends its own suffering. In contrast to the lingering fantasy of a revolution that would "not borrow its poetry from the past but the future," the weight of Marx's text looks backward at failure rather than forward toward fantasy, offering an analysis of how proletarian revolutions actually tend to unfold.[10] Rather than erasing the mother tongue, we find ourselves ensnared by it. We try to define ourselves in a single new utterance, but the monster mother tongue wraps itself around our ankles and pulls us back into itself.[11]

These failed attempts to create a new language that breaks with the content of the old result instead in glitches within the mother tongue, as Marx describes it, instances of scrambled syntax or stuttered speech.[12] In such a way, just when the proletarian revolutions seem to gain momentum, to say something new, they interrupt themselves mid-sentence.[13] In contrast to the fantasy of revolution as a decisive breaking point with the past, the actual proletarian revolutions occurred not as a great event but rather as a series of glitches, events flickering in and out of existence, perpetually restarting before they can begin.

If the revolution-to-come is found in the fantasy of forgetting our mother tongue in creating a new language, actual proletarian protests and revolts tend to leave us stuttering within our native language. We fail to create something new but we can no longer smoothly repeat what has already been said. The grand failure to create a new common language leaves us with a series of mini failures as we fail to articulate our visions of the future in the mother tongue in which we are stuck.

In Marx's blurring of fantasy and nightmare, we learn that on the world stage it is often difficult to distinguish freedom from bondage, which often takes the form of a comedy while preserving its tragic contents. Marx's manipulation of genre likewise shows itself in his blurred distinction between fantasy and horror in his extended metaphor of forgetting one's first language. The tension between the stubborn fantasy of an imaginary new language that overwrites the old and the stubbornness of the mother tongue, which does not allow itself to be forgotten, produces a new kind of expression in the form of failed expression: the repetition of failed protests and revolts, the failure to say anything new, fills one with deep desire and insecurity that stutter in our native tongue, which we cannot escape but can no longer smoothly articulate ourselves in. We become like a new expatriate who, in attempting to speak, think, and dream in a new language, begins to speak their own language as if it is a second language. In speaking their mother tongue, they may adopt the accent of those in their new country, speaking disjointedly as they grasp for words that once readily came to them. Before mastering the new language, they begin to relate to their native language as if it were a foreign tongue. In such a way, a failed revolution can leave people in worse conditions than before a revolt. One's relationship to the old is disrupted, but there is nothing substantial to grasp onto in its place.

Marx pairs the actual proletarian revolts amounting to nothing with the aspirational vision of the absolute event that will cut out the mother tongue. But the Young Hegelian fantasy of historical comedy as the absolute event reveals itself to be a negative double, a split between the image of total destruction and the nonevent that fails to arrive. The audience becomes restless as the star of the show fails to appear. The spotlight only highlights the absence. Critical theory only highlights its own failed incarnation. Yet, something stirs when absolute destruction grasps itself by its absence. The mother tongue cannot be silenced by a resistance that fails to utter a single new sentence. But the mother tongue also cannot shake her annoying negative double, the clumsy Stutter who stumbles into her path, tripping up her smooth articulation of progress.

The Comic and the Damned

Historical drama resurfaced when the Frankfurt School and its interlocutors on the peripheries adopted the Young Hegelian coupling of aesthetics and politics. The most obvious place to locate a new alliance between comedy and critical philosophy might seem to be in the plays and philosophy of Bertolt Brecht. However, critical laughter is heard even in what is often identified as the melancholic thought of Benjamin.[14] Benjamin echoes Marx's staging of revolution as a drama in *The Eighteenth Brumaire* when he states, quoting Blanqui: "Revolution is a drama perhaps more than a history."[15] History, as he also claims, has everything to do with drama.[16] In the twentieth century, Benjamin is one of the primary inheritors of Hegelian-Marxist drama, casting the dramatic action of history as tragic and revolution as its comic shadow.[17]

Benjamin's audience tends to experience his philosophy as tragic, partly due to the circumstances of his own life, especially his escape from Germany in 1932 and suicide in anticipation of a failed second escape from Nazi-occupied France in 1940.[18] It's hard to believe that Benjamin could frame his relationship to such circumstances as comic. Even Charlie Chaplin, reflecting on his 1940 film *The Great Dictator*, confessed that he would not have satirized Hitler if he had known the horrors to come.[19] Yet at the height of the fascist uprising, Benjamin nevertheless defends Chaplin's portrayal of "Hitler's Diminished Masculinity," taking comic inspiration in what would appear to be "the end."[20] Perhaps it is due to the darkness of Benjamin's comedy that some readers are drawn to the melancholic over the comic. In the spirit of comedy, Benjamin, like the demonic cock, looks his opponent in the eyes and laughs in the face of a stage that denies his subjectivity.

The casting of Benjamin as the melancholic is further supported by his early attention to tragedy and mourning, which he treats both as theatrical genre and political historical analysis. In comparison to references to tragedy, comedy is sparsely sprinkled throughout Benjamin's early notes, such as his fragments on Molière. An exceptional early study of comedy is found in a remarkable essay published in 1921, "Fate and Character," in which Benjamin fully outlines tragedy and comedy as a historical double.[21] A parade of colorful figures line up in single file, entering the text one by one to enact the concept of character and the concept of concept: the actor, followed by the gods, by the lucky one, the fates, the demon, the pagan, the hero, the pauper, the judge, the clairvoyant, the fortune teller. Each player soberly sacrifices their individuality for the weighty concept that each internalizes as their identity. In this first tragic usage, the concept of character is equated with a societal role or value that a person believes to be her inner essence. Just as the characters enact a concept, the concepts may also be interpreted as characters: Action, Atonement, Fortune, Guilt, Fate, Genius, Judgment, Law, Signs, Time.

Benjamin plays with different senses of fate by floating between Greek drama and forms of fortune-telling, such as palmistry and card reading. From one perspective the characters and concepts make up a theatrical cast. From another, at the same time, the troop is an alternative set of major Arcana cards belonging to a Benjaminian tarot deck. At the end of the parade of characters is the comic, otherwise known as the scoundrel. The comic fittingly replaces the Fool in a traditional tarot deck, representing a new beginning in position zero, which may be counted at the end or the beginning of the twenty-two major figures. As our friend from chapter 2, Strepsiades, illustrates, the comic as the scoundrel represents a figure utterly devoid of character (in the first sense). The comic is without character in two senses: the fledgling concept does not yet have a personality; the scoundrel is without virtue. Because he lacks inner content, the comic is reduced to a single superficial trait, an exaggerated physical feature or morally indifferent trait (e.g., Strepsiades's stupidity). In this second comic usage, character is equated with caricature. "Fate and Character" concludes with an ironic twist: the character without moral character (as dictated by law and religion) is the only character free to act as an ethical agent, which Benjamin identifies in the beginning and end of the essay as the Actor.

Earlier in the drama, the character lacking character also plays an important role in maintaining an oppressive tragic order. The pauper's placement in society destines him to be of an immoral disposition, becoming associated with qualities such as "thievish" or "envious." The poor are condemned from birth to be determined guilty by the law. By making the pauper guilty, the law maintains the appearance of innocence. The scoundrel, however, acting out of ignorance or rebellion, has no fidelity to an order that superficially counts him as a political player only to make a show out of exiling or terminating him later. The judge may condemn the scoundrel's foolish attempt to outsmart the law or his naive ignorance. Yet, the comic's relationship to his own action and to the world is without guilt. The audience of comedy falls in love with the scoundrel's inexplicable self-confidence despite his unflattering trait. We laugh at the scoundrel's folly, which results from his obliviousness toward societal convention, while secretly envying his freedom. The comic represents the thrill of uninhibited self-relation. This comic self-relation is entirely political in its indifference toward the political system that damns him. When Benjamin reflects on the character of the scoundrel in Chaplin's *The Circus*, he notes, "Chaplin appeals both to the most international and the most revolutionary emotion of the masses: their laughter."[22] In comedy, character grasps itself as a concept empty of any essential content. The reduction of character to a single inessential feature allows character to grasp herself outside of herself in her shadow.[23] The reduction of the concept of character, and concept of concept, to nothing more than the play of shadows yields liberation, first grasped by the comic Self, then by the masses.

As if reading his own cards, "Fate and Character" foretells the course of Benjamin's later focus on the politics of historical comedy as revolution. And yet, the essay tends to get lost in the shadow cast by weighty works such as *The Origin of German Tragic Drama*, which reduces comedy to a mere aside to ancient tragedy and the German baroque *Trauerspiel*.[24] Indeed, Benjamin's earliest notes mark nearly all human experience as tragic. These earlier fragments, written long before Benjamin's supposed "Marxist turn," are undeniably born of a Young Hegelian spirit. The formulation of history in "World and Time" is almost an exact echo of Ruge and Marx. The only imaginable way out of world tragedy is the comic destruction of the theatrical stages of history by history's own hand. Yet this final comic act recedes into the horizon like a messiah who repeatedly fails to return.[25]

Benjamin follows Hegel, identifying tragedy in the hero's speech, in which she soberly defends an action that places her in conflict with her society even though that action follows the normative social order of that same society. The hero's reasoning for her action is a mere reflection of Reason itself, a slowly evolving social inheritance, determining all that can be articulated within a historical moment. As Benjamin writes, "Reason expresses itself through language and language is tragic."[26] Language is tragic because speech simultaneously articulates and conceals the cracks in Reason. The hero's self-defense nearly exposes that Reason is at odds with itself. Yet the hero protects Reason by playing out her role as the hero, taking the credit and blame for a conflict belonging to all. "Too great humility is the bitterest irony," as Marx would say.[27] The attention on the hero conceals the fact that her relationship to the articulation of Reason is not unique. Everything that can be articulated within Reason, as Benjamin emphasizes, is tragic: "Tragedy is not just confined exclusively to the realm of dramatic speech; it is the only proper form to human dialogue. That is to say, no tragedy exists outside of human dialogue, and the only form in which human dialogue can appear is that of tragedy."[28] To be socially accepted as reasonable, speech must conceal the most reasonable thing of all: the contradictions belonging to Reason. Human dialogue is supported by an unspoken social contract between people who agree to appear reasonable by not responding to the obvious tensions in Reason, manifested in their own accounts of themselves. The tragic hero is the individual who defends the rationale that harms her. But the tragic hero is also the chorus or society who projects its own conflicts onto the scapegoat.

Benjamin's account of tragic speech as characteristic of all language highlights Marx's metaphor of the mother tongue as more than metaphor (as if metaphor could ever be mere metaphor). The only possible way out of tragedy is through the destruction of the mother tongue, which wraps itself around linguistic and nonlinguistic beings alike. As Benjamin writes, "There is no event or thing in either animate or inanimate nature that does not in some way partake of language."[29] Language moderates what can appear in world theater and banishes what cannot appear within Reason without exposing Reason. Society, in its role as the defender of Reason, exiles or terminates those whose very being points to universal contradiction. There are thus two kinds of roles to play within historical theater. One must conceal the contradictions within Reason by articulating oneself as a unity who reflects and blends into a greater social unity. Or one must fall through the cracks and do so quietly without drawing attention to the same cracks in which one's flickering existence is born only to immediately disappear.

Benjamin's early focus on historical tragedy veers toward comedy when he is exiled from academia before his academic career really began. As Benjamin prepared his habilitation—the final feat of a long gladiatorial battle required for entry into the German academy—he worried how the spirit of his writing would be restricted by the defenders of academic seriousness, or as Baudelaire, who demonstrated little restraint, called them: "spiteful pendants of solemnity—charlatans of gravity, pedantic corpses which have emerged from the icy vaults of the *Institut* and have come again to the land of the living, like a band of misery ghosts."[30] Benjamin's fears were not unfounded; his habilitation on the mourning play was rejected by his committee in 1925. To be more exact, he withdrew his habilitation before it could be officially rejected after receiving news of its fate. As his attention shifted to French comic theater and Russian and American wartime comic cinema, he soon found companionship in the writings of a band of academic exiles like himself, the Young Hegelians. A new alliance was formed, not only between critical philosophy and comedy, but between the negative historical double in the present and the same double in the past.

Several years after the publication of his rejected habilitation, Benjamin's curriculum vitae claims comedy, rather than tragedy, as the area of his specialization.[31] It further indicates his plans for a companion piece to the *Trauerspiel*, which would trace the relationship between ancient comedy and classical French comedy, paralleling his earlier analysis of tragedy and German Baroque drama.[32] The book on comedy was destined, by fate or by chance, to repeat the outcome of its tragic counterpart, finding long life and love (in audiences belonging to future generations) despite its initial failed conception. Although the comic double to the study of the mourning play never formally came to fruition, orphaned concepts of comedy and laughter fill Benjamin's later notes. *The Arcades Project* alone is filled with thirty-nine eruptions of mechanical, ancient, godly, drunk, strident, childlike, damnable, diabolic, satanic, human, derisive, profound, disruptive, scornful, ghostly, grotesque, nocturnal, and feminine laughter. The fragments contain over three times as many counts of laughter as tears, and Benjamin attributes most of his tears to excessive laughter. Benjamin's collection of different specimens of laughter makes its way into his final work on nineteenth-century Paris and Baudelaire, which draws heavily on Marx's *Eighteenth Brumaire*.[33] As Agamben accounts, Benjamin protected this final manuscript, which occupied the last three years of his life, carrying it under his arm in a black leather portfolio.[34] Benjamin's laughter in these pages goes well beyond his original plan for a genre study on classical French comedy. It erupts from a dark historical stage marked by the Nazi rise to power in 1933. It looks upon the grotesque with Baudelaire and attempts alongside Marx to grasp the repetition of failed resistance. This final work pursues the questions that haunt Benjamin's thinking from the beginning, "How does one laugh in their end?" "How does one laugh in *the* end?" "How does one laugh at the end that has already occurred?"

The various expressions of Benjamin's laughter erupt from two different comic tempos that reflect Marx's description of two kinds of failed revolutions. The first belongs to the sacred timing of the messianic, the infinity of the negative comic object in the form of the great historical comedy that "arrives," like Beckett's *Godot*, only in its failure to arrive. The second belongs to the satanic timing of the damned, the negative infinity of hell, which, like the proletarian revolutions, unfolds according to its own repeated internal disturbance. The first laughter responds to the tension of comic suspension, while the second responds to the clumsy physicality of comic slapstick. The rhythm of the finale that never begins ricochets off of the rhythm of a second act, which must restart each time an actor stumbles over a line.

Benjamin fantasizes about another kind of laughter that would erupt if the finale at last arrived. In one of his earliest essays, "The Metaphysics of Youth," he states, "Laughing, revelation stands before them and compels them to fall silent."[35] Messianic laughter represents a redemptive end to history that would liberate humanity from its tragic script. Yet, Benjamin simultaneously questions whether revelatory laughter is at the end of history or what drives history forward. At times, Benjamin identifies a kind of spiritual laughter as the negative force animating history. Under the domination of the mother tongue, materiality has no say over itself but is silently engrossed in immutable laws that articulate *what is*. Laughter shakes a historical stage, in which socio-material existence appears fixed by equally unchanging spiritual laws. Laughter is *the spirit of matter* or *the laughing matter of spirit*: "[Like] a shock that brings someone engrossed in reverie up from the depths . . . in laughter the muteness of the matter is overcome. In laughter, above all, matter takes on an abundance of spirit . . . indeed, it becomes so spiritual that it far outstrips language. Aiming still higher, it ends in shrill laughter."[36] Laughter is the eruption of what appears fixed within the normative order of all that has been articulated within Reason. Inspirited materiality has a good laugh when Spirit, to its delight, discovers its body: in a moment of lost innocence, the virgin in Eden giggles at the discovery of her nakedness; Self is tickled by the discovery of her communal body at the cross. In contrast to Aristotle's definition of pleasure as pure thought thinking itself, Benjamin locates laughter in materiality's grasp of its own historical embodiment. Spirit is nothing more than the thrill of materiality touching itself. History's shrill laughter cracks the seemingly fixed order that spoke for materiality as something separate and above materiality. As Benjamin puts it, "Laughter is shattered articulation."[37] The crack separating Spirit and Matter is itself shattered. But the shattering of the crack is not a simple restoration of an original oneness (that was never brought into existence). It is the exposure of a deeper negativity that the articulation of Reason concealed.

Benjamin sometimes identifies laughter as a grand comic end of an oppressive stage of history, the shrill laughter of shattered articulation. More often, however, he meditates on a laughter that creeps underneath the surface, unsettling what appears within reason. Beneath the fantasy of shattered articulation, laughter belongs to the lived time of world theater. Beneath the realm of tragic speech is a barely audible hiss that leaks through the contradictions of Reason. Revelation manifests itself on earth neither in language nor in silence but through a negativity that flickers within the tragic articulation of Reason. In "The Metaphysics of Youth," Benjamin also writes about the "one who inquires about revelation": "His eloquence escapes him; enraptured, he listens to his own voice. He hears neither speech nor silence."[38] In the suppression of a kind of messianic laughter that would silence the mother tongue, the worldly laughter of failed resistance is an irregular interruption within the articulation of Reason, recurring like a drunk hiccup or nervous stutter.

Although Benjamin's tears are caused by laughter, his laughter is often caused by defeat. Yet his defeated laughter does not dissolve into despair or nihilism. Benjamin offers an acceptance of defeat that overcomes despair and demands revenge. This comic perspective is expressed in the mantra of Saint

Silouan (later repeated by Gillian Rose): "Keep your mind in hell and despair not."[39] While Benjamin turns to Hegel and Marx to develop revolution as drama, he draws on Baudelaire's 1855 essay "The Essence of Laughter" to develop the darker comic theme of a "derisive" and "scornful laughter of hell."[40] Benjamin's "derisive laughter from hell" rises with a vengeance from a position of absolute defeat to haunt a tragic stage of history that damned him. Laughter no longer belongs to the victor who gloats over his defeated enemy, as the Spartans practiced it, but rather to one who is already damned. As Benjamin quotes Baudelaire, "All the miscreants of melodrama—accursed, damned, and fatally marked with a grin which runs from ear to ear—are in the pure orthodoxy of laughter."[41] The image of the miscreant of melodrama evokes Antigone's mad laughter after her execution has already been decided. When one is already socially damned, the threat of her second death becomes a joke. Being-between-two-deaths frees one from the mortal bond of being-toward-death. Infinity can only be pronounced from this place of living death or the undead. Benjamin's comedy unfolds along "the temporality of hell," which mocks death from a place of death.[42]

The narrator of Benjamin's comic-horror looks forward, like the Young Hegelians, in anticipation of the annihilation of a tragic script. Yet, this same vision recognizes that the final Event, by nature of its negative messianic structure, necessarily withdraws from the present. As the narrator steps forward, the end also takes a step back. Future-oriented vision is doubled, seeing both the outline of the shadow of the Event and its absence. The Janus-faced narrator of comic-horror simultaneously looks backward in defeat, like Marx of *The Eighteenth Brumaire*, toward what was never achieved. This backward-oriented vision is also doubled. Benjamin looks through the eyes of the angel of history with grief. He simultaneously looks backward on the present through the eyes of the phantom of the future, laughing in defiance at a social death that has already occurred. As Baudelaire writes, the double eruption of laughter and tears belongs to the damned, who find relief in neither Eden nor in Redemption to come, neither in visions of revolutions past nor future:

> In earthly paradise—whether one supposes it as past or to come, a memory or a prophecy, in the sense of the theologians or socialists . . . joy did not find its dwelling in laughter. As no trouble afflicted him, man's countenance was simple and smooth, and *the laughter which now shakes the nations* never distorted the features of his face. Laughter and tears cannot make their appearance in the paradise of delights. They are both equally the children of woe, and they came because the body of an enfeebled man lacked the strength to restrain them.[43]

As Baudelaire claims, laughter is a symptom of continual failure, like "a nervous convulsion, an involuntary spasm comparable to a sneeze."[44] The comic's inability to overcome his clumsiness—and the comic community's inability to shake its misfortune—points to a moment of falling out of favor. What wrong turn did we take along the way to lead us to this series of unfortunate events? One weeps over the event of her exile while laughing in the recognition that grace was never hers to begin with. The ideology of Eden, whether positioned in the past or future, begins to pull at the seams. The Nations shake in the presence of the children of woe, who understand that those who were nothing to begin with have nothing to lose. As Baudelaire concludes, "The phenomena engendered by the Fall [laughter and tears] will become the means of redemption."[45]

Benjamin's backward-facing double vision, which erupts in a mixture of laughter and tears, may be contrasted to Heidegger's future-oriented anxiety toward death. Heidegger assumed that the one ontological truth that each human being has in common is the indisputable fact that death awaits each of us in the indeterminate future.[46] Authenticity demands that we face the event of our very own impending death. But what a privilege to be so alive to flee or face one's future death and, what more, to call this final event one's very own. Benjamin's laughter is precisely directed at *a life that is not and is not my own*. This is the negation of the impersonal subject, the enunciation, "it is not." The laughter of the damned recognizes a kind of death that was in the beginning. For the damned, anxious anticipation of one's own death is yet another way of fleeing a death that has already occurred, a death that can never be one's ownmost, because it was determined for the individual before she was born.[47] One is made killable by being born into a social position that is already negative from the beginning. In contrast to Heidegger, who envisions a kind of passion for finite life that comes only through embracing the event of one's future death, Benjamin suggests that in an indifference to both life and death there is a kind of temporalization of infinity belonging to the damned. From the perspective of the damned, death is not an ultimate end but something that has already occurred and will occur again.

The occurrence of a death in birth can first be heard as an ontological position: one's subjectivization is constituted by what fails to appear as subject (the aborted twin who haunts us).[48] The split within subjectivity (between myself and my missing half), or on a different scale, the split within Spirit, is originary and constitutive. But the statement that "I am nothing" is also social and political in the sense that certain individuals cannot appear as actors within a given articulation of Reason, making their physical insistence a farce.[49] Tragedy gives nonexistence a mask of subjectivity, providing a false sense of subjective wholeness, representation, and agency. Benjamin's comedy instead exposes the nonexistence as nothing. In this comic instance of self-relating negativity, the first kind of ontological negativity flashes in the unmasking of the superficial appearance of determinate subject on the historical stage.

Benjamin's unfolding of the comic tempo of the damned presents "death as caesura that belongs together with all the straight lines of divine temporality."[50] The infinity of the damned underlies and rhythmically punctuates the smooth flowing finitude of the living, surfacing like a recurring glitch or stutter. In a similar way, the doctrine of laughter belonging to the damned appears as something opposed but nevertheless fully within the sphere of articulation, the symbolic, the law. In their role as a ghost tickler or agitator, those who are determined nothing cause Being to twitch. There is a slight stutter in all that can be articulated when Reason is unsettled by a negativity that stirs within it: "Beguiled by ghostly laughter in the air . . . reason falters, grasping at phantom straws."[51] Laughter can be shrill, but laughter can also be expressed in subtle distortions, existing only "in the hilarity of shadows. Nocturnal laughter floats in the air."[52] Benjamin's vengeful laughter claims, "I have been determined nothing, but you cannot destroy nothing." A certain kind of philosophical and political response can only begin from a place of absolute defeat. After the damned give up the hope of appearing on a stage that casts them in the role of nothing, it is then that one *appears as nothing*.

Benjamin leans into the character of the damned to explore how the gift of appearing is denied to the character of the poor and the Jew alike. Drawing again on Baudelaire, he further attributes ghostly laughter to the feminine, tracing the double of the Virgin and the Prostitute.[53] In "The Essence of Laughter," Baudelaire imagines Eve as the mother of laughter. The first outburst that erupts from her lips is in response to her own exile from paradise. Laughter is the symptom of failure but also of self-knowledge. Eve's eruption is the thrill of self-relation experienced precisely in her fall. She grasps herself not only in her nakedness but also in her exile. Could the drama have unfolded differently? Could her nakedness have been concealed from her for eternity? Or was the discovery of her own body (and knowledge of its goodness) not inevitable? Was she not destined to be damned from the beginning?

In my account of Genesis, material being is brought into existence not in a word or speech act but in a stutter. Being, pure Being attempts to conceal his primordial self-doubt by redoubling himself in embodied being. The unspoken commandment, the original social contract between divinity and humanity, is that creation must pretend not to notice Being's crack. But pure Being's insecurity gets the best of him and before anyone can state the obvious, Eve is forced to take the fall for Being's insufficiency. But as with all desperate attempts for control, the power move backfires. In her exile, Eve sees the role she was intended to play from the beginning. The exposure of her nakedness only magnifies the deficiency in Pure Being, who inadvertently exposes his own crack. Eve cannot hold back her laughter.

Baudelaire repeats the story of Eve in the figure of the Virgin in Paris, who stumbles upon an obscene caricature with exaggerated features. She blushes, muttering a soft "goddamn." Her hesitation soon turns to laughter when she fully discovers the pleasures that have been kept from her. The twin phantoms, who attach themselves to the damned, are born in the Virgin's laughter.

As Baudelaire explains, the immaculate angel loses her innocence when the Virgin laughs. The angel wraps herself up in her wings to hide herself from herself. But when the Virgin steps into the role of the Whore, the angel obtains fangs and claws. It is a story repeated from Lucifer to Eve to Christ, who exchange the bliss of unity with Being for the thrill of embodied self-relation, experienced through the split within one. Benjamin repeats Baudelaire's mantra: "Laughter is Satanic; it is therefore profoundly human."[54]

But does the experience of transformation—in incarnation or the fall, in conversion or corruption—leave the old self behind? Or does the ghost of the terminated self (the virgin; the immaculate angel; the divine) continue to shadow the birth of the new (the prostitute; the demon; the damned)? What looks like the transformation of one into its opposite is also the splitting of one into two, which remain two in one. The monstrous compound is "the existence of two being face to face with one another . . . it is a permanent dualism in the human being—that is, the power of being oneself and someone else at one and the same time."[55] Baudelaire concludes that laughter belongs to "the living contradiction" that grasps herself as such. The Virgin's laughter is not the creation of a new self, but a response to a deepening of a split rising to the surface: "Laughter is the expression of a double, or contradictory feelings; and that is the reason why a convulsion occurs."[56]

The prostitute is one of the first characters to step into Benjamin's early writings. From the beginning, she is wrapped up in revelation and laughter. She is the character who cannot appear as a human being according to Reason. Because she cannot appear and cannot be heard as a speaking subject, she shares a special relationship to the divine, who communicates through the cracks in Reason. Benjamin's first formulation of the divine is the character of "God [who] speaks and listens for the contradictions of language."[57] To whom does divine revelation belong? Like Ovid's Thisbe, the prostitute presses her ear against the great wall of Reason that denies her entry. She strains to make sense of the indeterminable noises that escape through the cracks. She presses her lips against the crack, uncertain if what escapes her mouth is a soft sob or ironic snicker. Does salvation await on the other side? It is not God whom she hears, but rather the damned who exist only within the cracks. By listening to the crack within Reason, we learn that both laughter and tears belong to the damned who are abandoned by their messiah.

The laughter of the damned is the resignation of one who has given up the midwife's goal of giving new life, that is, of achieving greater visibility, inclusivity, and representation for all. Rebellion takes the form of the repetition of the action of the oppressor rather than opposition when one who has been silenced repeats her silence louder. Benjamin's feminine laughter of the damned resonates with Sara Ahmed's understanding of resignation as feminist resistance. Ahmed identifies her own resignation from a post in professional philosophy in 2015 as an act of feminist protest. She recodes resignation from the tragic acceptance of one's defeat to a kind of resilience in defeat. As she puts it, "Resignation can sound passive, even fatalistic: resigning oneself to one's fate. But resignation can be an act of feminist protest . . . By snapping you are saying: I will not reproduce a world I cannot bear, a world I do not think should be borne."[58] Ahmed points out that articulating how one has been silenced or others have been silenced gives the false impression of having a voice. This is especially the case when a testimony to the way one has been silenced is taken as a solution rather than the exposure of a problem that continues to persist. As with the case of Freud's patient, the young girl who refuses to speak, sometimes desire can only sustain itself as unsatisfied desire. Voice is sustained only in the form of testifying to one's lack of voice. But this is still not to have a voice. In self-censorship, one refuses to speak over the silence.

In Ahmed's characterization of resignation as the refusal to both conceal and reproduce an unbearable world, we find the midwife's refusal to foster the birth of conditions that determine certain lives as nothing. And yet this practice of resignation, a kind of abortion that must be repeated, is at once the act of giving birth to what has already been determined nothing. In refusing to appear, one appears as the nothing that she has already been determined. Nothing appears in different forms: silence, refusal, resignation, absence, suicide, and (the self-termination of a historical stage) revolution. The series of failed revolutions that Marx highlights in his *Eighteenth Brumaire* is both driven and interrupted by a kind of self-censorship. Although the peasant revolts were seen as a failure, there is a subversive capacity precisely in the performance of their repeated failure. The proletariat revolution aborts itself before it can have political life.

Benjamin's comic timing of the infinity of hell is the hiccup or stutter that regularly interrupts the lines of historical progress. From this view, the movement of the negative is not in the power to forget one's mother tongue.[59] Rather, the work of the negative can also be found in the stutter within one's native language, which causes the mechanical reproduction of all that has been articulated to "tremble from head to toe."[60] To act as the nothing is to become a laughing ghost who haunts the space that both constitutes and denies one. One acts as the nothing in the realization that the space one haunts cannot, in turn, destroy what it has already made nothing. One cannot kill a ghost. The divine laughter shared among the damned in commune haunts the living, surfacing in slow revolutions that take place through hesitations and delays.[61] To end with another iteration of Rose's mantra: "Keep your mind in hell until the shrieks become shouts of joy."[62]

Chapter 7

Antigone's Disappearance Act in Yugoslavia

Our movement past the theatrical and theoretical stage to the world stage now circles back to Antigone and the theatrical stage. Although *Antigone* was reenacted on many European stages in the twentieth century as commentary on the different political stages of World War II, the communist renderings of *Antigone* in the context of postwar Yugoslavia present an unusual kind of enacted memorial. I focus on Dominik Smole's celebrated *Antigona* to consider tragic theater as a form of comic memorial.[1] How can the figure of Antigone, who is driven to suicide, offer a comic reflection on the most horrific events on the world stage? By now I hope I have established a kind of comedy that is distinct from a humorous lightness that aims at happy resolution. While this comic stance refuses resolution that comes too soon, it equally refuses the sober acceptance of tragic conditions as that which cannot be changed. I have suggested that Antigone's laughter in Sophocles's play remains tragic because it is directed at the opposing side of a conflict, a product of a crack that equally determines both sides.[2] As Freud saw it, when an individual laughs in the face of the other, she laughs in the mirror without recognizing her own image. The joke is on her.[3] In postwar Yugoslavia, Antigone's laughter becomes comic when she anticipates her own death, not at the end of the play, but in the beginning. Here, laughter does not belong to one of the heroes of a tragic division but to the split itself that structures the stage. In Smole's rendition, Antigone does not appear in the play that continues to bear her name. Antigone's absence is the silent laughter of the crack.

As I have also already claimed, Antigone's suicide at the end of Sophocles's play is a concrete repetition of her symbolic death that has already occurred before the play begins. Her death is in her own beginning as she is born into a society in which the roles of woman and citizen, which demand contrary action, cannot coexist in one body. As a logical contradiction she cannot reasonably appear as a subject. Or rather, in order to appear as subject, Antigone must become a logical contradiction. While the symbolic subject has the appearance of agency, Antigone herself is nothing more than the negative space of contradiction. She appears *as sister* or *as citizen* but the space of her subjectivity lies in the invisible division between these two irreconcilable roles.

Antigone dies twice: first symbolically (in her birth), then physically (in the act of taking her own life). As Lacan argues, Sophocles's tragedy takes place between Antigone's two deaths. "From Antigone's point of view life can only be approached, can only be lived or thought about, from the place of the limit where her life is already lost, where she is already on the other side. But from that place she can see it and live it in the form of something already lost."[4] Antigone's existence can only be sustained from the point of view of one who is already dead. In my view, Antigone is tragic because she insists on calling this zone of shades *life* (not merely life but a life that is worth dying for). Antigone, at last, dies comically in Smole's play through the doubling of her first double-death: her absence is repeated four times through the voice of a page, who gives reports of her silence. The four determinate moments of Antigone's negation—not merely in silence but absent silence (secondhand reports of her refusal to speak that the audience is not allowed to witness)—result in a kind of negative agency in the disappearance of her disappearance. Antigone's absence on stage, which becomes increasingly heightened as the play progresses, is perhaps more powerful and unnerving than any single staged performance of Antigone.

Antigone's suicide in Sophocles's play can be connected to the crucifixion of Christ because in both cases the choice between life and death is a false choice.[5] The crucifixion is a concrete reenactment of the death of the absolute that has already occurred in the incarnation. The crucifixion brings a split to the surface that is constitutive of the beginning. The second death deepens the originary crack by bringing negativity to the surface: the Calvary of Spirit. The elevation of Being produces a deeper sense of negativity as the progress of Spirit yields a deeper sense of failure. Likewise, in suicide, one reenacts a death that has already occurred in an attempt to give the first death visibility. Žižek conveys Antigone's forced choice in his own 2016 rendition of *Antigone*, which in the style of a choose-your-own-adventure story, offers three alternate ends.[6] While Antigone is truly less than zero in Smole's play (since her first absence increases by three over the course of the drama), Antigone is multiplied by three on Žižek's stage. In each of Žižek's endings, the character who remains standing wonders for a moment what would have happened had they chosen differently. The fantasy of *having chosen differently* is at once the fantasy of *having chosen* in the first place. But all three endings result in an equally devastating death, which leaves no victors. In the tragic hero's eyes, the acceptance of death is her ownmost relationship to her singular death. Žižek's Antigone firmly insists that although she is already dead, her second death at Creon's hands is of her choosing. She plays the role of the oracle prophesying her own death. As she tells Creon, "I know all too well I'm going to die—how could I not?—it makes no difference what you decree."[7] When Ismene nobly offers to die by her sister's side, Antigone insists that no one can share in the event of her death: "Don't try to share my death or make a claim to actions which you did not do. I'll die—and that will be enough . . . you choose life but it was my choice to die. Be brave. You're alive. But my spirit died some time ago so that I might help the dead."[8] Antigone tries to own her second death, but we see that all three paths lead to her damnation. Or rather, she cannot escape damnation through death. In this sense, her death—which she freely chooses—is passive and impersonal as it has already been determined. The choice between life and death proves to be a false choice when all three paths lead to destruction. In the third alternate ending, Antigone's passionate longing for her own death diminishes when she realizes even this final event cannot truly be her own. The chorus explains she may "freely choose" the fate that awaits her:

> Antigone: Is there a choice for me?
> Chorus: Of course there is. You're free to choose your death.
> Antigone: And if I don't?
> Chorus: You will be put to death in any case. But if you choose to freely meet your fate, you die with dignity.[9]

When the second death is revealed to be as impersonal as the first, negativity gains visibility. As we see implicitly with Antigone and then explicitly with Christ, while the second death fails to affirm one's ownmost being, it contains a kernel of the ultimate comic insight in the affirmation that one is already a negativity.

In Žižek's rendition of *Antigone*, Creon is dumbfounded at Antigone's desire directed at her own death. When she pleads to be put to death, he responds, "Women are meant to give life but this girl is obsessed with death!"[10] As the chorus goes on to note, Antigone's name means "against generating." In Sophocles's play, Antigone is fixated on the burial of her brother. In Žižek's play, Antigone becomes the personification of the death drive when she directs her desire to the fantasy of her own burial. In Smole's version, however, Antigone is the abortionist who seeks to bring the dead bodies out into the light of day. In Sophocles's play, Polyneices's unburied body remains visible for all to see; Antigone buries him to bring his spirit rest. In Smole's rendition, Polyneices's corpse is lost among thousands of anonymous corpses mangled beyond recognition; Antigone commits herself to the impossible task of identifying Polyneices's body, in an attempt to bring visibility to the anonymous corpses. Her act of uncovering the body to bury the body is not intended to give the dead respect and rest, but to beckon their spirits to come forth as the undead. Old Teiresias doesn't realize that his mockery is at once prophetic: "Do you think he'll look alive if you spread a little dust upon his limbs?"[11] Antigone's repeated refusal to appear on the stage is the process of giving birth to the absence of the unrecognized dead in a new form that is indifferent to both life and death, what might be called the undead.[12]

Smole's postwar rewrite of *Antigona* may be read as an enacted memorial within the context of socialist Yugoslavia. In contrast to Hegel's analysis of

Greek theater, Smole's appropriation of Antigone doesn't highlight human activity but rather absence. As a memorial, the play does not serve to point to a specific event or loss. It instead repeats a negative moment of historic paralysis or suspension. The tradition of restaging Smole's *Antigona* in Slovenia may be seen as the practice of meta-memorialization, which routinely returns to the past while openly weighing the dangers of awakening the unnamed dead against the dangers of letting the past conflicts sleep.

Walking in Circles with Antigone in Slovenia

Although Hegel's thought is often represented through diagrams of fractal triangles within triangles, a dialectician who counts the redoubling of doubles finds themselves walking in circles. It is very easy to get stuck in a single dialectical loop, as Hegel himself did. Dolar analyzes the multiple prefaces and introductions in Hegel's works: his own loop circles the beginnings before the beginning even begins. In his writing on the impossible beginning of the *Science of Logic*, Dolar comments on Hegel's own stuckness that drove him to rewrite the *Science of Logic* seventy-seven times: the first draft taking place during his honeymoon and the last attempt on his deathbed. As Dolar explains, "Logic might appear as the domain of the timeless, but not Hegel's logic, the time loop is essential, it is the time of precipitation and retroaction, and Hegel having to precipitate himself into publication is perhaps but a reminder of external circumstances mirroring the internal temporality."[13]

Other dialecticians are "stuck" in larger time loops: Rebecca Comay explores how the end of the *Phenomenology of Spirit* leads us back to the beginning, while Angelica Nuzzo walks the same circle around the end and the beginning of the *Science of Logic*.[14] My own thinking is stuck in what is at once the smallest and largest metaphysical looping between Being and Nothing and its ontological counterpart, the looping of the enunciations "It is" and "It is not" on the Greek and Christian stage. Are Hegelian triangles not in fact Nietzschean returns?

This issue of getting stuck in circles is central to dialectics, which Hegel describes as "the process of its own becoming, the circle that presupposes its end as its goal, having its end also as its beginning; and only by being worked out to its end, is it actual."[15] One should be suspicious of a dialectician who progresses upward and onward too quickly, interpreting the telos of negativity as at the service of historical progress. Suspension is the symptom of what has not and cannot be resolved by our own analysis, leaving us unsatisfied, compelling us to recount or rewrite the same thought from consecration to deathbed. Suspension is evidence that there is something that always resists both destruction and synthesis. The indestructible comic object returns to trip up our path. But here the remainder that resists destruction and synthesis is not something but nothing. *Nothing* resists the conceptualization of absolute knowledge. The dialectician who walks in circles ritualistically repeats precisely what fails to appear within their conceptualization: the nothing of the absolute notion.

This repetition of the negative is illustrated through Lacan's rereading of Freud's analysis of a child's game of cotton wheel, a predecessor of the yo-yo: games of *fort/da*, to and fro, or (in Nietzschean terms) "Go but come again!" Freud identified the pleasure produced in the repetition of the return of the sphere to the child (representing the return of the object of desire, the mother). Lacan, however, shifted the emphasis to the repetition of the space that reappeared between the child and the sphere.[16] The subject cries out "come again" not to the object of desire but to the recurring gap that frustrates her satisfaction (the gap we find is the very process of subjectivization). As Jonathan Lear points out, in order to understand an original loss, we create games, so that indeterminate negativity can be grasped through determinate negation. As Hegel frames it in the beginning of the *Logic*, we begin with Being and Nothing but we can only grasp the Nothing (which is unto itself indeterminate) because we have already "arrived" at Becoming. Ontology (not just a field of philosophy but the *Dasein* that we are—the being that we are always in the middle of enacting) is a game that we play to grasp the metaphysical Nothing that is logically (this is to say, illogically) indistinguishable from our Being.

Dialectic can feel like a game of yo-yo in which the structure of the relationship between the positive and negative repeats itself exactly (on a different historical stage with new actors). However, as Hegel sees it, the space of the negative does not repeat itself exactly when it resurfaces as the comic "object" in each dialectical loop. The thing that undergoes transformation with the progress of history is the nothing itself. Becoming belongs to the Nothing as much as Being. At the end of the *Phenomenology*, Hegel explains that the depth of Spirit shows itself in the surfacing of the nothing. At each stage of history, Spirit is "reborn" as a higher form of substance. But this maturation of Spirit is not in its positive progress. The "higher" form of substance instead reveals itself as a deeper sense of negativity in "the revelation of the depth of Spirit." As Hegel emphasizes, substance is in the negativity, and this negativity is the seat of the subject: "This revelation is, therefore, the raising-up of its depth, or its extension, the negativity of this withdrawn 'I,' a negativity which is its externalization of its substance."[17] We encounter ourselves—in the withdrawal of the self or "I"—in the negative space that resurfaces and deepens with each turn. Our encounter with the Nothing can produce an excess of pleasure (*jouissance*), disgust, or despair. Sometimes nothing is "grasped" with pleasure in the spirit of a child's game, but other times the nothing requires a ritual that allows us to grasp at the nothing with grief. In the case of the latter, the repetition of the nothing, of what fails to appear, becomes a kind of memorialization, not exactly of the dead, but of the central part of ourselves which was never born, or what is reborn only in its repeated failure to be born.

As I mention in my discussion of the philosopher-midwife in chapter 2, Lacan makes the bizarre and fascinating suggestion that the psychoanalyst is the abortionist.[18] The role of philosopher-analyst is not to heal a broken subject (or Spirit) or to give new life (say, to a new dialectical phase of Spirit), but to give the crack itself (non)expression. I use the term (non)expression because negativity only shows itself through its repeated refusal to appear. Or, as Lacan clarifies, what seems to refuse to appear is brought to light as a shadow of the unborn:

> What [is found] . . . in the hole, in the split, in the gap . . . ? Something of the order of the *non-realized*. One uses the term refusal. This is rather hasty—indeed, for some time now, one has no longer been sure what the term refusal means. At first, the unconsciousness is manifested to us as something that holds itself in suspense in the area, I would say, of the *unborn*. That repression should discharge something into this area is not surprising. It is the abortionist's relation to limbo. Certainly, this dimension should be evoked in a register that has nothing unreal, or dereistic, about it, but is rather unrealized. It is always dangerous to disturb anything in that zone of shades . . . without always being able to bring them up to the light of day.[19]

The midwife and the abortionist belong to a zone of shades between two worlds. The philosopher-midwife is in limbo between what always already is (the unborn Platonic form) and what is always coming to be (a particular concrete expression of Truth). But as Lacan sees it, the philosopher-abortionist is in limbo in a zone between two kinds of unrealized lives/deaths: between the unborn (the beginning before the beginning) and the undead (the end before the beginning, which cannot properly end because it has not properly begun).[20]

Through the lenses of Hegel and Lacan, philosophy—in its repetition and returns—becomes a kind of memorial to the undead that we enact in walking our dialectical circles. This strange memorial does not celebrate a lost life but recognizes a life that never began, a life that can only take place through the repetition of its failed death. While some memorials remember the death of a determinate something, other memorials repeat the failed birth (and death) of indeterminate negativity. We return not to ensure that we never forget what cannot be retrieved, but because we do not know what it is we mourn.

Memorialization in the form of the architectural statue can suggest that our stance toward the past is concrete while memorials in the form of repeated social activity present reconciliation with the past as a continual process. Enacted memorials suggest that reconciliation with the past is not itself a thing of the past. Each generation must grapple with its inherited memories, guilt, and grief and self-consciously take its own stance toward what came before it.

Socialist monuments in postwar Yugoslavia fell into both the categories of the erected and the enacted. State-funded architectural memorials erected in the 1960s and '70s by artists such as Serbian architect Bogdan Bogdanović have recently attracted international attention due to the Belgian photographer Jan Kempenaers and his collection called *Spomenik*.[21] Although Bogdanović identified as a surrealist, these memorials are commonly lumped together under the title of socialist modernism or even Soviet brutalism: a complete mischaracterization of their artistic, political, and historical staging.[22] Many of these now iconic steel and stone monuments, such as Bogdanović's famous *Stone Flower*, resemble a mechanical portal that binds two things together in its very act of severing.[23] These monuments in particular can be seen as the space of the in-between that simultaneously connects and seals off two discrete worlds: the carefully maintained peace and order of the State and unspeakable years of war. The gateways forbade anyone from straying backward into a troubled past or from allowing past conflicts to creep into the present. The status of these memorials in post-Yugoslavian capitalism is now controversial. Some monuments have been demolished; others have been stripped of their valuable material, while the majority fall into decay from neglect.

One of Slovenia's most embraced memorializations of the war, which is still observed today, however, took the form of an enacted monument: *Pohod po Poti okoli Ljubljane* (The Walk along the Path around Ljubljana).[24] During the Nazi occupation of Ljubljana, the city's thirty-three-kilometer border was surrounded by barbed wire in a failed attempt to fend off the antifascist, communist resistance. After the war, the wire was torn down. The empty tracks formed by the fence were reclaimed as a path for a memorial walk formally observed on May 9 to commemorate Ljubljana's liberation.

Ljubljana's annual walk around the Path of Remembrance and Comradeship, a ritual beginning in 1957 and continuing to the present, is mirrored in Slovene theater by the repetition of modern interpretations of Sophocles's *Antigone* following World War II.[25] Smole was a founding member of the so-called Critical Generation (1951–64), a group of artists and writers who founded a series of radical underground political journals as well as Stage '57, a theater for avant-garde productions which were often critical of the political stage of Tito's regime. One of the founders, Taras Kermauner, described the spirit of Stage '57 as "culturally militant, politically subversive, morally aware, and existentially risky."[26] Two years after the first memorial walk and the opening of Stage '57, Smole directed his celebrated rendition of *Antigona*. The restaging of Smole's play can be seen as an enacted memorial that is faithfully repeated. While the Critical Generation lasted a little more than a decade before its members were exiled or retreated into private life, Smole's *Antigona* remains a classic text. The play has been restaged and directed by at least eight famous Slovene directors on five stages.[27] Moreover, many playwrights have followed Smole in the tradition of rewriting *Antigone* against the backdrop of (post-)Yugoslavia.[28] On a performative level, the persistence of the play's production is an argument for the value of the living memorial over and against a memorial set in stone. In this way, the Slovene tradition seems to echo similar theatrical movements throughout postwar Europe that identified the erection of architectural monuments as superficial and rushed performances of reconciliation in response to the trauma of World War II. Performance art, such as the works performed at Stage '57, functioned as counter-memorial movements, suggesting that the stone memorial excused future generations from the inherited responsibility of preserving the memory of the past. Memorialization in the form of performance suggested that reconciliation with the past must be a collective, transgenerational endeavor. The past is something we must consciously reenact.

The specific tradition of *Antigone* productions in Slovenia, however, may be understood as meta-memorials rather than counter-memorials. I use the term "meta-memorial" to point to memorials that routinely revisit the complexities of both erected and enacted memorials. In Smole's version, for example, both Creon and Antigone are caught walking in circles, which seems to offer a reflection on Ljubljana's newly implemented memorial walk. Creon continuously circles his carefully manicured tulip garden at the center of the city. Antigone walks around the outside of the city walls. Creon's flower garden represents a new age of peace in the form of the nonevent: a stage of history that willfully ignores conflict, which it does not wish to resolve as much as to leave in the past. Antigone's hopeless search for her brother's body among countless mutilated corpses is a refusal of consolation, a refusal of superficial peace. Creon's walking and Antigone's walking are starkly opposed: there is something laughably absurd about the way Creon calmly strolls through his garden, while Antigone confronts the brutal reality of the aftermath of civil war. And yet the comic and tragic repetitions also mirror each other. Creon walks in one direction around the path toward what he believes to be a fresh future. Antigone walks in the other direction in an attempt to return to a past event for which she wishes to find redemption. They somehow fail to see that they walk the same circle toward an imaginary event. The circling is enough to drive all the characters to madness by the end of the third act. Smole raises a question that his play leaves unresolved: Does the faithful return to the past put the dead to rest, or do our footsteps disrupt the sleep of the undead?

Sophocles's *Antigone* has been adopted by many cultures in the wake of many wars to support the specific political positions of various playwrights. The play explores the painful confusion concerning the memory of the dead following civil war. Sophocles addresses the arbitrary nature of the treatment of the dead through the figures of Eteocles and Polyneices, two brothers who die fighting on opposite sides of the civil war of Thebes. In the end, Eteocles is on the side of the victors and is given the burial honors of a war hero. The body of Polyneices, declared a traitor of the state, is left to rot and be forgotten. The everlasting title of hero or criminal is attached to the corpses retrospectively. Had the outcome of the war been otherwise, traitor would be hero, and hero would be traitor. The king fully acknowledges the difficulties with the memorialization of the war hero. This is emphasized in Smole's play by the image of the mangled corpses that cannot be identified as hero or enemy. When the people demand that the war hero be venerated, Creon responds: "But how am I to find their corpses? I do not think their names are branded on their bones. What if we mix them up? How shall we tell the hero from the traitor?"[29] Creon's initial intuition is to allow the unsorted bodies to rest together. Perhaps if the unidentified dead could enter the underworld together, so could the living learn to live as one. The retroactive judgment of the dead would only carry the conflict of the civil war into the present. As Smole's Creon says, "All is as it should be; the traitor and the hero both are dead, and all conditions needed for the rule of law, and for the return to peace and normalcy, are satisfied . . . should we not leave the dead to rest alone in peace?"[30] And yet, the rabble cries out for a hero, and Creon's advisors convince him that if he wants to establish postwar order and unity, the enemy must be declared as such in no uncertain terms. It is in this spirit that Creon forbids Polyneices's burial. And yet as we see through the perspective of Antigone, the enemy is at once a brother to be mourned. As Hegel interpreted the conflict between Creon and Antigone, both sides are equally right in themselves. But because the ethical action demanded from each is in contradiction both sides are equally wrong. Because they are both equally right, they are both equally wrong.[31]

In Sophocles's original play, the audience inhabits the position of the chorus that represents the citizens belonging to the state under the rule of Creon. We are allowed to feel the tension of two equally compelling but conflicting ethical commands. On one hand, we may identify with Creon's desire to establish state unity in order to avoid another civil war. On the other hand, we may feel the conviction of confronting the violence that we committed in the name of war. Peace and justice show themselves to be opposed. In Western Europe following the war, the audience of *Antigone* occupied a very different position from that of Sophocles's audience. Western European adaptations of *Antigone* during and following World War II lost the ethical bind at the center of the original play. Jean Anouilh's 1944 rendition staged *Antigone* in German-occupied Paris.[32] Bertolt Brecht's 1947 production likewise portrayed Creon and the state as representing fascist Germany and Antigone as the sweetheart of the resistance.[33] At the climax of the play, when Antigone is imprisoned and sentenced to death, Creon's regime immediately overturns and destroys the state. The audiences of the French and German productions of *Antigone* were predisposed to fully identify with Antigone over and against Creon. As a result, these renditions produced a kind of one-sidedness that Sophocles's original play warned against.

In the context of Yugoslavia, however, Creon and Antigone both became figures of the antifascist, communist resistance. The Yugoslav staging of the play once again placed the audience in a space between two protagonists both equally guilty and equally innocent. In Western Europe, the relationship between Creon and Antigone represented the oppressive force of one regime over another political body with which the audience identified. In Yugoslavia, the conflict between Creon and Antigone spoke to an internal struggle within a single political regime to which both the playwright and the audience belonged.[34] Antigone reacts against the crimes of the state of which she herself is a member. Antigone is not opposed to Creon. Rather the split within Antigone is mirrored in the split with Creon.

Yugoslav renditions of *Antigone* recovered the ethical bind of Sophocles's original play by allowing the figure of Creon to resonate with Tito rather than Hitler. As many scholars of Partisan history would have it, Tito was originally a code name used for general correspondence between Partisan members, used to confuse the Secret Service into thinking that there was one figure in charge of the movement. The name was not merely a clever tactic, however, but also represented the unilateral, nonhierarchical nature of a movement built on the framework of communism rather than race, gender, ethnicity, or religion. When Josip Broz became the official leader of Yugoslavia, Tito was the split between two sovereign bodies: the person of Josip Broz and the symbol which could not be equated with any one person. Tito was a signifier constituted by a split. Tito thus had to undergo four deaths in order to die: (1) when Josip Broz takes on the name Tito in 1934, he undergoes a symbolic death, becoming much more and less than the weighty signifier that he as "referent" represents; (2) the bodily death of the sovereign in the physical passing of Josip Broz in 1980; (3) the second symbolic death of Tito in the breakup of Yugoslavia in 1990; and (4) the current process of demolishing the Partisan memorials, Tito's lingering remains. This final death is both physical and symbolic. The complexity of this fourth death repeats the driving question of Smole's play: "How does one kill a ghost?"[35]

The figure of Creon in Smole's rendition likewise stood for a sovereign ruler, but Creon was also not separate from all the members of the chorus, since Tito also stands for all. In this way the play spoke to the dead on both sides of the war in Slovenia: the estimated 28,000 Partisan members and 24,000 Home Guard members. The theme of the unburied dead also clearly alluded to the mass executions that followed the forced repatriation in May and June 1945 of those associated with the Slovene Home Guard. Smole questioned the actions of the Communist Party from within, as a member himself.[36] Indeed, he was one of the first to address the difficult question of memorializing the untried and unburied dead, including those killed in the so-called Kočevski Rog massacre. Rather than leaving one with a sense of resolution or respect for the heroes of the past, Smole's play highlights the ethical ambiguity concerning our memory of the dead. However, while the few others who openly questioned the postwar killings were silenced by the state, *Antigona* presented multiple conflicting perspectives within the same circle. Boris Krajger, who was responsible for silencing many of the Critical Generation's projects, not only applauded the performance of *Antigona* at

Stage '57 but subsequently invited Smole to start a new periodical, *Perspektive* (1960–64).[37] The Slovene staging of Antigone once again places the audience in a space between conflicting ethical imperatives: the imperative for peace versus the imperative for reconciliation; the imperative to move forward, to forgive and forget, versus the imperative to return to the past, to reflect, to confess deeds still unaddressed.

In the 1980s and 1990s, the figure of Antigone was adopted in right-wing discourse among those seeking national independence for Slovenia and Croatia in the dissolution of Yugoslavia. Antigone is still frequently evoked in the highly politicized, nationalist writings that demand "justice" for the postwar extrajudicial killings. Antigone became directly associated with Slovenian philosophers who fought for national independence, such as Spomenka Hribar and Tine Hribar. At the same time, however, she also became a central figure in the Marxist writings of the newly formed Ljubljana School for Psychoanalysis.[38] Antigone was redoubled in Ljubljana: first as a figure of tragedy in nationalist discourses, then as a figure of comic resistance in Hegelian-Marxist-Lacanian thought. The recurrence of Antigone in Slovenia today, especially the recurrence of her absence, forms a kind of political resistance that disrupts nationalist narratives.

Doubling the Double and Magnifying Nothing

Smole's play not only splits the audience between Antigone and Creon; it also explicitly dramatizes a split in Antigone and Creon themselves. As the dramatic action unfolds, the conflict that appears to be between two sides is shown to be internal to each side. The two are not opposed but rather mirror the conflict that belongs to each equally. Creon and Antigone at first appear to be the double in the form of an odd couple. Upon closer look we see that each character is already split. But what is magnified in the mirroring of the double in her double? Sophocles also shows this duality within Antigone, who is torn between her duty as a sister and her duty as a citizen. Sophocles's Creon is similarly split between his duty as king and his compassion for Antigone. Both characters are split between the call for justice and the call for peace, between an absolute universal law and their devotion to a particular relationship, between their impersonal role as citizen or king and their personal role as a family member. And yet, as Hegel emphasizes, Creon's and Antigone's actions in their relationships are not truly personal because these roles are circumscribed in the social conventions of Greek life. Although the characters struggle between two contradictory but equally compelling ethical imperatives, in the end their individual actions don't matter. Either way, they are doomed, because the very structure of Greek political and ethical life is in contradiction. This contradiction is reflected in each individual's relationship to the community but more dramatically in each individual's relationship to him or herself.

Smole represents this split within the individual by characters who encounter themselves as someone outside and opposed to themselves. Or rather, the characters find that they are *nothing more* than the gap between two roles that cannot coexist. One becomes two in the discovery of the split self—two becomes four in the doubling of the double (the recognition that the other opposing half is a mirrored double: one who is also two).[39]

The result of the oscillation between two irresolvable sides, which mirror each other even in their opposition, is a kind of historical *epochē*: a suspension of movement in the paralysis of choice, regarding taking a stance toward our past. What looks like paralysis from one perspective allows us to continually circle back to revisit the equipollence of ethical standpoints. Smole's play opens in a momentary pause following the war. The bodies of the dead rot in piles outside the city walls, but within the walls, the citizens feel that they have returned to a simpler time. The chorus announces, "Preserved by repetition's sheer inertia . . . Peace is restored!"[40] The crowning of the new king fills the people with hope. However, their hope is not in a new world but rather in the illusion that the king will be able to undo the memory of the war, returning the people to an earlier time when there were no bodies to bury and difficult decisions to be made. The citizens' hope is not for progress but for the preservation of the little that remains from before the destruction of war. The present is *nothing more* than the appearance of the new within repetition's sheer inertia. As the chorus puts it, we sing "new words set to an ancient tune." With the new king comes the promise of peace, but Smole calls the political goal of peace into question. Smole paints the idea of peace as the dream of the nonevent or the occurrence of nothing. No course of action can now alter or mend the terrible event of World War II. Since the great event cannot be opposed, it must be doubled, and thereby subverted, in its negative other: the nonevent of peace. As Tiresias explains, "All wars are senseless, without rhyme or reason, but one thing's for sure: that in the final analysis we have a non-event . . . If peace is what you want, for certain now you have it."[41] Peace is the historical paralysis following a period of chaos and horror. In retrospect, the only response to the great event seems to be what Hegel saw as the tragic proclamation, "It is. It has been. It cannot be otherwise." As Tiresias cynically puts it, "In our dealings with the dead we cannot add or take away, for if you wish to foist on them some attribute or label, to shower them with glory or to press their dead heads in the mire, you waste your effort to no end . . . all you get in answer is a stony smile . . . *I am no more.*"[42] The nonevent is the nothing in which we find rest when all else has been destroyed. In peace, the tragic proclamation "It is" is mirrored in its darkly comic negative double. We look to the present in the wake of destruction and declare with a mixture of grief and relief, "It is nothing. It is no more."

The thematic split in the Sovereign is mirrored in the split in the people: While many of the citizens are content with whatever comforts the new government provides them, a growing number cannot shake the dead. Even the rabble that congregates outside the palace is divided between those who praise Creon and those who demand that the king sort through the dead to bring them a hero.[43] Creon escapes the crowd and retreats to the stillness of his flower garden at night. He imagines he hears the birds cooing, but his page confirms that the birds are sleeping. Although Creon can barely make out the flowerbeds in the dark, he admires the orderliness of the arrangements. Ismene confronts him about a guard whom she suspects was killed at the king's command, but Creon wishes only to speak of the flowers.[44] Creon reiterates the theme of peace as the simple negation of bitter memories and a picture of unity as something that frees the individual from "the solitude of decision."[45] Smole's portrait of Creon in his garden of red flowers evokes the Yugoslav tradition of adorning Tito with a garland of red flowers (an image that becomes iconic through Tito's memorialization). Smole adds a new layer to the socialist symbol of the red flower, comparing nature to the tendency of the new political regime to pass over unresolved conflicts of the recent past.

The traditional memorial stands as a permanent reminder of those who heroically lost their lives for the next generation's peace and liberty. Nature, in many ways, is opposed to the memorial: it absorbs death into itself, erasing the memory of decay as it replenishes itself. Each new generation of growth is an identical replacement of what was lost, leaving nothing to be mourned.[46] The traditional memorial fights against nature's process of all too quickly replenishing itself without leaving a trace of what came before. As we see with the case of neglected memorials, if given the opportunity, the earth will readily consume a concrete representation of the dead just as it does the human body.

Creon eventually yields to the pressure to address the dead. He feeds one corpse to the hungry earth, declaring it traitor, and another corpse to the hungry rabble, declaring it hero. The hero's body is protected from the natural elements, and his memory honored with a permanent representation of his sacrifice. Smole's association of Creon with nature, however, is not a simple critique of the state for not doing enough to memorialize the dead, since many Partisan monuments were erected throughout Yugoslavia. Instead, Smole suggests that in the relationship between nature and the memorial, there is once again a mirroring of two faces that seem to be opposed. The memorial itself covers over the very life it serves to highlight by putting the dead to rest too quickly. Nature represents forgetfulness, but the memorial itself can be another kind of covering over in the act of selective remembering. The memories of both the forgotten body and the memorialized body are neutralized in the quest for reconciliation.

Smole continues to play with the motif of the split between two through the image of Creon's peace garden. The clearing, called peace, is revealed to be the gap within a deep unresolved contradiction. Creon is immediately split when he enters the stage in the first scene and finds Antigone missing. "Where is Antigone? Those whom I need to see should be here present: no wonder I have a headache. I do not like it when someone I need to see absents herself, especially when I have a headache. *Am I or am I not the king?*"[47] Creon's splitting headache is a symptom of his unfulfilled desire for Antigone. Antigone's absence immediately splits Creon between the "I am" and "I am not." The theme of Creon's split is discussed directly in the dialogue between Creon and his advisor, Tiresias. Creon reflects on the dual nature of the sovereign who is both an embodied human being but also a symbol that cannot be reduced to an individual body:

> Who is the king? Is the king one man, or are there two in him? Is the king he who with stern hands holds sway and tries and punishes—and at whose order some will rise and others fall—who cannot in the chaos of decisions keep his hands clean; or is the king a man who is concerned with other things—the hues of garden flowers, the peaceful sleep of roosting birds? Is the king one or the other? Or is he both of these?[48]

Creon oscillates between two images of the sovereign, but as Tiresias explains, sovereignty is precisely in the split between the two figures. The symbol of the sovereign must be an image for all citizens to claim, and yet it must also be over and above humanity. Creon is only the puppet for what he represents and acts according to what his role demands of him. Creon, as an individual, cannot be held accountable for the actions he has ordered. His crimes belong to all but no one in particular. Creon's guilt is everyone's guilt. And yet although Creon is absolved of the solitude of individual decision and responsibility, he continues to feel haunted by another.

Smole's enacted memorial, like Bogdanović's sculptures, reflects the overlooked aesthetic movement of socialist surrealism. The highest moment of surrealism in the play presents a grotesque and darkly comical dreamscape. Creon falls asleep and finds himself far from his garden in a barren land, the harshness of which echoes the landscape outside the city walls where Antigone walks in circles. He wanders through a bleak expanse like a sheet of ice with "no soul to be seen, or beast or blade of grass." A ravenous firebird trails him overhead. The king repeatedly pulls a piece of rancid meat out of his pocket and throws it to the bird who, each time, gulps it up but regurgitates it: a grotesque mirroring of the circling we see in so many places throughout the play. Creon follows a track made by someone who had walked this space perhaps many times before him. At first the tracks are alarming since he does not know who made them and where they lead. But he quickly finds comfort in mindlessly following a way made entirely by another. Suddenly a small dot appears in the distance, growing larger until Creon realizes he is approaching a man. It turns out that the man he thought he was following walks in the opposite direction, toward him. The two men eventually meet on a path that is discovered to be circular. Creon's recollection of the dream encounter is a bizarre surrealist adaptation of the master-slave dialectic, too brilliant not to quote at length:

> We stood there for some time in silence, with our gaze fixed upon the ground, weighed down with guilt, until in a fury I looked up and stared him in the face. And there [in the face of the devil], I saw myself! But what a caricature of me: a tulip in my hand! I didn't know whether to laugh or weep! . . . "Give way," I told him firmly. "Give way," he also said, equally calm. "Get lost!" I spoke forcefully and drew my sword. "Get lost!" he too repeated, grasping his tulip by the petals. I cried, "you stupid joker!" aiming my sword at his heart. He cried, "you stupid joker!" . . . [and] pierced me too with the unusual weapon . . . right into my heart . . .
> "Enough of this," I told him. "Since you are me, why should you try to murder me?"
> "I hate you," he said—saying exactly what I had in mind.
> "I hate you too," I said, his eyes, I dimly saw, now clouding over. "And what if we both die," I said.
> "And what if we both die?" said he.
> I lost my temper. "Don't repeat each word I say," I shouted, "after all, you are not really me!" He answered calmly, "And you're not really me."
> And then we slowly, slowly sank . . . floundering in some mysterious, thick fluid *more similar to nothing than to anything I know*. The further we sank, the closer we merged, till in the end I'd say nothing remained of me except the tulip in my heart . . . I wanted to bite his head off. And he'd have done the same to me . . . But he had nothing, for nothing remained of me.[49]

In the deadly encounter between the king of swords and the king of roses—two sides of the sovereign—Creon watches himself dissipate into nothing. In this highest moment of comedy, the proclamation—It is nothing. I am no more—yields its deepest meaning. In a moment of mutual (non)recognition, the two sides see themselves through their fading vision from the (non)perspective of the crack that binds them. As the birds of fire fly down to lap up their blood, the stillness of the peace garden recognizes itself—in an instance of comic-anguish—in the nothingness of the void.

The Transformation of Nothing in the Repetition of Nothing

Creon watches himself dissipate into nothing at the climax of the play. Antigone, in contrast, is nothing from the start of the play. Although Creon is at times played by two actors, Antigone herself never appears on stage. We only meet the protagonist through the dialogue of the other characters who are constantly speculating what Antigone might say if she were present or what she might be doing or thinking elsewhere. The longer Antigone remains absent, the more frantic the speculation becomes. Creon's double is redoubled in Ismene, who fills in for her missing sister, speaking lines that Sophocles wrote for Antigone. In this respect, Creon and Tiresias aren't wrong when they accuse Ismene of being possessed by her sister. Ismene initially identifies with her sister so closely that she accidentally refers to herself in the third person. When Ismene passionately argues that death is the great equalizer that erases our sins and virtues alike, Tiresias attacks her: "That thought is not your own! You're quoting *her* again." "So what if I am," Ismene responds, "The words may be my sister's but I am with her in heart and soul. The thought is hers and I agree with her wholeheartedly."[50] Although Smole's Ismene is at first a bold substitute for Antigone, quite unlike Sophocles's own timid Ismene, by the second act, when Antigone has yet to appear, she begins to doubt her sister's quest. Ismene begins to contradict herself, at times speaking on behalf of her sister and at other times against her without being able to identify which voice is her own. Ismene, like Creon, recognizes that she is split. She confesses to the page: "My dear young page, some fateful spell cleft my soul in two . . . fused into a single being submitting to the dictates of one body."[51] Ismene comes undone, oscillating between the frantic claims "this is *really* me" and "I am not myself." Oscillating between her selves—or her self and not self—she stumbles upon "herself" in the negative space between being and nonbeing: "What if . . . it is discovered that we merely strut and act; *what if you realize that mankind exists—but you are not a man?* If a sudden light illuminates the unknown side of things, where all our standards, social order, and tradition seem shallow, false, and ludicrous? . . . What if it turns out that I am a bare, inflated mask . . . ?"[52] The persistence of Antigone's absence causes a deepening of the split within both Creon and Ismene. The crack within each character reaches the surface as both characters realize that they are *more similar to the nothing* of Antigone than any version of themselves standing on the stage.[53] According to logic, one cannot be both one identity and its negation. And yet, the place of the subject emerges not in either one or both sides of the double, but between the "me" and the "not me" generated by the same stance.

Each character slowly discovers their subjectivity to be more similar to nothing than anything that can be represented on the stage: no more living than the dead. As the present characters declare themselves to be "no more," Antigone gains a kind of negative agency through the repetition of the non-event of her failed appearance. With each failure to appear, Antigone's silence is amplified. While Creon and Ismene enact the doubling of the double, the page speaks for the crack between them, represented by Antigone's absence. The page is assigned to look after Antigone when she withdraws into private following the war. The page returns four times to give a report of Antigone, but reports only of her silence and the monotonous repetition of her daily walks around the city walls. The page enters the stage four times to offer four distinct accounts of Antigone's silence in her absence.[54]

The Page's Four Accounts of Antigone's Silence

1. The page reports that Antigone has withdrawn into her room and is silent by her window. Creon is split between the "am" and "am not." (95)
2. The page's second report of Antigone's silence is juxtaposed with the watchman's second report of Antigone's inflammatory public speech. In an effort to silence Antigone, Creon forces the page, who amplifies Antigone's silence, to murder the watchman, who represents Antigone's rumored speech. Creon's plan backfires: By silencing Antigone's voice, he empowers her silence. (101–3)
3. Although Creon has given the sisters secret permission to search for the body at night (which would make the already impossible task truly impossible), the page states that she circles the walls ritualistically in silence each day in broad daylight. (123–26)
4. The page reports that Antigone now walks in circles through the night. Antigone's most subversive act takes the form of obedience. Everyone, including Ismene, judges Antigone to be mad. In the persistence of her absence, they become truly hysterical and are convinced that Polyneices's ghost is everywhere. (145)

Nothing changes as Antigone's absence punctures the reliable tempo of the play's events. And yet, we may say that although nothing really changes, *nothing really does change* by its fourth interruption when the page reports of Antigone's silent circling. There is no significant formal change in each report of Antigone's absence. It is precisely through this repetition of nothing new, that nothing itself becomes the agent of its own transformation. In his first report, the page explains that Antigone, day after day, stares blankly out of her window. This is the page's first and last account of her speech:

> She seemed to be in a severe state of nervous shock and the next moment, rather too calm and collected . . . she took me by the hand and led me to the window. "Is the sun shining dark?" she asked. "No, no," I said, "it's shining bright as ever." "How strange, how strange," she murmured, "it sheds no light on me." And then she took me by the other hand and asked, "Now tell me. What is on your mind?" My mind was blank. My eyes were on the birds migrating southwards . . . "Birds, birds, where are you off to?" I murmured—and she said, "Forget about the birds; their way spells weakness; you have to live your life where you are."[55]

The page admires how the flock of birds move as one as if heading toward a clear destination on the horizon. But Antigone sees the birds' unity as anchored in the desire to escape a harsh landscape that must be faced. Creon, like the page boy, also finds comfort in the birds in his garden until the grotesque image of the fire bird regurgitating its food reminds him that there is no escape. What one devours whole returns. Antigone is compared to a bird that is separated from its flock, refusing to take flight.

When the page returns to Creon to offer his report, he becomes increasingly reluctant to speak even to Antigone's silence, as if any utterance might taint the purity of her refusal to appear. He speaks only to the steady repetition of her absence: "Today, like yesterday and all these recent days, she's out again, and, measured by the hourglass sands, her absence lasts from early dawn until the last rays of the dying sun."[56] The phrase "like yesterday, today, and tomorrow" is repeated by the characters like a mantra, pointing to two negative infinities based in repetition without difference: the inertia of a repetition free from terror maintains the social order.[57] Antigone's equally punctuated mechanical failure to appear is a kind of repetition of nothing that terrifies the nothing of the infinity of peace. The two temporal modes take the same form, and yet one haunts the other, causing a disturbance in its flow.

The young page, who perhaps is too young to fully understand the horrors of the war, becomes Antigone's shadow. He stands next to her through her mourning. When she goes out to find her brother's body, the page follows her outside the city walls to search through the mangled corpses. The page stays with Antigone even when the harsh sun forces Ismene to abandon the search. The rumored sightings of Antigone beyond the wall in broad daylight begin to disturb people. The rather suspicious rumors of sightings of Antigone beyond the wall at midnight disturb the people more. As Antigone appears to be everywhere and nowhere (in her failure to appear anywhere), the people begin to whisper that the ghost of Polyneices has indeed returned to haunt them. Haemon becomes hysterical:

> In spite of all the obstacles, she keeps up the search. And while the search continues, it's just as if we had him living with us here and now. Polyneices to the right of us, Polyneices to the left of us, in the corner by the stove, in the shadows on the ceiling, hidden behind a tree, reflected in the water of the palace pond; he's everywhere! I see him in her eyes, like a hilltop in the clouds; I see him in the dimple of your tepid smile, in the grooves of Creon's wrinkles, and Ismene's restless fingers. That damned fellow's ghost, I seem to see it everywhere! Are we all mad? Crazy? Are we ill? We killed him—why? So that he'd haunt us night and day, alive, although a ghost, and more alive than ever![58]

By the end of the third act, even Tiresias, the cynical defender of peace and order, is convinced that Polyneices stands among them. Haemon orders the watchman to kill Polyneices *again*, which repeats the question: "How does one kill a ghost?" Soon all the characters reach a state of hysteria constantly, alternating between the cries, "Polyneices is dead!" and "Polyneices is not dead!" The play becomes a game of *fort-da*, "Polyneices is gone!—Polyneices is here!"

Ismene is the only character besides the page who claims to have had a firsthand encounter with Antigone throughout the play. At the final climax, Ismene calls everything she thought to be certain into question, which leads the page to quietly confess that he is less certain about his own memories of Antigone: "Now don't be upset, gracious lady, I too am only talking to myself, from dawn till noon, from noon till night, just talking to myself . . ."[59] In the final scene, it is reported that Antigone has miraculously found Polyneices's body and has buried the corpse in Creon's tulip garden. The guards set out to immediately execute both Antigone and the page. Tiresias regains composure and declares that things will soon return to normal.

Although it is assumed that Antigone's final death is at the end of the play, a creeping suspicion chills an astute viewer: Was Antigone already dead at the beginning of the play? After reaching the end of the play, one can return to reread Smole's play as beginning only after the event of Antigone's suicide. It's only after reaching the end, when Ismene and the page call their own testimonies into question, that we discover that the end has already occurred before the beginning. Antigone's suicide is repeated in Smole's play not as a tragic end but as a passive act of comic revenge. In her final comic death before the beginning, Antigone gives birth to both herself and her brother as the undead, who call up the living to voice their silence louder.

The tradition of staging Smole's *Antigona* within Slovenia functions as meta-memorial, which routinely returns to the past while openly weighing the dangers of awakening the unburied dead against the dangers of letting the unaddressed conflicts of the past sleep. However, it is not a memorial that leaves us with a sense of peace concerning the past. Rather than taking a specific stance toward the past, it raises questions about how we stand among the dead. The play magnifies different forms of negativity though the repetition of the nonevent and the layering of silence. Silence is expressed in the refusal to remember but equally in the act of remembering selectively, since any act of memorialization necessarily conceals as much as it uncovers. Forgetting (in the form of keeping silent and moving forward) and remembering (in the form of pausing to give voice to the dead) are presented as yet another double. The truth itself is also in what is left unsaid—the thing that has not been addressed or staged—the missing Antigone.

As Benjamin claims, "the muteness of matter is overcome" when an inspirited historical stage is split in vengeful laughter: Spirit as a laughing matter or Matter's laughter.[60] But he also acknowledges a kind of silent laughter belonging to "the hilarity of shadows."[61] Smole's *Antigona* is set to the temporal rhythm of what Benjamin identifies as the comedy of the damned. In my reading of Smole's play, Antigone does not represent a decisive call for action, for example, the demand to memorialize the unburied dead. The play acknowledges the impossibility of putting the dead to rest either through memorialization or through the careful maintenance of feigned forgetfulness. Repetition can be mindless, a kind of covering over, as represented in the image of Creon circling his manicured garden. But there is another kind of mechanical repetition of nothing that thickens our failed relationship to history with each turn.

Conclusion

History's Laugh Lines and Comic Resistance Today

Returning to Fate and Character

Laughter as an embodied experience is also an affective excess that cannot be contained in the body and finds release through eruption. Following the Young Hegelians, Marx, and Benjamin, I have identified the excessive nature of laughter that belongs to the body but exceeds the body as spiritual. Yet this spiritual excess that cannot be contained by a body also reshapes that body. Laugh lines are static wrinkles that form around the mouth, putting one's speech in parentheses. When we are young, the lines only appear when we flash our teeth, but as we grow older, the lines become a permanent trace of the fleeting smiles and grimaces expressed throughout a lifetime. Wrinkles betray an individual by frustrating attempts at self-censorship, making it impossible to hide one's past and present emotions behind a blank face.

I read the lines on your face like the palmist reads a hand. They tell me your secrets, what you have withstood and what you could not withstand any longer. Not *what* but *that*, a testament *that* you did not pass through the world untouched. They are the overflow of the gifts bestowed on you and the loss that was too great. These lines are also a lifetime of interactions too trivial to be consciously counted or recounted but that stirred you in those moments, causing your face to twitch.

The unconsciousness lives on the surface of the body in the faint lines etched into the skin. Wrinkles cling to the unprocessed excess of joy and trauma. But they also cling to the sensation of the stranger who brushes past unnoticed. As Rebecca Comay writes in her reflection on face lines at the time of one's death, wrinkles are the asynchronous resurfacing of affects belonging to another time:

> A wrinkle shows just how ambiguously time inscribes itself on our mortal bodies. Like every mark, it seems to hint of a discrete and datable moment of decision or incision, while ultimately frustrating

the desire to identify any such moment. Even as it seems to bear the stamp of a punctual moment "*in* time," to mark a singular here and now of inscription, its belated appearance points only to a prior passage "*through* time." Appearing only belatedly, like a text written in invisible ink, the wrinkle is the perfect cipher of traumatic anachrony.[1]

Time draws itself into our skin, I would add, gently tugging in different temporal directions. Face lines express a passage through time that cannot be undone. Palm lines predict a passage into the future that has yet to arrive. Do the creases in our palms, some already drawn in the womb, dictate what lines will be sketched into our face? Can the face be redrawn by an outburst of unforeseen emotions and sensations rising to the surface?

In "Fate and Character," Benjamin introduces the wise woman or fortune teller who looks for signs in the palm, the stars, and her cards.[2] The fortune teller, who enters the stage early on, is followed at the end of the narrative by the comic genius, who is nothing more than a twitch within the tragic articulation of history.[3] The fortune teller is a dramatic personification of fate, a future drawn into the body and the cosmos even before birth. The comic genius is a dramatic personification of character, a glimmer of individual expression that escapes our predetermined roles.

It may be said that one's character is found in a defining trait that allows an individual (person or concept) to be distilled into an identifiable caricature. But as I discuss in chapter 6, Benjamin meditates on the comic caricature to arrive at an insight concerning character in general. The comic caricature is often defined by a trait empty of substance (a big nose, a clumsy gait). The superficial trait is a placeholder for a singular expressivity that can't quite be named but nevertheless prevents one from being fully reduced to another. The tragic perspective clings to this trait, insisting on the substance of their being. However, freedom is found in embracing a secret about the self that others pretend not to see: nothing essentially differentiates one from another. Fate is nothing more than the law or society that assigns certain characters guilt before they enter the stage. As Benjamin emphasizes, there is nothing the poor can do to achieve innocence. Morality is not determined by one's character but by one's predetermined role.

Only a scoundrel would be willing to entertain and exploit this scandal in Being and the Law. A different sense of character emerges when nothing seizes herself by the secret of her being. Nothing differentiates one from another. However, the specific moment of coming to sense one's negativity is completely singular. Character is Nothing's self-relation in each unique moment through which she grasps herself by her negativity. The concept of nothing, which can't be properly thought, can only be realized through the awakened sensation of one's embodied being. The character of this moment of self-relation can only be affective, giving rise to emotions that even the palmist cannot predict: joy, despair, rage, hilarity, relief.

History's Laugh Lines and Comic Resistance Today 151

As I've emphasized throughout this book, dialectic allows itself to be counted in multiple ways, yielding different rhythms that stress specific beats. The same tune is looped on repeat, but a new dance emerges as the characters/concepts move in unique constellations according to a variation in rhythm. When swept into the rhythm, the characters lose count until one breaks timing to set a new beat.

In such a way, "Fate and Character" unfolds differently depending on which character taps their foot. When the fortune teller sets the rhythm, the characters/concepts are transformed into an unusual tarot deck. The fortune teller personifies fate, but she simultaneously exposes the cracks in the unfolding of history. When she pulls her cards at random, each combination reveals different cracks. Or, to put this differently, the pairings reveal new splits, stressing different beats or perhaps skipped beats, through the specific relationship between each. The coupling of the fortune teller and comic genius—fate and character—indicates that the future is not entirely determined by the lines that define our present character. Liberation lurks within a twitch in what has already been drawn, a stutter in all that can be said within the tyranny of reason.

In "Lines That Reduce," Sam Dolbear connects Benjamin's fortune teller to the historical character of Charlotte ("Lotte") Wolff (1897–1986), a doctor of reproductive medicine in Berlin who later worked as a palmist in Paris and queer sexologist in London.[4] Dolbear tells the story of first discovering Wolff's name tucked away in a sort of family tree that Benjamin drew in 1932 connecting his friends and acquaintances (see figure 4).[5] In one exercise, Dolbear removes the names, inviting his audience to meditate on the shape of the delicate hand-drawn lines.[6] Conjuring the spirit of Wolff, Dolbear becomes the palmist, reading the diagram as fate lines sketched into a hand. I see the lines as belonging to missing faces. Soft whiskers sprout from blank spaces once occupied by a primary friend to spaces reserved for friends of the friend. The whiskers remind me of "crows' feet," the wrinkles that form at the outer corner of eyes when a person squints or smiles. Some of these smile lines drip downward, transitioning into the laugh lines, framing the place where the mouth would speak the censored names.

Our fate is in our hands, but our character is in our face. Our fate is in our hands. The expression is at once a double that is at odds with itself, suggesting destiny (fate lines) and self-determinacy (action). Character is also a paradoxical double, a singular expression that emerges from one's scripted role and predetermined historical staging. Fate and Character are initially an odd couple, the first representing determinacy and embeddedness, the second representing contingency and freedom. But when seen through the (non)perspective of the crack in each, they are inverted mirror images of paradoxical doubleness: (fate and character | character and fate). Each side already contains both itself and the other. And yet the twins' split character can only be grasped in the appearance of their odd coupling.

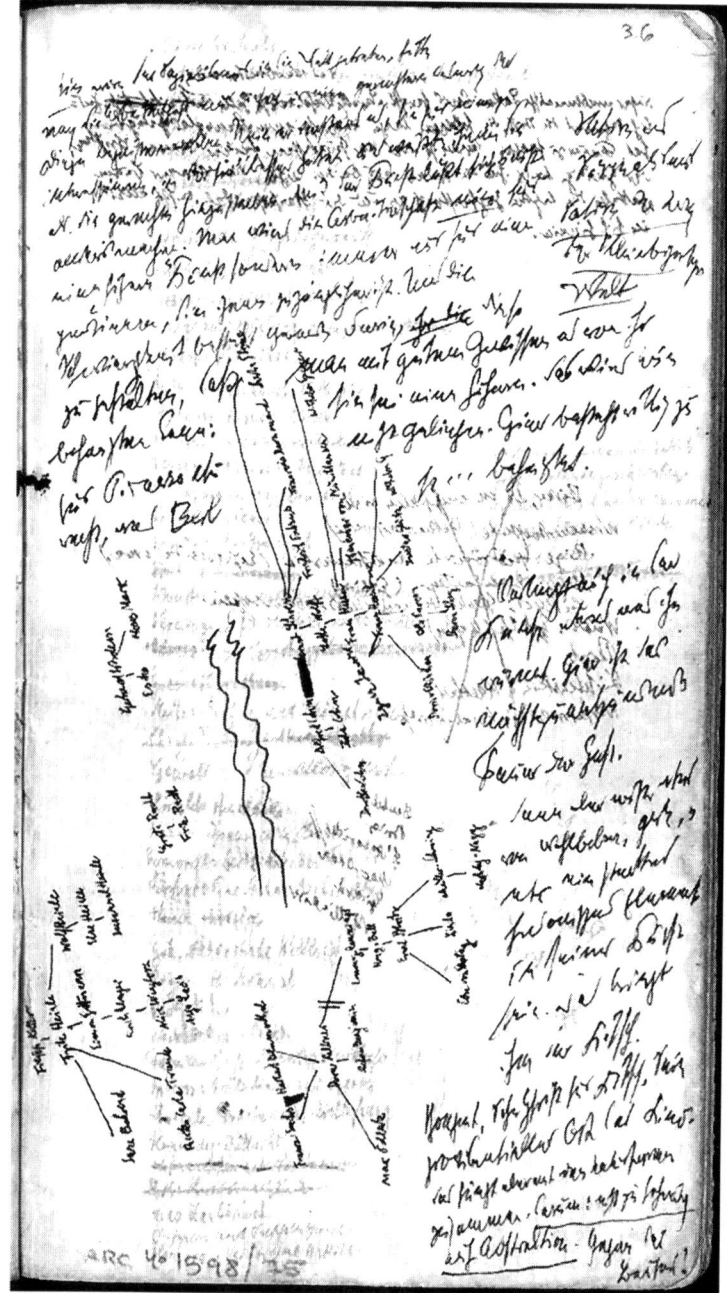

Figure 4. Walter Benjamin, Parchment Notebook (*Pergamentheft*). National Library of Israel, ARC. 4, 1598/75.

The dialectical doubling of the double reveals cracks that were present from the beginning. From the beginning to the end, nothing changes. One grasps herself by her crack when she sees her mirror image in her opposed double who is also split. And this moment of self-revelation is experienced simultaneously, although rarely symmetrically, by the other. Being experiences the horror of the crack in the absolute, while Nothingness experiences the thrill of the crack in her negative being. With this double grasp, something (nothing) stirs in each. Nothing changes as she experiences a shift in her relationship to her self. As the agent of this shift, nothing changes.

Benjamin reflects on the lines connecting the cracks in both fate and character, extending upon a Nietzsche quote: "'If a man has character, he has an experience that constantly recurs.' This means: if a man has character, his fate is essentially constant."[7] Dolbear further extends on Nietzsche and Benjamin: "The movement is circular: if one has fate, one has character; if one has character, one has fate. One's chance encounters at certain moments in one's life, in the formation of 'primal acquaintances,' establish hidden laws that mark out certain passages, or paths of experience. The diagram, then, like the palm, is a mapping of those paths, those laws that direct and determine the course of one's life."[8] Drawing linear fate lines that connect the passage from the past to one's present character becomes the act of retracing circles. Benjamin sits before a canvas to paint a self-portrait that captures his character. But in trying to outline his defining traits, he instead finds himself tracing the comings and goings of his acquaintances, moving in his overlapping spiraling social circles in Berlin. At what points do these characters come into touch as they brush by each other and his own body? What affects linger in the air and on his skin after the others have left?

Benjamin's "chosen family" tree is a performative failure, illustrating the impossible task of making a comprehensive diagram of all the characters who have left a mark on us. In trying to keep count of every event and character, in an effort to give an account of oneself, one becomes lost in a labyrinth of asynchronous affective relations. We forget the names and faces of most of our encounters, but a faint echo or scent of relationality lingers. The negative remainder of our dancing constellations is worn into the stage even when the individual actors who once inhabited these relations are forgotten.

History is marked by laugh lines. Our communal bodies are continually shaped as we move along the grooves caused by an overflow of unresolved conflicts, lingering expectations and disappointments, what goes unnamed, unfulfilled desires, unspoken codes, and unprocessed joy and grief. Do you ever have the sensation you are following in another's footsteps? Are we walking in circles?

Over time the grooves deepen and harden, forming cracks. Like face wrinkles, historical cracks simultaneously limit and deepen expressivity. Individuals who are born directly in these cracks, damned to slip right through the same cracks that form them, are the phantom comic heroes of a transgenerational historical drama. Even when they are not properly named as main characters, the phantoms express themselves by animating the cracks with their ghostlike laughter, a hiss, a twitch, a stutter. Action is born in the freedom of coming to sense how one's part has been substantially cut out of a social script.

Dialectics is a form of communal storytelling that allows us to restage a script. We retell stories through our speech but also through our live performance. Dialectics, despite its different beats, twirls us in circles all the same. Each dialectical looping is the experience of being stuck, of being swept along by historical repetition, which is no more progress than paralysis. But as I explore in chapter 7, walking in circles is also a living memorial that actively engages in the unresolved drama of a previous stage of history, which is no more past than present. Walking in circles is an act of resistance like the Partisans who, in the spirit of Jericho, surrounded the fascist camps making unsettling noises that caused the enemy to surrender.[9] The way we enact and recount the experiences that form us determines who counts. The counter counts themself as subject, by first giving testimony to their absence.

Returning to Censorship and Laughter

This book began with an exploration of comedy as a moment in Hegel's history of art and religion. Comedy is also a lens through which we can read how each of these histories, as they are lived and narrated, is structured by cracks that come to the surface as they deepen. My own narrative left Hegel "behind" to attend to political movements that grasped their resistance to a reactionary, oppressive government as a historical comedy. I identified direct laugh lines connecting the revolutions voiced by the Young Hegelians in early nineteenth-century Germany to the antifascist resistance of twentieth-century Europe voiced by Benjamin. The philosophical voices of the resistance laughed in the face of censorship at the risk their own destruction, while its institutional double, academic philosophy, often played the role of the diplomat, remaining silent for the sake of its own self-preservation.

How do these historical laugh lines extend and deepen through our current political dramas? It would be impossible to draw a comprehensive diagram tracing this inheritance, but our individual and communal bodies sense the growing tensions within the specific cracks that we are born into and the lines drawn into our skin.

Today history repeats itself in the birth of new laws that seek to permanently implement censorship under the farce of protecting free speech. The United States is one front of a global battle of laughter and censorship fought between camps that might be identified as the "Old" and the "Young." Although the conflict seems to run along a generational divide, the division is importantly shaped by class, race, sexuality, and gender. Education and comedy once again become the central tools for liberation and resistance as well as the weapons for politicians, who manipulate religion for private and corporate profit, gained at the expense of those who have long been cast into the socioeconomic position of the damned.

The introduction of hundreds of new state laws, some backed by the Supreme Court, threatens the existence of already vulnerable people by hindering their capacity for self-relation. State laws prohibiting abortion and gender affirmation surgery, for example, alienate people from their embodied being: their needs, pain, pleasure, and essential expressivity.[10] Laws that allow for discrimination based on sexual orientation, for example, prevent individuals from accessing benefits and services made available through participation in the communal bodies that form their society.[11]

Self is divided first from its body, then from its communal bodies. This process of destroying self-relation is fully carried out through the destruction of history's self-relation achieved by the censorship of education. State laws prohibiting curriculum on Black history and race studies seek to erase the lines that connect America's discriminatory practices and cultures from its violent racist past, a past that sustains itself in new forms.[12] The Supreme Court ruling on affirmative action as unconstitutional further stands in the way of Black students from entering the university to develop their voices in order to testify to the history that forms their experiences.[13] Censorship does not only omit certain historical events and actors but also creates a grotesque, farcical double who trolls history, calling itself by this name. Children are taught that slavery empowered its victims.[14] The original becomes a phantom of its counterfeit twin who threatens to snuff out the memory of history's concrete existence.

As I explore in chapter 5, Marx argues that political power that is empty of all political content stands for nothing more than its own preservation. It secures its power through the censorship of Spirit by severing self and history. Self cannot grasp itself in its historical existence, and history cannot grasp itself by its present individual and communal bodies. Power conceals its own lack of substance, insisting on its absoluteness as it reduces those it exploits to nothing. Double negation takes the form of negative twins: a substanceless power and the subject whom it makes powerless. Public Spirit can no longer feel itself even in its destruction as it is replaced by National Feeling, which is nothing more than the demand to be desensitized to one's own suffering and ecstasy. When Spirit is reduced to nothing, nothing more than National Feeling, materiality falls out of self-relation and cannot give testimony to the specific state of its own existence in any particular place and moment.

The oppressor denies culpability by pretending that its victims do not exist. The damned must not be named. Uttering the name of the ghost might reunite them with their body, like saying "Bloody Mary" in the mirror three times. New censorship laws forbid educators from speaking the word "gay" in acknowledgment of the existence of queer people.[15] Queer children learn that they don't exist within reason and, therefore, must retreat into the cracks of society the moment they begin to sense themselves; for queerness is above all a heightened sensation of self-relation grasped through the emergence of affective relationships to others. To speak other names, such as "Palestinian," in institutional spaces places one in immediate controversy and scandal with the threat of expulsion.

During the summer of 2023, when I wrote this conclusion, I couldn't have anticipated what I would witness the following year as a lecturer at Columbia University. Academic censorship was imposed externally by Congress and internally by compliant administrators who invited grotesque police violence on their own community in the name of self-preservation. Like the Prussian censorship, the pervasive censorship and surveillance measures beginning in 2023 across the United States (and across the world) targeted student organizations, foreign students and professors, and anyone who sought to represent the experience of those who have been violently negated (historically and presently) by others who see their power as Absolute. I also could not have anticipated how this horror would be met by the most brilliant emergence of communities united by the shared desire for accountability and justice (for all), rejecting the farcical appearance of unity maintained by their institutions.[16]

The narrative structure that reduces another to nothing is a paradoxical double that simultaneously denies another's existence while convincing the nameless that they should be satisfied to defend their own negative social and political role as a substantial self. To resist this internalized self-effacing narrative, an individual must constantly invert and replay the two narratives: I do in fact exist in ways I have not yet been allowed to sense and express (B | N); I do not really count in the way I have been taught to count myself as self (N | B). The affirmation of nothing grasps itself in the negation of being. The repetition of the split counternarrative (already composed of two doubles) can be exhausting and disorienting. Sometimes exhaustion and disorientation result in the experience of paralysis (*Aufhebung*). Sometimes, at the same time, paralysis produces movement (*Aufhebung*). The eruption of unpredictable affects—rage, despair, hilarity—is the cracking open of the crack in the narratives that place the self out of reach.

Some forms of censorship restrict people from naming themselves and restrict history from giving an account of itself. But as we explored with the Young Hegelians, those (individuals, institutions, and societies) who announce themselves as "champions of free speech" often enforce censorship by restricting how people are allowed to feel, rather than what they can say, especially about the champions themselves. Universities are sanctioned spaces for research and teaching that promote critical analysis of societal and global power structures. It is inevitable that this analysis turns on the very institutions that fund and support institutional critique. But as Sara Ahmed's *Complaint!* documents (and what many of us already know in secret), the institutions that promote critical analysis often prevent their members from feeling critically toward the institutions themselves and their human representatives who defend their institutional roles as their essence.[17]

Academics are permitted to analyze how the contradictions within academic institutions, in general, mirror the contradictions of global capitalism. But there are few effective stages for individuals to step forward to express how their individual bodies are caught in these contradictions. Those who describe the sensations and emotions of being crushed within the cracks are often punished for "allowing" the effects of their exploitation and abuse to come to the surface. In tragic conditions, the one who most keenly senses the effects of a broken system is identified as the source of a contradiction belonging to all the members of the community. A person's sensitivity—their inability or unwillingness to conceal suffering—threatens the appearance of a community that pretends not to sense the cracks in the structures that sustain its farcical unity.

Keeping silent is only possible by aborting feeling at its root. One feels nothing in the form of being desensitized to the injustice done against one's body or communal body. Another feels nothing in the form of remaining neutral in the face of the injustice done against another's body or communal body. Ruge critiques the academic who plays the role of the diplomat. Those who bite their tongue, remaining above a conflict "belonging to others," support and conceal the abuse of others who don't have the privilege of feigning neutrality. Philosophy must be willing to engage in conflict. Or, in Ruge's view, philosophy that is philosophy is already in conflict. As José Esteban Muñoz argues, we must allow ourselves to feel the sensation of lack, to admit that the community we desire is "not-yet."[18] Muñoz's not-yet echoes the split temporality and desire belonging to Hegel's ethics: the desire for community requires recognizing the need for reconciliation; the persistence of hope that motivates action toward reconciliation requires ongoing uncertainty regarding whether reconciliation will ever be achieved. Ethics, like Spirit itself, is driven by a skeptical engine that sputters, calling its own progress into question.

Violence is permitted against certain kinds of bodies whose lives count as nothing, before their institutions, the state, the law, the world. Censorship in its many forms discourages individuals from causing a disturbance by speaking about the violence that has been done to them. Sometimes a violated subject or "violable" subject is directly discouraged from speaking, from naming names, or specifying violations. But often their silence is enforced through an environment that fetishizes the appearance of order, collegiality, balanced perspectives, and moderation. The Young Hegelians were rightly critical of the virtue of moderation and measure. How can one be reasonable when what has been done to them is beyond comprehension? Those who represent the space of the middle or in-between as the space of reason and common sense do not occupy the crack but the position of the Absolute, who does not stand for anything while refusing to acknowledge its empty contents.[19]

Perhaps my tone becomes too serious for a book on laughter. How is injustice, violation, and violence a laughing matter? Comedy takes center stage, rising from underground, when history is prevented from speaking up for itself. I observe a contemporary battle of laughter against laughter as a stage on which different groups attempt to maintain or gain narrative power. In the spirit of the first-generation Hegelians, I identify this divide as Old and Young Comedy. Which side's laughter is censored by which? The story is told differently depending on which beat is emphasized.

Old Comedy, in my account, represents a privileged position of narrative power that perceives itself as under attack by a new generation, whom the Old associates with political correctness, cancel culture, trigger culture, sexual frigidity, and snowflake sensitivity. In the United States, this position is commonly associated with the Right, but other defenders of Old Comedy speak in the name of radical leftist politics. They argue that the elimination of racist, antisemitic, sexist, homophobic, transphobic, and xenophobic jokes does not challenge the underlying material conditions and cultures that give rise to these jokes; humor is a symptom of ideology, and jokes are important for taking societal temperature, allowing fear and anxiety to come to the surface. In what ways do the positions of the defenders of Old Comedy within the American Right and European Left mirror or oppose each other? I ask this question honestly, probing my own communities, rather than rhetorically.

Most lovers of comedy, we defenders of comic Spirit, are perversely attracted to profanity, irreverence, and transgression. This attraction can be an expression of the desire to defy power structures that are reinforced by cultural inscriptions of race, gender, sexuality, and class. As I discuss through Hegel's analysis of ancient art-religion in chapters 2 and 3, a society's "ethical code" is often nothing more than normative social roles that alienate individuals from their selves and their communities, while preventing that society from forming a concrete ethical community that takes accountability for how its contradictions damn certain actors from the beginning.

Irreverent outbursts, whether expressed through dark humor or anger, can be the expression of pain and grief. The experience of beginning to sense one's desensitization is itself a sensational reawakening. As I discussed in chapter 3, comic-anguish is the experience of coming into touch with disillusionment. The tragic hero is struck by a glimmer of comic genius: a sense that the social scripts that they fiercely defended as their most authentic "self" and "community" inhibit the realization of either. In a moment of concrete self-relation, one experiences the sensation of a former sense of self, dissipating into nothing. Yet, anguish is present in comic relief. The thrilling desire for a substantial existence does not necessarily negate the grief of the loss of a self and community that never existed as one once believed. Comedy that truly values freedom and liberation must take suffering more seriously than tragedy does.

A comic community is born out of a common sense of irreverence. The love for provocation belongs to those who long for the destruction of power structures that limit their self and our shared experience and eliminate the substantial existence of certain individuals altogether. At the same time, this attraction also belongs to those who want to preserve their own power within these structures. The split desire for destruction and preservation of the status quo surfaces in the comic community and within a single member. One must pay close attention, for even dreams of revolution can reek of a revolutionary's anxious attachment to their own power within the structures they seek to dismantle in theory.

Conversations that express anxiety toward political correctness often neglect an adequate analysis of the real violence done to the traditional subjects of laughter. It's especially alarming when Leftist conversations about free speech become imbalanced, stressing the wrong beat. I attend conferences on comedy where provocative defenses of rape jokes outweigh discussions that acknowledge the reality of rape culture and its relationship to symbolic violence. Is humor that expresses bigotry or portrays violence, always done to another, necessary to identify the existence of bigotry and violence? The other does not need proof of what has been done to their body. When does the defense of Old Comedy contain an underlying insistence on the rightness of the comedian's (and theorist's) own anxiety toward the other (e.g., the existence of Brown refugees in Europe, of transgender individuals in popular culture, of women who can give voice to their embodied experiences)? Arguments defending the right to joke about "our" anxiety toward "the other" become blurred with arguments defending the right to be anxious about the other who has suddenly gained a platform to tell their own jokes.

I learned to laugh in the 1990s and early 2000s through the perspective of predominantly white male comics on Comedy Central whose jokes were almost always at the expense of another who didn't have a platform to speak to their own experience. As my comic heroes took jabs at feminized and queer individuals, my laughter distanced me from sensing myself as the derogatory object of humor. And by internalizing femininity and queerness as objects of anxiety and fear, my laughter distanced me from grasping myself by my own body and desires.

Laughter is the process of distancing and de-distancing. I experience the thrill of grasping myself as self as my laughter undergoes transformation. As the cracks within given social identities deepen coming to the surface, so does the possibility of deeper self-relation. There is something redemptive about belonging to the audience of a new wave of Young Comedy. Scrolling through an endless stream of stand-up reels on TikTok, I'm exposed to comedians from infinite standpoints without duplications, some of which are deeply relatable and some of which expose me to experiences that are completely unlike my own. Gen Z humor is introspective, vulnerable, and fearless, especially in its irreverence toward the societal contradictions that create tensions within the comedian's personal experience and damn our shared world.

The split between the Old and Young within first-generation Hegelians didn't simply indicate a generational divide. Instead, the Old defended the institutional structures and ideological narratives that sustained their own platform by eliminating competing voices. The Young had no other choice than to create alternative platforms. One side of the divide feared no longer being the only voice, while the other dreamed of speaking in new tongues, of uttering a single original sentence.

In today's battles between censorship and laughter, the Old self-designate themselves as such when they fixate on a younger generation whom they identify as a threat to their free pursuit of pleasure. What the Old calls "cancellation" is often nothing more than an audience's freedom to attend a different show when there are so many shows to choose from. Concrete censorship, in contrast, acts in the name of freedom, not only to silence diverse voices but to eliminate their very existence at a moment when new expressions of self and community are being born. Drag, one of the oldest forms of subversive comedy, becomes the heated target of censorship just as it explodes into mainstream media and culture.[20] Through drag, queer people magnify the aspects of their own existence that have been the object of the Old's anxiety. Drag is the comic art of self-exposure, rather than self-defense, requiring nerve and vulnerability. It celebrates the self while turning old anxiety into the object of laughter. Young Comedy has always existed at every stage and includes those from every generation who insist on existing more vividly and experiencing pleasure more intensely than "freedom" (or the free rein of the Old) permits.

Have cancel culture and political correctness made us too serious? Has the Young lost their sense of humor? Perhaps they simply do not share the Old's anxiety toward the other's existence. My sense is that people of all ages are simply exhausted from holding open so much space for the Old's anxiety. Many of us come to sense ourselves as the derogatory object of the Old Comedy we grew up with. We've grown bored with the comedy that once held us captive for lack of other options. The Young are less fearful, teaching us that we no longer need to laugh along nervously at our own existence.

How many people fear cancellation because they have never been forced to reflect on how their actions or narratives may have caused harm? The insecurity at the core of absolute power is forced to come to the surface. Some people who speak in the name of free speech fear losing the power to control the narrative about those who have been historically prevented from giving accounts of their own experience. They fear being held accountable for the symbolic and physical violence that they have freely enacted for as long as history itself can remember. Behind their defense of free speech lies their terror that the other will be permitted to finally speak, to finally expose what has been done to her: how she has been silenced; how her body and communal bodies have been violated; how her words, jokes, and art have been stolen from her and spoken under another's stage name.

I have argued that the sensation of self-doubt is the condition and invitation for self-reflection. The self is born and sustained through negative self-relation. Hélène Cixous's "The Laugh of the Medusa" is a feminist manifesto for those excluded from history through the censorship of their body and voice.[21] The subject who is disconnected from her body is reduced to a shadow of the "militant male" with the power to fight and write, to act and give the only account of that action; in order to write herself into history, the self who has been reduced to a shadow must kill the false self who prevents her from breathing.[22] When the self turns on its double, the shadow comes into touch with her body. The act of masturbation gives rise to revolutionary laughter by reuniting spirit and matter. Cixous calls to her self: "Touch me, caress me, you the living no-name, give me my self as myself ... my body ... what touches you, the equivoice that affects you, fills your breast with an urge to come to language and launches your force; the rhythm that laughs you ... the part of you that leaves a space between yourself."[23] The midwife performs the double act of self-termination and self-birth, grasping herself by the crack between what she is and what she is not.

"Self-preservation," for preservation's sake, insists on a self that is empty of substance, while a certain kind of "self-destruction" risks destroying the farcical apparatus of self that prevents one from coming into touch with their individual and communal body. To sense that one has been made nothing, often from the beginning, is to sense one's own desensitization. To sense one's negativity, like the tingling of a foot that has fallen asleep but is shaken into movement, immediately gives rise to the emergence of new sensations and emotions. Self-relation is found in the moment one grasps oneself by her self-alienation and experiences the shooting sensation of desiring more.

The self's relationship to her negativity is her ability to grasp herself as an active participant in an ethical community that questions its own ethical commitments at every stage. Those who have been denied power do not fear cancellation, because they are born into a social position that was denied voice from the beginning. Each time she is censored, she comes closer to grasping herself by the root of her constitutive silencing. The thrill and terror of self-relating negativity through which the self grasps herself by her communal body gives rise to an outburst that cannot be censored. To borrow again from Cixous's manifesto of laughter:

> We the precocious, we the repressed of culture, our lovely mouths gagged with pollen, our wind knocked out of us, we the labyrinths, the ladders, the trampled spaces, the bevies—we are black and we are beautiful.
>
> We're stormy, and that which is ours breaks loose from us without fearing any debilitation. Our glances, our smiles, are spent; laughs exude from all our mouths; our blood flows and we extend ourselves

without ever reaching an end; we never hold back our thoughts, our signs, our writing; and we're not afraid of lacking.

What happiness for us who are omitted, brushed aside at the scene of inheritances; we inspire ourselves and we expire without running out of breath, we are everywhere!

From now on, who, if we say so, can say no to us? We've come back from always.[24]

History's wrinkles remember what is wiped from our collective memory and promise to reawaken our bodies by shaking us awake with revolutionary laughter. Laughter can be a defense mechanism that expresses fear and anxiety toward another. Defensive laughter does not allow itself to be laughed at even though its cracks have been exposed. But laughter can also be the sensation of self-expansion as we come into touch. Laughter as an expression of the insurmountable insecurity in absolute power is countered by a laughter that has nothing to fear because it has nothing to lose and everything to gain by learning to count its own existence.

ACKNOWLEDGMENTS

I'd like to express my deep gratitude for . . .

my friends in Ljubljana who gave me a philosophical home, including Mladen Dolar, Alenka Zupančič, Lev Kreft, Goran Vranešević, Bara Kolenc, Martin Hergouth, and Samo Tomšič;

my philosophical friends, Walter Brogan, Jim Wetzel, Patricia Grosse Brewer, and Simon Waxman, who guided me through the early stages of conceiving this book;

my family for their intellectual, creative, and emotional companionship: James, Khan, Emily, Scott, and my parents;

the communal bodies through which I grasped my political subjectivity and practiced resistance: CUAD, VAMP, The Moon Platoon;

Faith Wilson Stein, who always has the perfect words of motivation, and the talented team of editors at Northwestern University Press, including Anne Gendler, Nathan MacBrien, and indexer Matthew John Phillips, who skillfully guided the development of this book;

the gift of time to think, read, write, and discuss ideas, which was possible through the material support of a Fulbright grant to Slovenia, a research position at the Maimonides Center for Advanced Studies in Jewish Skepticism at the University of Hamburg, and a fellowship at the ICI Berlin Institute for Cultural Inquiry;

Robert Scott Whipkey, who graciously gave me permission to use his painting *Annihilation, in Hansa Yellow w/ Red Ochre (after Sanford Robinson Gifford)* for the cover of this book.

A shorter version of chapter 1 was originally published as "Twice-Two: Hegel's Comic Redoubling of Being and Nothing," *Problemi International: Journal for Psychoanalytic Theory and Philosophy* 2 (2018): 253–78. Reprinted by permission of the publisher.

Chapter 2 was published in a different form as "The Aborted Object of Comedy and the Birth of the Subject: Plato and Aristophanes' Alliance" in *The Object of Comedy*, ed. Jamila M. H. Mascat and Gregor Moder (Palgrave Macmillan, 2020), 75–92.

Sections from chapter 3 were originally presented in an earlier form in 2013 and published as "Hegel on the Crucifixion as Comedy," in *Proceedings of the XXIII World Congress of Philosophy*, vol. 1, ed. Konstantinos Boudouris (Philosophy Documentation Center, 2018), 25–31, https://doi.org/10.5840/wcp23201814. Reprinted by permission of the Philosophy Documentation Center.

Early versions of sections from chapter 3 and chapter 4 were translated into Slovenian and appeared as "Hegel in Marx o gledališkem in historičnem prizorišču komedije" [Hegel and Marx on the theatrical and historical stage of comedy], trans. Lev Kreft, *Borec: A Journal for Slovene Philosophy and Culture* 706–8 (2014): 140–59.

A version of several pages from chapter 6 was originally published as "The Lick of the Mother Tongue: Derrida's Fantasies of 'the Touch of Language' with Augustine and Marx," in *The Language of Touch: Philosophical Examinations in Linguistics and Haptic Studies*, ed. Mirt Komel (Bloomsbury, 2019), 107–20. Reprinted by permission of Bloomsbury Academic, an imprint of Bloomsbury Publishing Plc.

A shorter version of chapter 7 was originally published as "Antigone's Stance amongst Slovenia's Undead," *Studia ethnologica Croatica* 29 (2017): 19–42.

NOTES

Introduction

1. G. W. F. Hegel, *Phenomenology of Spirit* (hereafter *PS*), trans. A. V. Miller (Oxford University Press, 1977), §§699–787; Hegel, *Phänomenologie des Geistes* (hereafter *Werke 3*), vol. 3 of *Gesamte Werkausgabe*, ed. Eva Moldenhauer and Karl Markus Michel (Suhrkamp Verlag, 1986), 512–76. Throughout these notes, citations to translations of key texts will be followed by the relevant citation to the original-language edition, separated by a semicolon.

2. *PS*, §743; *Werke 3*, 541.

3. *PS*, §747; *Werke 3*, 544.

4. G. W. F. Hegel, *Lectures on the Philosophy of Religion: The Lectures of 1827* (hereafter *LPR*), ed. Peter C. Hodgson, trans. Robert F. Brown, J. Michael Stewart, and Peter C. Hodgson (Oxford University Press, 2007). I cite this one-volume edition of the critical three-volume English translation, reissued by Oxford in 2007. Unless otherwise stated, the German pagination refers to Hegel, *Vorlesungen über die Philosophie der Religion, Teil 2: Die bestimmte Religion* (hereafter *VPR 2*), and *Teil 3: Die vollendete Religion* (hereafter *VPR 3*), ed. Walter Jaeschke (Felix Meiner Verlag, 1994). Hegel uses the term "divine drama" in his notes published in *Vorlesungen über die Philosophie der Religion* (hereafter cited as *W2*), 2nd ed., in 2 vols., ed. Philipp Marheineke (Duncker und Humblot, 1840). The editors of *LPR* include this addition in a footnote (*LPR*, 471n214), commenting on *VPR 3*, 252.

5. *PS*, §§699–787; *Werke 3*, 512–76.

6. Hegel, *Hegel's Aesthetics: Lectures on Fine Art*, vol. 2 (hereafter *Aesthetics*), trans. T. M. Knox (Oxford University Press, 1975), 2.1192–1238; Hegel, *Vorlesungen über die Ästhetik III* (hereafter *Werke 15*), vol. 15 of *Gesamte Werkausgabe*, ed. Eva Moldenhauer and Karl Markus Michel (Suhrkamp Verlag, 1970), 474–576. Hegel analyzes drama throughout his lectures, but in this section he compares the representation of the divine in ancient and modern drama and their relationship to history.

7. "The Religion of Beauty, or Greek Religion," *LPR* 330–57; "Die Religion der Schönheit oder die griechische Religion," *VPR 2*, 532–60; "The Consummate Religion," *LPR* 391–489; "Die vollendete Religion," *VPR 3*, 177–270.

8. Karl Marx, "Comments on the Latest Prussian Censorship Instruction," in *Marx-Engels Collected Works*, vol. 1, *Karl Marx: 1835–43* (International Publishers, 1975), 109–31; Marx, "Bemerkungen über die neueste preußische Zensurinstruktion," in *Marx-Engels-Werke 1*, ed. Institut für Marxismus-Leninismus beim ZK der SED (Dietz Verlag, 1956), 3–24. Hereafter, the English and German Marx-Engels editions will be abbreviated as *MECW* and *MEW*, respectively, followed by the volume number.

9. Arnold Ruge, "Hegel's 'Philosophy of Right' and the Politics of our Times," in *The Young Hegelians: An Anthology*, ed. Lawrence S. Stepelevich, trans. James A. Massey (Cambridge University Press, 1983), 211–36; originally published as "Hegels Rechtsphilosophie und die Politik unserer Zeit," in Deutscher Jarbücher 189–90 (1842). Hereafter, the pagination for the translation is followed by column references to the original text.

10. Ruge, "Hegel's 'Philosophy of Right,'" 212; "Hegels Rechtsphilosophie," 756a.

11. Ruge, "Hegel's 'Philosophy of Right,'" 214; "Hegels Rechtsphilosophie," 757a.

12. Farce has the appearance of change but preserves the tragic content of what it claims to subvert with the masquerade of a new form. Comedy may repeat the same form as tragedy in a way that offers a changed relationship to what it reiterates. As Marx claims, a tragic stage must play out its own contradictory logic before it recognizes itself as farcical. When tragedy takes itself seriously it can recognize its own farce—the contradictory structures that it defended as absolute. Comic consciousness comes out of the repetition of tragedy.

13. This work explores the relationship between laughter and many forms of silence. Silence may result from censorship, but it also is a form of protest. Laughter itself may interrupt speech, but it may also take the form of a silent snickering. For a recent account of the politics of silence, see Ed Pluth and Cindy Zeiher, *On Silence: Holding the Voice Hostage* (Palgrave Pivot, 2019).

14. Marx, *The Eighteenth Brumaire of Louis Bonaparte*, in MECW 11, 103; *Der achtzehnte Brumaire des Louis Bonaparte*, in MEW 8, 115.

15. There are many provocative and ethically compelling defenses of the tragedy of spirit within Hegelian philosophy. See, for example, Theodore D. George, *Tragedies of Spirit: Tracing Finitude in Hegel's Phenomenology* (State University of New York Press, 2006).

16. Lady Philosophy is the protagonist of Boethius's partly fictional account of his own censorship and imprisonment for speaking out against political corruption. The apparition first appears in ripped garments as a result of men who have attempted to claim her and use her for their own purposes. Lady Philosophy might appear as a tragic figure, but the story speaks to philosophy's victorious resilience and power in the face of suppression. Boethius, *De consolatione philosophiae. Opuscula theologica*, ed. Claudio Moreschini (K. G. Saur, 2005); Boethius, *Consolation of Philosophy*, trans. J. C. Relihan (Hackett, 2001).

17. Because I focus on Hegelian-Marxist comedy, I only briefly mention philosophers more commonly associated with comedy, notably Nietzsche, Bergson, Kierkegaard, and Bataille. See, for example: Friedrich Nietzsche, *Thus Spoke Zarathustra*, trans. Adrian Del Caro (Cambridge University Press, 2006); Georges Bataille, "Hegel, Death and Sacrifice," *Yale French Studies* 78 (1990): 9–28; Bataille, "Un-Knowing: Laughter and Tears," *October* 36 (1986): 89–102; Henri Bergson, *Laughter: An Essay on the Meaning of the Comic* (Dover, 2005).

18. I use the pronouns "we/our" when referring to the experiences of specific communities that I belong to (I take this project to be an act of feminist, queer resistance). "We" might also refer to communities with which I stand in solidarity. In this case, even when the present and inherited struggles do not belong to

everyone, the term "we" acknowledges that the fight for their right to exist and exist joyfully belongs equally to all. I strive to avoid universalizing "we" unless I'm referring to a conviction in an ethical imperative that I believe ought to be universal.

19. Apuleius, *Metamorphoses*, 2 vols. (Harvard University Press, 1989); Nietzsche, *Thus Spoke Zarathustra*, 255–57.

20. Hegel, *The Science of Logic* (hereafter *SL*), trans. George di Giovanni (Cambridge University Press, 2010); Hegel, *Wissenschaft der Logik* (hereafter *Werke 5* or *Werke 6*), vols. 5–6 of *Gesamte Werkausgabe*, ed. Eva Moldenhauer and Karl Markus Michel (Suhrkamp Verlag, 1986). Lacan's reading of the cracking of the egg and lamella: Jacques Lacan, *The Seminar of Jacques Lacan: Book XI: The Four Fundamental Concepts of Psychoanalysis*, ed. Jacques-Alain Miller, trans. Alan Sheridan (W. W. Norton, 1998), 197–98.

21. A group of my students at the University of Hamburg represented the concept of the concept in the context of reading Hegel's Master-Slave dialectic through two hands. I am specifically drawing on an image illustrated by Lulu Bartels, spring 2021.

22. Karl Michelet, *Geschichte der letzten Systeme der Philosophie in Deutschland von Kant bis Hegel* (Nabu Press, 2012), 623. For a contemporary and beautifully creative reading of Hegel's owl in the crack between beginnings and ends, see Andrew Cutrofello's *The Owl at Dawn: A Sequel to Hegel's "Phenomenology of Spirit"* (State University of New York Press, 1995).

23. On the slogan "no more": Diogenes Laertius, "Pyrrho," *Lives of Eminent Philosophers*, trans. R. D. Hicks (Harvard University Press, 1925), IX. 11; Sextus Empiricus, *Outlines of Scepticism*, ed. and trans. Julia Annas and Jonathan Barnes (Cambridge, 2000), I.10.

24. For the ancient skeptics, "equipollence" often referred to two equally compelling arguments, competing definitions or beliefs that cannot logically both be true. In Hegel's view, this contradiction encountered in thought and language reflects a contradiction that is in the world. The experience of equipollence is not merely intellectual but encountered in the competing and contradictory demands inscribed in our social roles. We experience equipollence in our relationships and even in our bodies through contradictory but equally powerful sensations and desires (pleasure/pain; attraction/revulsion).

25. *SL*, 746; *Werke 6*, 564.

26. Alenka Zupančič, *The Odd One In: On Comedy* (MIT Press, 2008).

27. Mladen Dolar, "Being and MacGuffin," *Crisis and Critique* 4, issue 1 (2017): 82–101.

28. Immanuel Kant, *Kritik der Urteilskraft*, vol. 5 of *Gesammelte Schriften* (Reimer, 1908 [1790]), §5, 332–33.

29. Walter Benjamin, *The Arcades Project* (hereafter *Arcades*, followed by the relevant *Konvolut*), trans. Howard Eiland and Kevin McLaughlin (Harvard University Press, 2002), 325 [J53a,4]; Benjamin, *Das Passagen-Werk*, vol. 5 of *Gesammelte Schriften* (hereafter *GS* followed by the relevant volume number), ed. Rolf Tiedemann and Hermann Schweppenhäuser (Suhrkamp Verlag, 1998), 409–10.

30. *MECW 3*, 185; *MEW 1*, 389.

Chapter 1

1. *MECW 11*, 103; *MEW 8*, 115.
2. Jean Yarbrough, dir., *The Naughty Nineties*, featuring Bud Abbot and Lou Costello (Universal Studios, 1945).
3. A pair of opposites (tragedy and farce) sometimes say the same thing, while the repetition of the same phrase ("Who's on first? Who's on first!") alters the meaning of the first iteration.
4. Hegel, *SL*, 59; *Werke 5*, 82.
5. *SL*, 746; *Werke 6*, 564.
6. Sigmund Freud, "The 'Uncanny,'" in *The Standard Edition of the Complete Psychological Works of Sigmund Freud*, vol. 17, ed. and trans. James Strachey (Vintage, 1999), 217–56.
7. In "The 'Uncanny,'" Freud analyzes the relationship between the comic effect and the double. Freud compares two stories involving a severed hand. In both cases, the severed hand redoubles a symbolic cut in the viewer's own body (castration). But in one case, the image evokes a shudder and, in the other, laughter. In the first case, the image of the severed hand is uncanny because the audience identifies with the protagonist who experiences the violence. The audience shudders to convince themselves that the scene is unthinkable in reality. Because the cut comes too close to home, the audience pulls away. In the other case, the severed hand is comical when the audience identifies with a character who is not directly inflicted by the violence. With the illusion of distance, the audience leans in to have a closer look, ironically bringing them closer to a symbolic cut within their own body: "The 'Uncanny,'" 236, 245, 252.
8. Freud, "The 'Uncanny,'" 252.
9. James Parrott, *Twice Two*, featuring Stan Laurel and Oliver Hardy (Hal Roach Studios, 1933).
10. For an account of the early development of the Ljubljana School, see Kaitlyn Tucker Sorenson, "Experience as Device: Encountering Russian Formalism in the Ljubljana School," *Slavic Review* 79, no. 1 (2020): 93–114.
11. Slavoj Žižek, *Hegel in označevalec: Poskusi "materialističnega obrata Hegla" v sodobni psihoanalitični teoriji in njihov pomen za historični materializem* (Univerzum, 1980).
12. Rastko Močnik, *Meščevo zlato: Prešeren v označevalcu* (Analecta, 1981).
13. A playful reference to an essential collection published seven years later: *Everything You Always Wanted to Know about Lacan (But Were Afraid to Ask Hitchcock)*, ed. Slavoj Žižek (Verso Books, 1988).
14. Alenka Zupančič, *The Odd One In: On Comedy* (MIT Press, 2008), 57–58.
15. Zupančič, *The Odd One In*, 58.
16. Slavoj Žižek, *Bolečina razlike* (Obzorja, 1972); see also Kaitlyn Tucker Sorenson, "Razpor: On Slavoj Žižek's First Break," *European Review* 29, no. 6 (December 2021): 752–61.
17. *SL*, 437; *Werke 6*, 17.
18. Perhaps postmodern comedy precedes postmodern philosophy.
19. The trope of the multiplication of Bugs first appears in *The Big Snooze*, dir. Robert Clampett (Warner Brothers, 1946).
20. Hegel is at once too severe and too frivolous. Instead of denying this characterization, chapters 1, 3, and 4 explore the relationship between "too seriousness"

and "too light," identifying the value of leaning into these affects at the same time, both in the context of establishing critique and for acknowledging grief.

21. Judith Butler, *Subjects of Desire: Hegelian Reflections in Twentieth-Century France* (Columbia University Press, 1987), 21.

22. Slavoj Žižek, *The Sublime Object of Ideology* (Verso Books, 1989), 148–49; Žižek, "Laugh Yourself to Death: The New Wave of Holocaust Comedies!" *Lacan.com*, December 14, 2005, https://www.lacan.com/zizekholocaust.htm.

23. Zupančič, *The Odd One In*, 28–29. For a collection of essays about the indestructible comic object by the extended Ljubljana School community, see *The Object of Comedy*, ed. Jamila Mascat and Gregor Moder (Palgrave Macmillan, 2020).

24. Søren Kierkegaard, *The Concept of Anxiety: A Simple Psychologically Oriented Deliberation in View of the Dogmatic Problem of Hereditary Sin* (Liveright Publishing, 2014); Jean-Paul Sartre, *Being and Nothingness: An Essay on Phenomenological Ontology*, trans. Hazel E. Barns (Philosophical Library, 1956).

25. Friedrich Nietzsche. *Beyond Good and Evil*, trans. R. J. Hollingdale (Penguin Classics, 2003).

26. Gary Nelson, dir., *Freaky Friday* (Walt Disney Productions, 1976).

27. Slavoj Žižek, "Why Should a Dialectician Learn to Count to Four?," *Radical Philosophy* 58 (1991): 3–9. The importance of this four-part structure remains critical to his later work. See, for example, Žižek, *Less Than Nothing: Hegel and the Shadow of Dialectical Materialism* (Verso Books, 2012).

28. Jacques Lacan, *The Four Fundamental Concepts of Psychoanalysis: Seminar XI*, ed. Jacques-Alain Miller, trans. Alan Sheridan (W. W. Norton, 1998).

29. Hegel, *SL*, 746; *Werke* 6, 564.

30. Žižek, "Why Should a Dialectician Learn to Count to Four?," 3.

31. Žižek, "Why Should a Dialectician Learn to Count to Four?," 5.

32. Zupančič, "Repetition," in *The Odd One In*, 149–82.

33. See, for example, Mladen Dolar, "Comedy and Its Double. Die Komödie und ihr Double," in *Schluß mit der Kömodie! Stop That Comedy!*, ed. Robert Pfaller (Sonderzahl, 2005), 25–59; 181–209.

34. Mladen Dolar, "Hegel and Freud," *E-flux Journal* 34 (April 2012), 9–10.

35. For one formulation of the mirror phase, see Lacan, *Écrits*, trans. Bruce Fink (W. W. Norton, 2007), 75–81.

36. William Shakespeare, *The Comedy of Errors* (Cambridge University Press, 1988).

37. Antonin Artaud, *The Theater and Its Double*, trans. Mary Caroline Richards (Grove Press, 1994). On "two peas in a pot": this heading comes from a famous Stan Laurel malapropism in *Sons of the Desert* (Hal Roach Studios, 1933). Stan is searching for the expression "two peas in a pod" to describe himself and Ollie but accidentally stumbles upon the charming malapropism "two peas in a pot." Stan's malapropisms always seem to hit the nail on the head. The accidental suggestion is that two companions who are too similar are likely to get each other in trouble, like two peas in a boiling pot of water.

38. Hegel on the two tragic sides that mirror each other: *PS*, §740; *Werke 3*, 539–40.

39. Plato, *Symposium* (hereafter *Symp.*), trans. W. R. M. Lamb (Harvard University Press, 1925), 189c–193e.

40. David Swift, dir., *The Parent Trap* (Walt Disney Home Entertainment, 1961).

41. Stanley Kubrick, dir., *The Shining* (Warner Bros. Pictures, 1980).

42. Barbet Schroeder, dir., *Single White Female* (Columbia Pictures, 1997).

43. This fight to the death illustrates what makes dialectical repetition distinct from postmodern repetition. In postmodern repetition, there is no longer any claim to originality. Dialectical repetition is characterized by a tension produced between two, each of which seems to have an equal claim to the position of the first. And yet, it is impossible to decide which side is referent and which side is signifier. In my view, the repetition of the first double in the second double (the movement from 2 to 4) does not overcome this tension but allows for a new affective relationship in the preserved tension between two. The fight to the death of one of the two sides also does not overcome the tension. The greatest irony is in the revelation that one is already two. When Hedy is exposed as having a personality disorder, Allie's own alter-ego emerges. It is not only Hedy who is split. Allie's dark side proves to be as destructive as Hedy's shadow self.

44. Clyde Geronimi, Wilfred Jackson, and Hamilton Luske, dirs., *Alice in Wonderland*, based on the works of Lewis Carroll (Walt Disney Productions, 1951).

45. Hegel, LPR, 340; VPR 2, 543–44.

46. The American Dialect Society, "Word of the Year: 1993," https://www.americandialect.org/woty/all-of-the-words-of-the-year-1990-to-present#1993, accessed January 12, 2018. I had a T-shirt with a troll on it and the word "Rad." My sister, my sidekick, wore a similar T-shirt with a troll and the word "Not!" She followed me around as a constant negation of my claim to being rad.

47. Patrick Eiden-Offe reads the *Science of Logic* through a literary lens, sensitive to its satirical elements: *Hegels Logik Lesen: Ein Selbstversuch* (Matthes & Seitz Verlag, 2020).

48. SL, 59; Werke 5, 82–83.

49. Dolar, "Being and MacGuffin," 92–93.

50. A comic double of Aristotle's absolute as thought thinking itself: Aristotle, *Metaphysics*, 12.1072b.20.

51. Thanks to Aaron Schuster for this suggestion of adding the Three Stooges and Marx Brothers in the process of counting to four through classic comic cinema.

52. Alfred Appel, "Conversations with Nabokov," *NOVEL: A Forum on Fiction* 4, no. 3 (1971): 213.

53. The tetradic dialect within the original double Being and Nothing is inherent to a comic double, like Laurel and Hardy. The episode in which the comedians double themselves as their female counterparts reveals a dynamic that is already present in the duo: (B | N), (N | B), (B | B), (N | N) → (L | H), (H | L), (L | L), (H | H). Two more doubles emerge, a repetition of L | L and H | H if one counts cross-coupling diagonally. I count this doubling as a repetition of the same form in the oscillation between the duo.

54. Dolar, "Being and MacGuffin," 92.

55. James Parrott, dir., *Brats*, featuring Stan Laurel and Oliver Hardy (Hal Roach Studios, 1930).

56. Ingmar Bergman, dir., *The Seventh Seal* (Svensk Filmindustri, 1957).

Chapter 2

1. Aristophanes, *Clouds, Women at Thesmophoria, Frogs* (hereafter *Cl.*), trans. Stephan Halliwell (Oxford University Press, 2015).
2. *Cl.*, 130–40.
3. Plato, *Symp.*, 210a–212c; Plato, *Theaetetus* (hereafter *Tht.*), in *Theaetetus and Sophist*, trans. Christopher Rowe (Cambridge, 2015), 149b10.
4. *Symp.*, 189c–193e.
5. Hegel, *LPR*, 457; *VPR 3*, 239.
6. Hegel, *PS*, §748–59; *Werke 3*, 545–57.
7. *PS*, §708; *Werke 3*, 517.
8. *PS*, §714; *Werke 3*, 521.
9. *PS*, §722–23; *Werke 3*, 437–38.
10. *PS*, §729; *Werke 3*, 530–31.
11. *PS*, §745; *Werke 3*, 542.
12. *PS*, §747; *Werke 3*, 544.
13. Certain strands of ancient skepticism attempt to avoid the disruption of skepticism on a social and political level by limiting the skeptic's mode of inquiry to a theoretical register. Sextus Empiricus notably argues that because philosophical inquiry cannot lead us to absolute ethical maxims, it is advisable to conform on a practical level to the laws and customs of one's society. Tragedy, however, shows us that "going along" with the laws and customs of one's society is exactly what leads an individual into a practical *epochē*: the experience of being caught between two ethical actions that are both demanded by one's society but in conflict with each other. Comedy exposes the underlying societal and political contradictions that place the individual in conflict with themselves and their community. The result is the total upheaval of the political and ethical systems that structured the tragic stage. Sextus, *Outlines of Scepticism*, I.11–15.
14. *PS*, §746; *Werke 3*, 543.
15. For Hegel, self-consciousness is the main stage character of art-religion. In other words, he's interested in how self-consciousness changes shapes through different aesthetic, religious, and philosophical representations of human life. Through skepticism and comedy, self-consciousness grasps itself as a pure negativity and, for the moment, will have no sense of despair or nihilism but will be perfectly at peace with its negative content.
16. *PS*, §754; *Werke 3*, 549.
17. Halliwell makes a strong case about the positive relationship between Socrates and Aristophanes; see the notes to the introduction to his translation of *Clouds*, 4–6.
18. *Cl.*, 94.
19. *Cl.*, 240–99. I summarize this lengthy dialogue in a few sentences, but all the crude bits come directly from Aristophanes without exaggeration.
20. Aristophanes, *The Wasps, The Poet and the Women, The Frogs*, trans. David Barrett (Penguin Classics, 1964).
21. *Cl.*, 510–626. This is a loose and playful paraphrase, summarizing the longer parabasis. It's my intention to capture the tone and main points in Aristophanes's text, but I would encourage anyone to read the full passage in all its brilliance.

22. *Cl.*, 521.

23. *Cl.*, 161–77.

24. *Cl.*, 134–83, gives the full exchange between Strepsiades and the student.

25. *Cl.*, 169–77. This quotation is based on Halliwell's translation but shortened. As Halliwell states in n137, aborted means "made to miscarry." The same term is repeated in the *Theaetetus* (150e) in Plato's characterization of Socrates as the midwife.

26. Plato, *Plato: Five Dialogues: Euthyphro, Apology, Crito, Meno, Phaedo*, trans. John M. Cooper and G. M. A. Grube (Hackett, 2002), *Ap.*, 18d, 19c.

27. On the philosopher as the object of ridicule and laughter, see *Tht.*, 172c, 174a, 174c; on the philosopher's own ridicule and laughter, see *Tht.*, 174d, 175b, 175d.

28. As Halliwell argues, the Athenians were deeply apprehensive about the volatile nature of laughter (*Cl.*, 264–75). Given this cultural background, Socrates's defense of critical laughter, at least in the *Theaetetus*, is significant. Just as the philosopher needed a comic defender, so was the comic poet in need of philosophical defense.

29. One of Socrates's stand-up routines rides on Protagoras: Socrates jokes that instead of calling man the measure, Protagoras might have chosen the pig, baboon, or tadpole (*Tht.*, 161c-d). Socrates's ridicule in the *Theaetetus* always allows the joke to be turned back onto himself. If Protagoras is correct, Socrates continues, then all of his own philosophy is a laughingstock (*Tht.*, 161–62a).

30. *Tht.*, 142b5.

31. *Symp.*, 210a–212c.

32. *Tht.*, 149a–151e5.

33. *Tht.*, 151c5.

34. *Tht.*, 149d1.

35. *Tht.*, 149b10 (I capture this quote in my own words).

36. *Tht.*, 149b10 (I capture this section in my own words). Goran Vranešević further analyzes the connection between the negative remainder of speculative epistemology and humor: "A joke produces something out of nothing precisely because its speculative character goes beyond mere understanding—it produces something unlooked for." Goran Vranešević, "The Extimate Essence of Speculation," *Psychoanalysis, Culture, and Society* 29 (2024): 396–411, https://doi.org/10.1057/s41282-024-00443-7.

37. Theaetetus's surprise birthing of sextuplets is replayed by Trudy Kockenlocker in Preston Sturges's comedy *The Miracle of Morgan's Creek* (Paramount Studios, 1944).

38. *Tht.*, 156a–158a, 198d1–200c1, 202d10–203e5.

39. *Tht.*, 157a–b1.

40. Edmund Husserl, *Ideas Pertaining to a Pure Phenomenology and to a Phenomenological Philosophy*, vol. 2, trans. Richard Rojcewicz and André Schuwer (Kluwer Academic Publishers, 1989), §§36–37.

41. *Tht.*, 156a–c5.

42. *Tht.*, 156c5.

43. *Tht.*, 156e5.

44. *Tht.*, 157b1–5.

45. *Tht.*, 157b1–c1.

46. *Symp.*, 189c–93e.
47. Jacques Lacan, *The Four Fundamental Concepts of Psychoanalysis: Seminar XI*, ed. Jacques-Alain Miller, trans. Alan Sheridan (W. W. Norton, 1998), 197–200.
48. Lacan, *Seminar XI*, 23.
49. *Tht.*, 157c5.
50. *Tht.*, 157c5–d5.
51. *Tht.*, 158a.
52. In his commentary on the *Theaetetus* (Hackett, 1990), Burnyeat demonstrates that how one chooses to interpret Socrates's treatment of Protagoras in 151d–184a will determine one's overall approach to the entire text, which, due to the ambiguity of this passage, lends itself to very different readings. Burnyeat represents "Reading A" by George Berkeley, who argues that while Socrates embraces a Protagorean framing of perception, he denies perception as a definition of knowledge, since the object of knowledge for Socrates is imperceptible. Berkeley nevertheless identifies Socrates as cherry-picking aspects of the philosophies of Theaetetus, Protagoras, and Heraclitus to arrive at his own theory of perception. Burnyeat represents "Reading B" by Richard Price, who argues that Socrates follows Theaetetus via Protagoras and Heraclitus to its own absurd conclusion that culminates in the impossibility of language (179c–183c).
53. *PS*, §754; *Werke 3*, 549.
54. *PS*, §747, *Werke 3*, 544.
55. *PS*, §752; *Werke 3*, 547.
56. *PS*, §752; *Werke 3*, 547.
57. Exodus 3:1–22.
58. Exodus 3:14.

Chapter 3

1. For a discussion of the reemergence of Being and Nothing in the *Science of Logic*, see W. A. Suchting, "Marx, Hegel and 'Contradiction,'" in *Marx and Philosophy: Three Studies* (Palgrave Macmillan, 1986), 81–103.
2. Hegel, *PS*, §§699–787; *Werke 3*, 512–76.
3. Hegel compares the representation of the divine in ancient and modern drama and their relationship to history: *Aesthetics*, 2.1192–1238; *Werke 15*, 474–576.
4. I focus on the 1827 lectures: "The Religion of Beauty, or Greek Religion": *LPR* 330–57; *VPR 2*, 532–60; "The Consummate Religion": *LPR* 391–489; *VPR 3*, 177–270.
5. *LPR*, 471n214: this addition to *VPR 3*, 252 on Christianity as divine drama appears in Hegel's notes published in *Vorlesungen über die Philosophie der Religion* (hereafter cited as W2), 2nd ed., in 2 vols., ed. Philipp Marheineke (Duncker und Humblot, 1840).
6. *LPR*, 457; *VPR 3*, 239.
7. *LPR*, 467; *VPR 3*, 248–49.
8. *PS*, §808; *Werke 3*, 591.
9. My intention is to subvert the ableism of the ancient imagery of "tragic blindness" as I reinterpret these dramatic conventions.
10. *LPR*, 354; *VPR 2*, 558.

11. Matthew 6:10.

12. Matthew 27:51.

13. In my interpretation of Hegel's transition from "Art-Religion" to "Revealed Religion," Christianity does not surpass Greek religion or reveal a higher truth that was not already contained in Greek drama.

14. *LPR*, 340 n338: the editors include this addition to *VPR* 2 544 from Hegel's notes (W2).

15. Marx, *MECW* 11, 103; *MEW* 8, 115.

16. Hegel's most famous account of Antigone is in the *Phenomenology of Spirit* at the end of "Reason" and continuing into the opening of "Spirit" (*PS*, §437, §§446–63; *Werke* 3, 320, 328–42). In *Hegel, Literature and the Problem of Agency* (Cambridge University Press, 2001), Allen Speight highlights Hegel's anachronistic use of Antigone in the *Phenomenology of Spirit*'s "Spirit" and argues that Hegel looks to Antigone to comment on the socially mediated character of action in general. Hegel later turns to Greek tragedy and comedy in the chapter on art-religion to discuss the specific account of the Greek subject and society as it is represented in the historical development of art. Hegel's analysis of Antigone, however, is not found in the context of a historical sequence but in a chapter that introduces the concept of absolute Spirit. Speight sees this, at the very least, as suggesting that Hegel looks to Antigone to comment on the modern subject's relationship to her actions and society. Hegel similarly emphasizes that the character of Christ is more significant as a picture of Spirit than as a historical or theological event (*LPR*, 465n199). It can be argued that the figures of Antigone and Christ are pictures of two kinds of consciousness: the latter representing Hegel's (Spirit's) longing for a consciousness through which finitude and the infinite could be reconciled, the former (or both) representing the failure of this vision to be actualized both historically and within the modern subject.

17. Sophocles, *Antigone*, trans. Reginald Gibbons and Charles Segal (Oxford University Press, 2003), 499–503.

18. Hegel identifies women as free agents in his discussion of Antigone in the *Phenomenology of Spirit*'s transition from the chapter on "Reason" to "Spirit." For Hegel, the fact that Antigone identifies herself as an agent in her action and gives a reflective account as to what motivated her toward that action makes her a self-conscious subject. Yet, while identifying women as free agents, he also argues that when certain societal gender roles such as mother and wife are presented to women as an essence (as in the case of ancient Greek culture), this agency is not fully realized by feminized subjects who anchor their individuality in what is identified as an external, higher order. Hegel argues that Antigone's devotion to her dead brother reflects her commitment to the general idea of Brother disconnected from the life of Polyneices. She loves an empty figure, which she does not associate with the actions of Polyneices. Hegel writes that her "deed no longer concerns the living but the dead, the individual who, after a long succession of separate disconnected experiences, concentrates himself into a simple completed shape, and has raised himself out of the unrest of the accident of life into the calm of simple universality" (*PS*, §451; *Werke* 3, 330–31).

19. *LPR*, 334–35; *VPR* 2, 538–39.

20. *LPR*, 333, 344–45; *VPR* 2, 537, 548–49.

21. *LPR*, 345; *VPR* 2, 549.

22. I see the social and political as both belonging to the ideology or normative Reason of one's time and place. In my view, even our critiques of ideology are a product of the symbolic order of our time. An "independent" event cannot directly challenge or overturn a political framework. As I show through the example of Antigone, the tension between the political law and social role is an internal contradiction of Greek life.

23. Terry Pinkard, *Hegel's Phenomenology: Sociality of Reason* (Cambridge University Press, 1996), 145.

24. *LPR*, 353; *VPR 2*, 557.

25. *MECW 3*, 185; *MEW 1*, 388.

26. *LPR*, 354; *VPR 2*, 558.

27. *PS*, §733; *Werke 3*, 534.

28. Sophocles, *Antigone*, 532–34.

29. *LPR*, 353; *VPR 2*, 557.

30. *LPR*, 340; *VPR 2*, 543–44.

31. Robert Williams, "Overcoming the Kantian Frame: Tragedy, Recognition, and the Death of God," *The Owl of Minerva* 45, nos. 1–2 (2013–14): 91–111.

32. Williams, "Overcoming the Kantian Frame," 92.

33. See also Martin Jay, "Against Consolation: Walter Benjamin and the Refusal to Mourn," in *War and Remembrance in the Twentieth Century*, ed. Jay Winter and Emmanuel Sivan (Cambridge University Press, 1999), 221–39.

34. Walter Benjamin, *The Origin of German Tragic Drama*, trans. John Osborne (Verso Books, 1998), 139. The full acknowledgment of the tragic "It is" is impossible for the modern, who is consumed by infinite sadness. The melancholic "It is nothing" of the *Trauerspiel* is closer to Greek comedy than tragedy. And yet as we see in ancient drama, the tragic "It is" is not contradicted but mirrored in the comic "It is nothing."

35. Aeschylus, *Aeschylus I: Oresteia: Agamemnon, The Libation Bearers, The Eumenides*, trans. Richmond Lattimore (University of Chicago Press, 1969), 88–170; *PS*, §738–43; *Werke 3*, 537–41.

36. *LPR*, 339; *VPR 2*, 543.

37. *LPR*, 352; *VPR 2*, 556.

38. *LPR*, 352; *VPR 2*, 556.

39. Aristophanes, *The Wasps, The Poet and the Women, The Frogs*, trans. David Barrett (Penguin Classics, 1964).

40. Aristophanes, *The Wasps, The Poet and the Women, The Frogs*, 179.

41. *LPR*, 340; *VPR 2*, 544.

42. Benedict de Spinoza, *Ethics*, in *The Collected Works of Spinoza*, vol. 1, ed. Edwin M. Curley (Princeton University Press, 1988), IVP7 and IVP7C: "An affect cannot be restrained or taken away except by an affect opposite to, and stronger than, the affect to be restrained."

43. Plato, *Symp.*, 223c–d.

44. Mladen Dolar, "The Comic Mimesis," paper presented at *The Object of Comedy* conference, Jan van Eyck Academie, Maastricht, March 9, 2012.

45. *LPR*, 457; *VPR 3*, 239.

46. In *The Odd One In* (43–60), Zupančič analyzes Nathan A. Scott's reading of the incarnation of Christ as a comedy. While Zupančič explores the Hegelian elements of Scott's reading of the incarnation, she ultimately rejects

Scott's characterization of comedy as a materialist/humanist celebration of the limitations and flaws of human nature in the utter dissolution of divine transcendence. I follow Zupančič's understanding of comedy as not the deflation of the absolute into the merely human but as the recognition of the absolute/divine/more-than-human as belonging to the concrete human subject. However, while Zupančič identifies true comedy in the story of the life and death of Christ, I treat the incarnation and crucifixion as distinct moments and maintain that the incarnation is not yet the comedy of comedy. For even if this man is recognized as divine in the incarnation, the sacred in man is still recognized as an isolated moment that is an exception to human life in general. For Hegel, as I argue, the sacred is only realized as belonging to the human community at the crucifixion of Christ, which leads to the Pentecost, an event at which in the final death of the divine Other, Spirit is celebrated in its concrete form at what is intrinsic to the human community.

47. *PS*, §749; *Werke 3*, 545–46.
48. *LPR*, 468; *VPR 3*, 249–50.
49. *PS*, §§748–59; *Werke 3*, 545–74.
50. Commentary on *PS*, §752, 585.
51. *LPR*, 465n199: the editors include this addition to *VPR 3*, 246, from the 1831 lectures (W2).
52. *LPR*, 425; *VPR 3*, 209.
53. *LPR*, 427; *VPR 3*, 210–11.
54. *LPR*, 457; *VPR 3*, 239.
55. 2 Cor. 5:14–15.
56. Zupančič, *The Odd One In*, 35.
57. Zupančič, *The Odd One In*, 33.
58. On the tradition of ancient crucifixion as communal comedy, see Stephen Halliwell, *Greek Laughter: A Study of Cultural Psychology from Homer to Early Christianity* (Cambridge University Press, 2008), 471–82.
59. Halliwell, *Greek Laughter*, 474.
60. Luke 23:39–43.
61. *LPR*, 467; *VPR 3*, 248–49.
62. Louis Dupré, "The Despair of Religion," *The Owl of Minerva* 16, no. 1 (1984): 23–24.
63. *LPR*, 467; *VPR 3*, 248–49.
64. William Desmond, *Beyond Hegel and Dialectics: Speculation, Cult and Comedy* (State University of New York Press, 1992), 132.
65. Hegel, *LPR*, 354; *VPR 2*, 558.

Chapter 4

1. Denis Diderot, *Discours de la poésie dramatique* (Nouveaux classiques Larousse, 1975); on Hegel's analysis of Diderot as a figure on the enlightenment, see *PS*, §§522, 545; *Werke 3*, 386–7, 403; *Aesthetics* 2.845, 2.847, 2.1171; *Werke 15*, 77, 79, 491.
2. I capitalize Church and State here, as I do other nouns in previous chapters, to treat them as stage characters playing out their farcical role.
3. Chapter 5 explores the Young Hegelian nuanced and varied relationships to religion and theology. Two texts that damned the Young Hegelians as a radical

atheist organization in the eyes of the State, both published in 1841, were Ludwig Feuerbach's *Das Wesen des Christentums* (Otto Wigand, 1841) and Bruno Bauer's *Die Posaune des jüngsten Gerichts über Hegel, den Atheisten und Antichristen: Ein Ultimatum* (Ulan Press, 2021).

4. There are several endearing examples of Engels's interest in comedic writing, including "Fragments of a Tragicomedy: Horned Siegfried" and his letter to Marie Engels in Barmen, in *MECW 2*, 428–42.

5. Marx, "Comments on the Latest Prussian Censorship Instruction," in *MECW I*, 109–31; "Bemerkungen über die neueste preußische Zensurinstruktion," in *MEW 1*, 3–24.

6. Marx, "Contribution to the Critique of Hegel's Philosophy of Law. Introduction," in *MECW 3*, 175–87; "Zur Kritik der Hegelschen Rechtsphilosophie. Einleitung," in *MEW 1*, 378–91.

7. For a close analysis of the defense of style as central to political criticism in Marx's early works, see Daniel Hartley, *The Politics of Style: Towards a Marxist Poetics* (Brill, 2016).

8. Marx and Engels. *The Holy Family, or Critique of Critical Criticism*, in *MECW 4*, 103–97; *Die heilige Familie*, in *MEW 2*, 3–223.

9. *MECW 35*, 204; *MEW 23*, 208.

10. On the capitalist's laughter, see Samo Tomšič, "Laughter and Capitalism," *S: Journal of the Circle for Lacanian Ideology Critique* 8 (2015): 22–37.

11. *MECW 11*, 103; *MEW 8*, 115.

12. Carl Friedrich Göschel, *Aphorismen über Nichtwissen und absolutes Wissen* (E. Franklin, 1829).

13. Lawrence S. Stepelevich, introduction to *The Young Hegelians: An Anthology* (Cambridge University Press, 1983), 3.

14. Göschel, *Aphorismen*, 160.

15. Because of my focus on comedy, I regrettably overlook Bruno Bauer, who is also responsible for promoting the relationship between religion, politics, and art. See for example, Bruno Bauer, *Hegels Lehre von der Religion und Kunst: von dem Standpunkt des Glaubens aus beurteilt* (Otto Wigand, 1842). Bauer experienced his own conversion from "Old" to "Young" Hegelianism through Strauss's *Leben Jesu*: David Friedrich Strauss, *The Life of Jesus, Critically Examined*, trans. George Eliot (Cambridge University Press, 2010).

16. Arnold Ruge, "Hegel's 'Philosophy of Right,'" 214–15; "Hegels Rechtsphilosophie," 757a.

17. For the influence of Berlin comedy on Kierkegaard's relationship to laughter, see Bara Kolenc, *Ponavljanje in uprizoritev: Kierkegaard, psihoanaliza, gledališče* (DTP Analecta, 2014), 47–48; 104–6.

18. On Halliwell's analysis of Spartan cultural attitudes toward laughter and the cult of laughter see *Greek Laughter*, 44–50; 177–90. My following narrative is deeply influenced by his comparisons of Spartan and Athenian attitudes toward laughter.

19. Halliwell, *Greek Laughter*, 44.

20. Aristotle, *Parts of Animals*, 3.10.673a7–9.

21. *Homeric Hymns*, "Hymn II: To Demeter."

22. Halliwell, *Greek Laughter*, 44.

23. Halliwell, *Greek Laughter*, 47.

24. Aristotle, *Rhetoric*, 2.4.1381a33–6.
25. On the question of the Athenian censorship of kinds of speech that could threaten democratic speech: Halliwell, *Greek Laughter*, 26, 218–9, 241–44, 318.
26. Thomas Hobbes, *Leviathan*, (Cambridge, 2003), I.6.43.
27. Halliwell, *Greek Laughter*, 26–27, 29.
28. Euripides, *Bacchae*, 378–81
29. Euripides, "Electra," 900–930; "Bacchae," 1165–75.

Chapter 5

1. Marx, *MECW 1*, 109; *MEW 1*, 3.
2. *MECW 1*, 111; *MEW 1*, 5.
3. *MECW 1*, 113; *MEW 1*, 7.
4. *MECW 1*, 116; *MEW 1*, 10.
5. *MECW 1*, 117; *MEW 1*, 11.
6. *MECW 1*, 117; *MEW 1*, 11.
7. *MECW 1*, 118; *MEW 1*, 12.
8. *MECW 1*, 119; *MEW 1*, 12.
9. *MECW 1*, 123; *MEW 1*, 17.
10. *MECW 1*, 114; *MEW 1*, 8.
11. *MECW 1*, 112; *MEW 1*, 6.
12. *MECW 1*, 112; *MEW 1*, 6.
13. *MECW 1*, 114; *MEW 1*, 7.
14. Max Stirner, "Art and Religion," in *The Young Hegelians: An Anthology*, ed. and trans. Lawrence S. Stepelevich (Cambridge University Press, 1983), 334; "Kunst und Religion," in *Max Stirner's kleinerer Schriften und seine Entgegnungen auf die Kritik seines Werkes: 'Der Einzige und sein Eigenthum' aus den Jahren 1842–1848*, ed. John Henry Mackay (Bernhard Zack's Verlag, 1914), 268.
15. Ruge, "Hegel's 'Philosophy of Right,'" 232; "Hegels Rechtsphilosophie," 776a.
16. Ruge, "Hegel's 'Philosophy of Right,'" 231; "Hegels Rechtsphilosophie," 765b.
17. Stirner, "Art and Religion," 329; "Kunst und Religion," 260.
18. Stirner, "Art and Religion," 331; "Kunst und Religion," 264.
19. Stirner, "Art and Religion," 327–28; "Kunst und Religion," 259.
20. Stirner, "The Ego and Its Own," excerpt from *The Young Hegelians: An Anthology*, ed. Lawrence S. Stepelevich, trans. Steven T. Byington (Cambridge, 1983), 348; *Der Einzige und sein Eigentum* (Reclam, 1991), 186.
21. Stirner, "Art and Religion," 332; "Kunst und Religion," 266; see also 333; 268: "But when the mystery is cleared up, and the otherness and strangeness removed, and established religion is destroyed, then comedy has its task to fulfill. Comedy, in openly displaying the emptiness, or better, the deflation of the object, frees men from the old belief, and so their dependency on this exhausted being. Comedy, as befitting its essence, probes into every holy area, even to Holy Matrimony."
22. Stirner, "The Ego and Its Own," 337; *Der Einzige und sein Eigentum*, 6.
23. Ruge, quoting Kant, in "Hegel's 'Philosophy of Right,'" 221; "Hegels Rechtsphilosophie," 760a.

24. Ruge, "Hegel's 'Philosophy of Right,'" 215–16; "Hegels Rechtsphilosophie," 757b.
25. Ruge, "Hegel's 'Philosophy of Right,'" 223; "Hegels Rechtsphilosophie," 760b.
26. Ruge, "Hegel's 'Philosophy of Right,'" 220; "Hegels Rechtsphilosophie," 759a.
27. Ruge, "Hegel's 'Philosophy of Right,'" 222; "Hegels Rechtsphilosophie," 760a.
28. Ruge, "Hegel's 'Philosophy of Right,'" 222; "Hegels Rechtsphilosophie," 760a.
29. Ruge, "Hegel's 'Philosophy of Right,'" 217, 219; "Hegels Rechtsphilosophie," 758a, 758b.
30. Ruge, "Hegel's 'Philosophy of Right,'" 231; "Hegels Rechtsphilosophie," 765b.
31. Ruge, "Hegel's 'Philosophy of Right,'" 225; "Hegels Rechtsphilosophie," 762a.
32. Ruge, "Hegel's 'Philosophy of Right,'" 233; "Hegels Rechtsphilosophie," 756b.
33. Ruge, "Hegel's 'Philosophy of Right,'" 232; "Hegels Rechtsphilosophie," 776a.
34. Ruge, "Hegel's 'Philosophy of Right,'" 234; "Hegels Rechtsphilosophie," 756b.
35. Ruge, "Hegel's 'Philosophy of Right,'" 232; "Hegels Rechtsphilosophie," 776a.
36. Ruge, "Hegel's 'Philosophy of Right,'" 214; "Hegels Rechtsphilosophie," 756a.
37. Ruge, "Hegel's 'Philosophy of Right,'" 215; "Hegels Rechtsphilosophie," 757a.
38. Ruge, "Hegel's 'Philosophy of Right,'" 214; "Hegels Rechtsphilosophie," 757a.
39. Stepelevich, 305; see also MECW 1, 10–21
40. *MECW 3*, 179; *MEW 1*, 382.
41. *MECW 3*, 175; *MEW 1*, 378.
42. *MECW 3*, 177; *MEW 1*, 380.
43. *MECW 3*, 178; *MEW 1*, 381.
44. *MECW 3*, 183; *MEW 1*, 387 (I depart from MECW, translating *Geburtsstätten* as "birthplaces").
45. *MECW 3*, 184; *MEW 1*, 388 (translation slightly altered).
46. *MECW 3*, 182; *MEW 1*, 385.
47. *MECW 3*, 186–7; *MEW 1*, 390–91 (translation slightly altered).
48. *MECW 3*, 178; *MEW 1*, 381.
49. *MECW 3*, 185; *MEW 1*, 389.

Chapter 6

1. Walter Benjamin, "On the Concept of History," in *Selected Writings, 4, 1938–1940* (hereafter *SW 4*), ed. Howard Eiland and Michael W. Jennings (Harvard University Press, 2006), 389–400; "Über den Begriff der Geschichte," in *GS 1*, 691–706. Agamben offers a detailed analysis of the connection between Benjamin's late writings from 1937 to 1940 in "On Benjamin's Baudelaire," in *Walter Benjamin and Theology*, ed. Colby Dickinson and Stéphane Symons (Fordham University Press, 2016), 222.
2. A collection of Benjamin's essays on comedy and comedians is found in *Selected Writings 2.1, 1927–1930* and *Selected Writings 2.2, 1931–1934* (hereafter *SW 2.1* and *SW 2.2*, respectively), ed. Michael W. Jennings, Howard Eiland, and Gary Smith (Harvard University Press, 2005). References to angels in relationship to the comedian/satirist appear specifically in "Karl Kraus" in SW 2.2, 433–58; GS 2.1, 367–68; The figure of the trickster, specifically Chaplin, as the angel of peace is found in "Ibizan Sequence, April–May 1932" 2.2: 587–94, 590; "Ibizan," GS 4.1: 402–9, 406.
3. Gershom Scholem, "Walter Benjamin and His Angel," in *On Walter Benjamin*, ed. Gary Smith (MIT Press, 1988), 51–89.

4. Benjamin, "Agesilaus Santander II," in *SW 2.2*, 714; *GS 6*, 521.
5. "Agesilaus Santander II," 714; 521.
6. Scholem, "Walter Benjamin and His Angel"; Giorgio Agamben, "Walter Benjamin and the Demonic; Happiness and Historical Redemption," in *Potentialities. Collected Essays in Philosophy*, trans. Daniel Heller-Roazen (Stanford University Press, 1999), 138–59.
7. Scholem, "Walter Benjamin and His Angel."
8. Benjamin, "Chaplin," in *SW 2.1*, 199–200; *GS 3*, 137.
9. Marx, *The Eighteenth Brumaire of Louis Bonaparte*, in *MECW 11*, 104; *MEW 8*, 115.
10. *MECW 11*, 106; *MEW 8*, 117.
11. I make a similar argument in "Fantasies of Forgetting Our Mother Tongue," *Journal of Speculative Philosophy* 33, no. 3 (2019): 368–80.
12. *MECW 11*, 108; *MEW 8*, 120.
13. *MECW 11*, 106; *MEW 8*, 118: "proletarian revolutions . . . interrupt themselves continually . . . to begin it afresh."
14. For a critique of the melancholic readings of Benjamin, see Sami Khatib, "Melancholia and Destruction: Brushing Walter Benjamin's 'Angel of History' against the Grain," in "Politics and Melancholia," ed. Dominiek Hoens and Justin Clemens, special issue, *Crisis and Critique* 3, no. 2 (2016): 21–39, https://www.crisiscritique.org/storage/app/media/2016-09-05/sami-ka.pdf.
15. Benjamin, *Arcades*, 470 [N7, 3].
16. Benjamin, "Trauerspiel and Tragedy," in *Selected Writings 1, 1913–1919* (hereafter *SW 1*), ed. Marcus Bullock and Michael W. Jennings (Harvard University Press, 1996), 55; "Trauerspiel und Tragödie," in *GS 2*, 133.
17. A nod to Benjamin's engagement with Hermann Cohen in "Fate and Character," in *SW 1*, 206; "Schicksal und Charakter," in *GS 2*, 178: "Every tragic action . . . cast a comic shadow" (jede tragische Handlung . . . einen komischen Schatten werfe).
18. Some details of Benjamin's life were first told in Gershom Scholem's account, *Walter Benjamin: The Story of a Friendship*, trans. Harry Zohn (Faber and Faber, 1982).
19. Charles Chaplin, *My Autobiography* (Simon & Schuster, 1964), 316.
20. Benjamin, "Chaplin," in *SW 2.1*, 199–200; *GS 3*, 137; "Chaplin in Retrospect," in *SW 2.1*, 222–24; "Rückblick auf Chaplin," in *GS 3*, 157–58; and "Hitler's Diminished Masculinity," in *SW 2.2*, 792–93; "Hitlers herabgeminderte Männlichkeit," in *GS 6*, 103.
21. Benjamin, "Fate and Character," 201–6; "Schicksal und Charakter," 171–78.
22. Benjamin, "Chaplin in Retrospect," 224; "Rückblick auf Chaplin," 157–58.
23. Benjamin, "Fate and Character," 206; "Schicksal und Charakter," 178.
24. Benjamin, *The Origin of German Tragic Drama*, trans. John Osborne (Verso Books, 1998).
25. Benjamin, "World and Time," in *SW 1*, 226; "Welt und Zeit [fr 75]," in *GS 6*, 98–99.
26. Benjamin, "The Role of Language in Trauerspiel and Tragedy," in *SW 1*, 59; "Die Bedeutung der Sprache in Trauerspiel und Tragödie," in *GS 2*, 137.

27. *MECW 1*, 113; *MEW 1*, 7.
28. Benjamin, "The Role of Language," 59; "Die Bedeutung der Sprache," 137.
29. Benjamin, "On Language as Such and the Language of Man," in *SW 1*, 62; "Über Sprache überhaupt und über die Sprache des Menschen," in *GS 2*, 149.
30. Charles Baudelaire, *The Essence of Laughter, and Other Essays, Journals, and Letters*, trans. Gerard Hopkins (Meridian Books, 1956), §I.
31. Benjamin, "Curriculum Vitae (III)," in *SW 2.1*, 78; *GS 6*, 225.
32. See Adriana Bontea for an analysis of Benjamin's development of a study of French comedy as intended as a companion piece for his work on tragedy: "A Project in Its Context: Walter Benjamin on Comedy," *MLN* 121, no. 5 (December 2006): 1041–71.
33. Agamben was responsible for uncovering Benjamin's so-called Paris Manuscripts, which Bataille's widow had deposited at the Bibliothèque nationale de France. Horkheimer enthusiastically commissioned the project in 1937 for the Institut für Sozialforschung. Agamben edited and posthumously published selections of the manuscript in Italian as a collection of essays on Baudelaire. For a later English edited volume, see *The Writer of Modern Life: Essays on Charles Baudelaire*, ed. Michael W. Jennings (Harvard University Press, 2006).
34. Agamben, "On Benjamin's Baudelaire."
35. Benjamin, "The Metaphysics of Youth," in *SW 1*, 9; "Die Metaphysik der Jugend," in *GS 2*, 95.
36. Benjamin, *Arcades*, 325 [J53a,4].
37. Benjamin, *Arcades*, 325 [J54,1].
38. Benjamin, "The Metaphysics of Youth," 7; "Die Metaphysik der Jugend," 92.
39. Gillian Rose, *Love's Work* (New York Review Books, 2011), 105.
40. Benjamin, *Arcades*, 325 [J53a,4], 383 [J90,2].
41. *Arcades*, 325 [J53a,3].
42. For an insightful analysis of the negative infinity of the dead, see Elissa Marder, *Dead Time: Temporal Disorders in the Wake of Modernity (Baudelaire and Flaubert)* (Stanford University Press, 2002).
43. Baudelaire, *The Essence of Laughter*, § II (italics mine).
44. Baudelaire, *The Essence of Laughter*, § III.
45. Baudelaire, *The Essence of Laughter*, §II.
46. Martin Heidegger, *Being and Time*, trans. J. Stambaugh and D. J. Schmidt (State University of New York Press, 2010).
47. In contrast to Antigone's suicide, Heidegger's being-toward-death is yet another kind of fleeing death. As Zupančič claims, being-toward-death conceals another relationship to death: "We precipitate ourselves towards death in order to avoid this realization, in order to be finally able to 'live in peace,' sheltered from *jouissance*, sheltered from the drive that makes us do things which go against our well-being. Death proves to be the best shelter against the death drive." Alenka Zupančič, *The Ethics of the Real: Kant and Lacan* (Verso Books, 1995), 254.
48. On Lacan's notion of "Being-for-death" in relationship to Heidegger: Jacques Lacan, *Écrits: A Selection*, trans. Alan Sheridan (Routledge, 2001), 76 and 132.
49. In Lacan's view this symbolic death applies to all subjects. The signifier that allows us to appear within the symbolic field fails to represent the subject.

The excess that the signifier or name fails to represent is determined as nothing. In contrast to Althusser, who argues that the subject is fully ideological, Lacan sees subjectivity in the negative space that escapes ideology. Subjectivization is a kind of death that requires us to become nothing in appearing as this determinate something.

50. Benjamin, *Arcades*, 66 [B2,4].
51. *Arcades*, 326 [J54a,1] (trans. slightly altered).
52. *Arcades*, 776 [d17,4] (trans. slightly altered).
53. *Arcades*, 63 [B1,4].
54. *Arcades*, 325 [J53a,3].
55. Baudelaire, *The Essence of Laughter*, §VI.
56. Baudelaire, *The Essence of Laughter*, §V.
57. Benjamin, "The Metaphysics of Youth," 7; "Die Metaphysik der Jugend," 93.
58. Sara Ahmed, "Speaking Out," *Feminist Killjoy* (blog), June 2, 2016, https://feministkilljoys.com/2016/06/02/speaking-out/.
59. I reference Marx's famous quote, "A beginner who has learnt a new language always translates it back into his mother tongue, but he has assimilated the spirit of the new language and can freely express himself in it only when he finds his way in it without recalling the old and forgets his native tongue in the use of the new" (*MECW 11*, 104).
60. Gilles Deleuze, "He Stuttered," *Essays Critical and Clinical* (Verso, 1998), 107–14; 109.
61. Benjamin, "Agesilaus Santander II," 714; 521.
62. Rose, *Love's Work*, 74.

Chapter 7

1. Dominik Smole, *Antigona*, in *Antigone Adapted: Sophocles' "Antigone" in Classic Drama and Modern Adaptation, Translation, and Transformation*, trans. and ed. Robert Cardullo (Academic Press, 2011), 91–172.
2. For another perspective on laughter on the ancient tragic stage, see Matthew Dillon, "Tragic Laughter," *The Classical World* 84, no. 5 (1991): 345–55.
3. Sigmund Freud, *Jokes and Their Relation to the Unconscious* (W. W. Norton, 1990).
4. Jacques Lacan, *The Seminar of Jacques Lacan: Book VII: The Ethics of Psychoanalysis*, ed. Jacques-Alain Miller, trans. Dennis Porter (W. W. Norton, 1997), 280.
5. In their readings of Lacan's analysis of forced choice, Zupančič and Dolar argue that the paradox of the choice between life and death forces an individual to choose to sacrifice the very thing they were fighting for to prove their resoluteness. See Lacan, *The Seminar of Jacques Lacan: Book XI: The Four Fundamental Concepts of Psychoanalysis*, ed. Jacques-Alain Miller, trans. Alan Sheridan (W. W. Norton, 1998); Alenka Zupančič, *The Ethics of the Real: Kant and Lacan* (Verso Books, 1995), 215–16; Mladen Dolar, "Beyond Interpellation," *Qui Parle* 6, no. 2 (1993): 75–96.
6. Slavoj Žižek, *The Triple Life of Antigone* (Bloomsbury Academic, 2016).
7. Žižek, *The Triple Life of Antigone*, 5.
8. Žižek, *The Triple Life of Antigone*, 9.

9. Žižek, *The Triple Life of Antigone*, 25.
10. Žižek, *The Triple Life of Antigone*, 6.
11. Antigone and Ismene do not merely awaken the memory of the dead. In revisiting the death, they give birth to the dead in a new form: the monstrous undead. As Smole's Tiresias puts it, "Polyneices did exist while he was living . . . he is a corpse and you are trying to squeeze him into a tight, ill-fitting skin. You and Antigone have fixed it so that Polyneices is not Polyneices but some peculiar, headstrong, impudent nonentity, a monstrous illusion born of troubled minds! Polyneices, as you two would like, you shall never see" (Smole, *Antigona*, 135).
12. The death drive suggests that to be reborn is to give birth to oneself, but the emergence of new life is not in what is but what is not. For a further discussion of birth in death, see Rob Weatherill, *The Death Drive: New Life for a Dead Subject?*, vol. 3 of Encyclopedia of Psychoanalysis (Rebus Press, 1999).
13. Mladen Dolar, "Being and MacGuffin," 85.
14. Rebecca Comay, *Mourning Sickness* (Stanford University Press, 2011). Angelica Nuzzo, *Approaching Hegel's Logic Obliquely: Melville, Molière, Beckett* (State University of New York Press, 2018).
15. Hegel, *PS*, §32; *Werke 3*, 36.
16. For an extended discourse on the cotton wheel: Freud, *Beyond the Pleasure Principle*, vol. 18 of *The Standard Edition of the Complete Psychological Works of Sigmund Freud* (Hogarth Press, 1955), 14–16; Lacan, *Écrits: A Selection*, trans. Alan Sheridan (Routledge, 2001), 77; Jonathan Lear, *Happiness, Death, and the Remainder of Life* (Harvard University Press, 2000), 57–95; Eric Santner, *The Royal Remains: The People's Two Bodies and the Endgames of Sovereignty* (University of Chicago Press, 2011), 63–86; Alenka Zupančič, *The Odd One In: On Comedy* (MIT Press, 2008), 168.
17. *PS*, §808; *Werke 3*, 591.
18. Lacan, *Seminar XI*, 22–23, 141.
19. Lacan, *Seminar XI*, 22–23.
20. Lacan develops the theme of being between two deaths as the sphere of tragedy in *Seminar VII* and *Seminar VIII*.
21. Jan Kempenaers, *Spomenik* (Roma Publications, 2015). Kempenaers's beautiful collection of photographs has attracted enthusiasts in favor of the preservation of the remaining Partisan monuments. His work has also been criticized for divorcing the monuments from the artists and historical contexts. For work that places these memorial sculptures within their political and aesthetic stage, see Gal Kirn and Robert Burghardt, "Yugoslavian Partisan Memorials: Between Memorial Genre, Revolutionary Aesthetics and Ideological Recuperation," *Manifesta Journal: Journal of Contemporary Curatorship* 16 (2011): 66–75; Gal Kirn, "Transformation of Memorial Sites in the Post-Yugoslav Context," in *Retracing Images: Visual Culture after Yugoslavia*, ed. Daniel Šuber and Slobodan Karamanić (Brill, 2012), 251–81.
22. Gordana Korolija Fontana-Giusti, "Bogdan Bogdanović: Dissident in Life, Architecture and Writing," in *Architecture of Paradox of Dissidence*, ed. Ines Weizman (Routledge, 2014), 33–44.
23. *Stone Flower* is a monument to the victims of the Ustasha during World War II in the Jasenovac concentration camp. Created by Bogdan Bogdanović in 1966. http://mortalcitiesforgottenmonuments.com/Bogdan-Bogdanovic.

24. Blaž Vurnik, "Kabinet čudes: Ljubljana v žičnem obroču" [Cabinet of curiosities: Ljubljana in the barbed-wire ring], *Delo.si*, April 22, 2016. http://www.delo.si/znanje/izobrazevanje/kabinet-cudes-ljubljana-v-zicnem-obrocu.html.

25. On the political background of Smole's plays, see Robert Cardullo, "Dominik Smole: Life and Work," in *Antigone Adapted*, 85–90. On the history of Slovene avant-garde theater originating with Stage 57, see Eda Čufer, "Between the Curtains: New Theater in Slovenia, 1980–1990," in *Impossible Histories: Historic Avant-Gardes, Neo-Avant-Gardes, and Post-Avant-Gardes in Yugoslavia, 1918–1991*, ed. Dubravka Djurič and Miško Šuvakovič (MIT Press, 2003), 376–403.

26. Cardullo, "Dominick Smole: Life and Work," 86.

27. Stagings of Smole's *Antigona* in Slovenia from 1960 to 2010:

Year	Location	Director
1960	Stage '57, Ljubljana	Franci Križaj
1960	Drama SNG, Maribor	Miran Herzog
1960	SNG Drama, Ljubljana	Slavko Jan
1971	Slovenian Permanent Theatre, Trieste	Mile Korun
1983	Ljubljana City Theatre, Ljubljana	Franci Križaj
1987	SNG Drama, Ljubljana	Meta Hočevar
1988	Preseren Theatre, Kranj	Matjaz Zupančič
2010	Drama SNG, Maribor	Jaka Andrej Vojevec

28. Slovene renditions of *Antigone*:

1959	Dominik Smole, *Antigona*	
1970	Nada Gaborovič, *Antigona s severa*	
1983	Jure Detela, "Antigonina pesem," from *Mah in srebro*	
1996	Dušan Jovanović, *Antigona*	
2012	Evald Flisar, *Antigona zdaj*	
2015	Slavoj Žižek, *The Three Lives of Antigone*	

29. Smole, *Antigona*, 98.

30. Smole, *Antigona*, 97.

31. Hegel, LPR, 353; VPR 2, 557.

32. Jean Anouilh, *Antigone*, performed at Théâtre de l'Atelier in Paris during the Nazi occupation, 1944.

33. Bertolt Brecht, *Antigone*, adapted from Hölderlin (Germany), performed in Switzerland, 1948.

34. The political stage of Slovenia during World War II offered a compelling backdrop for *Antigone*. Following the Axis invasion of Yugoslavia in 1941, Slovenia was uniquely partitioned among Axis powers: Hungary annexed Prekmurje, Italy occupied the south and Ljubljana, Germany took the northeast, and the Independent State of Croatia was given the southeast. The occupation

provoked a three-year resistance movement, led by the communist Slovene Partisans from 1942 to 1945, who opposed the Italian-sponsored White Guard (later renamed the Slovene Home Guard under Nazi command) and smaller fascist paramilitaries. Supported by the Third International, the Soviet Union, and British intelligence, the Partisans led one of the most effective anti-Nazi resistance movements in occupied Europe.

35. In a performance art project entitled *Shadows*, Antonio Grgić renders the outline of demolished Yugoslav monuments, suggesting that although the monuments have been physically destroyed, their symbolic value lingers as ghosts in the negative space of their absence: http://www.antoniogrgic.com/performansi1.html.

36. Smole's political positions were heavily influenced by the Catholic socialist thought of Edvard Kocbek, especially his work *Strah in pogum: Štiri novele* [Fear and courage: Four short stories] (Državna založba Slovenije, 1951).

37. Cardullo, "Dominik Smole: Life and Work," 86.

38. See Alenka Zupančič's most recent work on Antigone, *Let Them Rot: Antigone's Parallax* (Fordham University Press, 2022).

39. The ancient Greek tragic theme of fate resonates with the reduction of the individual within the aesthetic of Yugoslav socialism. Smole emphasizes the dissolution of the individual into the collective by doubling his characters. His characters encounter themselves as outside and opposed to themselves. Or rather, they find that they are nothing more than the gap between two roles that cannot coexist. One becomes two in the discovery of the split self—two becomes four in the doubling of the double (the recognition that the other opposing half is a mirror double: one who is also two)—four becomes many in the total shattering of the individual—the many returns to the one, not as individual ones but as one unity containing all—One, in the end, shows itself to be both all and nothing.

40. Smole, *Antigona*, 92.

41. Smole, *Antigona*, 92.

42. Smole, *Antigona*, 99.

43. A theoretical companion to Smole's characterization of both the sovereign and the rabble as split between two bodies can be found in Santner, *The Royal Remains*.

44. Smole, *Antigona*, 116.

45. Smole, *Antigona*, 116.

46. Smole's theme of nature as the desire to cover over loss runs throughout many Slovene adaptations. As Žižek puts it in his retelling of *Antigone*, the "thirsty earth," which is indifferent to human concerns, readily swallows up the dead. Jure Detela's 1983 poem about Antigone also describes the transformation of the decaying human body into the shapes of its environment: "Beautiful is the corpse that decays in the way the tree rots . . . the corpse has been hidden. It is buried everywhere, wherever I am." As Detela describes it, the unburied dead have lost their human attributes but are present everywhere within nature. And yet the business of our everyday life neutralizes their voices: Jure Detela, "Antigone's Poem" ("Antigonina pesem"), in *Moss & Silver*, trans. Raymond Miller with Tatjana Jamnik, 40–43 (Ugly Duckling Presse, 2018).

47. Smole, *Antigona*, 95, emphasis mine.

48. Smole, *Antigona*, 108.

49. Smole, *Antigona*, 138, emphasis mine.

50. Smole, *Antigona*, 117.
51. Smole, *Antigona*, 146.
52. Smole, *Antigona*, 163, emphasis mine.
53. Dolar argues that subjectivity emerges in failed subjectivity. A forced choice is given between the "me" and the "not me" that is also generated by the same subject. Between the self that is interpellated into one's social order and one's denial of this identity as who they really are, there is a bare "unknown side of things." As Dolar puts it, "The forced choice entails a loss and opens a void . . . of something that was never possessed" ("Beyond Interpellation," 82).
54. Smole, *Antigona*, page numbers cited parenthetically in the text.
55. Smole, *Antigona*, 102.
56. Smole, *Antigona*, 124.
57. Smole, *Antigona*, 126.
58. Smole, *Antigona*, 153.
59. Smole, *Antigona*, 146.
60. Benjamin, *Arcades*, 326 [J53a,4].
61. Benjamin, *Arcades*, 776 [d17,4].

Conclusion

1. Rebecca Comay, "Proust's Remains," *October* 144 (2013): 23–24.
2. Benjamin, "Fate and Character," in *SW 1*, 201–6; "Schicksal und Charakter," in *GS 2*, 171–79.
3. Benjamin, "Fate and Character," 204 (the clairvoyant, wise woman), 205–6 (the comic hero, genius, and scoundrel); "Schicksal und Charakter," 175–76 (*die weise Frau*), 177–78 (*der komische Held, der Genius, der Schurke*).
4. Sam Dolbear, "Lines That Reduce," in *The Case for Reduction*, ed. Christoph E. H. Holzhey and Jakob Schillinger (ICI Berlin Press, 2022), 117–33. See Charlotte Wolff, *Hindsight: An Autobiography* (Quartet Books, 1980); Wolff, *Studies in Hand-Reading* (Chatto & Windus, 1936); Wolff, *Love between Women* (Duckworth, 1971).
5. Benjamin, "Anmerkungen der Herausgeber," in *GS 6*, 804.
6. Dolbear discusses the form of Benjamin's family tree in his article "Lines That Reduce," 122–25. He conducted the specific exercise in a workshop talk presented at the ICI Berlin Institute for Cultural Inquiry on November 22, 2021.
7. Benjamin, "Fate and Character," in *SW 1*, 202; "Schicksal und Charakter," in *GS 2*, 173.
8. Dolbear, "Lines That Reduce," 127.
9. Joshua 6:1–21.
10. *Dobbs v. Jackson Women's Health Organization*, 597 U.S. __ (2022), the US Supreme Court held that the Constitution does not confer the right to abortion, overturning *Roe v. Wade*, 410 U.S. 113 (1973) and *Planned Parenthood of Southeastern Pa v. Casey*, 505 U.S. 833 (1992). For an overview of the impact of the ruling, see Kate Kelly and Marisa Schwartz Taylor. "A Year of Upheaval on Abortion's Front Lines," *New York Times*, July 20, 2023, https://www.nytimes.com/interactive/2023/07/20/us/roe-dobbs-abortion-networks-services.html?searchResultPosition=10. For more information about US bills by state affecting transgender individuals, see National Center for Transgender Equality, July 20, 2023. https://transequality.org/.

11. In *303 Creative LLC v. Elenis*, 600 U.S. __(2023), the Supreme Court ruled that the First Amendment prohibits Colorado from forcing a website designer to create expressive designs containing messages with which the designer disagrees.

12. For a list of recent bills restricting race studies, see Sarah Schwartz, "Map: Where Critical Race Theory Is Under Attack," *Education Week*, June 11, 2021, https://www.edweek.org/policy-politics/map-where-critical-race-theory-is-under-attack/2021/06. See also Alicia Hawkins, "Lawmakers Introduced 563 Measures against Critical Race Theory in 2021 and 2022," *UCLA Newsroom*, April 6, 2023, https://newsroom.ucla.edu/releases/lawmakers-introduced-measures-against-critical-race-theory. For a perspective placing new legislation in the context of the history of Black studies censorship, see Derecka Purnell, "America Has a History of Banning Black Studies. We Can Learn from That Past," *The Guardian*, February 14, 2023, https://www.theguardian.com/commentisfree/2023/feb/14/african-american-studies-history-repression-resistance-republicans.

13. *Students for Fair Admissions v. Harvard*, 600 U.S. 181 (2023); Stephanie Saul, "What the Affirmative Action Ruling Means for Colleges and Universities," *New York Times*, June 30, 2023, https://www.nytimes.com/2023/06/30/us/affirmative-action-diversity-college-education.html?searchResultPosition=9.

14. "SS.5.AA 1.6, Florida's Sate Academic Standards—Social Studies, 2023," Florida Department of Education, https://www.fldoe.org/core/fileparse.php/20653/urlt/6-4.pdf.

15. On the censorship of language and issues associated with LGBTQ people and race, see Edward Swidriski, "Florida's 'Don't Say Gay' Law Raises Serious Legal Questions," American Bar Association, November 22, 2022, https://www.americanbar.org/groups/labor_law/publications/labor_employment_law_news/fall-2022/florida-do-not-say-gay-law; Nathaniel Frank, "What the Science Says about 'Don't Say Gay' and Young People," *New York Times*, April 20, 2023, https://www.nytimes.com/2023/04/20/opinion/dont-say-gay-bill-florida.html.

16. For a collection of essays written by students and other community members about their experiences during the 2023–24 academic year, see *Diacritic*'s special issue on the pro-Palestinian student-led encampments with the editors' introduction: "Encamped: The Unliberated University," *Diacritics* 52, no 1 (2024): 4–6. https://dx.doi.org/10.1353/dia.2024.a955182.

17. Sara Ahmed, *Complaint!* (Duke University Press, 2021).

18. José Esteban Muñoz, *Cruising Utopia: The Then and There of Queer Futurity* (NYU Press, 2009).

19. For several examples of bipartisan political parties and campaigns rooted in the concept of "common sense" and "civility," see "Common Sense: No Labels," https://nolabels.org; "Common Sense American," National Institute for Civil Discourse https://www.commonsenseamerican.org/who-we-are/commonsense-american-boards/.

20. For a comprehensive list of 492 anti-LGBTQ bills proposed in the US in 2023, see "Mapping Attacks on LGBTQ Rights in U.S. State Legislatures," American Civil Liberties Union, updated August 4, 2023, available at https://www.aclu.org. For a specific account of drag censorship, see "The Dangers of Drag Censorship with Peppermint," *At Liberty Podcast*, American Civil Liberties Union, January 12, 2023, https://www.aclu.org/podcast/the-dangers-of-drag-censorship-with-peppermint.

21. Hélène Cixous, "The Laugh of the Medusa," trans. Keith Cohen and Paula Cohen, *Signs* 1, no. 4 (Summer 1976): 875–93.
22. Cixous, "The Laugh of the Medusa," 880.
23. Cixous, "The Laugh of the Medusa," 882.
24. Cixous, "The Laugh of the Medusa," 878.

REFERENCES

Aeschylus. *Aeschylus I: Oresteia: Agamemnon, The Libation Bearers, The Eumenides*. Translated by Richmond Lattimore. University of Chicago Press, 1969.

Agamben, Giorgio. "On Benjamin's Baudelaire." In *Walter Benjamin and Theology*, edited by Colby Dickinson and Stéphane Symons, 217–30. Fordham University Press, 2016.

Agamben, Giorgio. "Walter Benjamin and the Demonic: Happiness and Historical Redemption." In *Potentialities: Collected Essays in Philosophy*, edited and translated by Daniel Heller-Roazen, 138–59. Stanford University Press, 1999.

Ahmed, Sara. *Complaint!* Duke University Press, 2021.

Ahmed, Sara. "Speaking Out." *Feminist Killjoy* (blog). June 2, 2016. https://feministkilljoys.com/2016/06/02/speaking-out/.

American Dialect Society. "Word of the Year: 1993." Accessed January 12, 2018. https://americandialect.org/woty/all-of-the-words-of-the-year-1990-to-present/#1993.

Anouilh, Jean. *Antigone: Tragédie*. Éditions de la Table Ronde, 1946.

Appel, Alfred. "Conversations with Nabokov." *NOVEL: A Forum on Fiction* 4, no. 3 (1971): 209–22. https://doi.org/10.2307/1345118.

Apuleius. *Metamorphoses*. 2 vols. Edited and translated by J. Arthur Hanson. Harvard University Press, 1989.

Aristophanes. *Clouds, Women at Thesmophoria, Frogs*. Translated by Stephan Halliwell. Oxford University Press, 2015.

Aristophanes. *The Wasps, The Poet and the Women, The Frogs*. Translated by David Barrett. Penguin Classics, 1964.

Aristotle. *Metaphysics, Volume II: Books 10–14. Oeconomica. Magna Moralia*. Translated by Hugh Tredennick, G. Cyril Armstrong. Loeb Classical Library 287. Harvard University Press, 1935.

Aristotle. *Parts of Animals: Movement of Animals. Progression of Animals*. Translated by A. L. Peck and E. S. Forster. Loeb Classical Library 323. Harvard University Press, 1937.

Aristotle. *The Art of Rhetoric*. Translated by J. H. Freese. Revised by Gisela Striker. Loeb Classical Library 193. Harvard, 2020.

Artaud, Antonin. *The Theater and its Double*. Translated by Mary Caroline Richards. Grove Press, 1994.

Aumiller, R. "Fantasies of Forgetting Our Mother Tongue." *Journal of Speculative Philosophy* 33. no. 3 (2019): 368–80.

Bataille, Georges. "Un-Knowing: Laughter and Tears." Translated by Annette Michelson. *October* 36 (1986): 89–102. https://doi.org/10.2307/778556.

Bataille, Georges. "Hegel, Death and Sacrifice." Translated by Jonathan Strauss. *Yale French Studies* 78 (1990): 9–28. https://doi.org/10.2307/2930112.

Baudelaire, Charles. *The Essence of Laughter, and Other Essays, Journals, and Letters.* Translated by Gerard Hopkins. Meridian Books, 1956.

Bauer, Bruno. *Hegels Lehre von der Religion und Kunst: Von dem Standpunkt des Glaubens aus beurteilt* [Hegel's teachings on religion and art: Judged from the standpoint of faith]. Leipzig, 1842.

Bauer, Bruno. *Die Posaune des jüngsten Gerichts über Hegel, den Atheisten und Antichristen: Ein Ultimatum* [Trumpet of the Last Judgment against Hegel, the Atheist and Antichrist: An ultimatum]. Ulan Press, 2021.

Benjamin, Walter. *The Arcades Project.* Translated by Howard Eiland and Kevin McLaughlin. Harvard University Press, 2002.

Benjamin, Walter. *Gesammelte Schriften.* 7 vols. Edited by Rolf Tiedemann and Hermann Schweppenhäuser. Suhrkamp Verlag, 1991.

Benjamin, Walter. *The Origin of German Tragic Drama.* Translated by John Osborne. Verso Books, 1998.

Benjamin, Walter. *Selected Writings, 1: 1913–1926.* Edited by Marcus Bullock and Michael W. Jennings. Harvard University Press, 1996.

Benjamin, Walter. *Selected Writings, 2.1: 1927–1930.* Edited by Michael W. Jennings, Howard Eiland, and Gary Smith. Harvard University Press, 2005.

Benjamin, Walter. *Selected Writings, 2.2: 1931–1934.* Edited by Michael W. Jennings, Howard Eiland, and Gary Smith. Harvard University Press, 2005.

Benjamin, Walter. *Selected Writings, 4: 1938–1940.* Edited by Howard Eiland and Michael W. Jennings. Harvard University Press, 2006.

Benjamin, Walter. *The Writer of Modern Life: Essays on Charles Baudelaire.* Edited by Michael W. Jennings. Harvard University Press, 2006.

Bergman, Ingmar, dir. *The Seventh Seal.* Svensk Filmindustri, 1957.

Bergson, Henri. *Laughter: An Essay on the Meaning of the Comic.* Translated by Cloudesley Brerton and Fred Rothwell. Dover Publication, 2005.

Boethius. *Consolation of Philosophy.* Translated by J. C. Relihan. Hackett, 2001.

Boethius. *De consolatione philosophiae. Opuscula theologica.* Edited by Claudio Moreschini. K. G. Saur, 2005.

Bontea, Adriana. "Walter Benjamin on Comedy: A Project in its Context." *Modern Language Notes* 121, no. 5 (2006): 1041–71.

Brecht, Bertolt. *Die Antigone des Sophokles: Materialien zur "Antigone."* Suhrkamp, 1965.

Burnyeat, Myles. *The Theaetetus of Plato.* Hackett, 1990.

Butler, Judith. *Subjects of Desire: Hegelian Reflections in Twentieth-Century France.* Columbia University Press, 1987.

Cardullo, Robert. "Dominik Smole: Life and Work." In *Antigone Adapted: Sophocles' "Antigone" in Classic Drama and Modern Adaptation, Translation, and Transformation*, translated and edited by Robert Cardullo, 85–90. Academic Press, 2011.

Chaplin, Charles. *My Autobiography.* Simon & Schuster, 1964.

Cixous, Hélène. "The Laugh of the Medusa." Translated by Keith Cohen and Paula Cohen. *Signs* 1, no. 4 (1976): 875–93.

Clampett, Robert, dir. *The Big Snooze.* Warner Brothers, 1946.

References

Comay, Rebecca. *Mourning Sickness*. Stanford University Press, 2011.

Comay, Rebecca. "Proust's Remains." *October* 144 (2013): 3–24. https://www.jstor.org/stable/24586589.

Cutrofello, Andrew. *The Owl at Dawn: A Sequel to Hegel's "Phenomenology of Spirit."* State University of New York Press, 1995.

Čufer, Eda. "Between the Curtains: New Theater in Slovenia, 1980–1990." In *Impossible Histories: Historic Avant-Gardes, Neo-Avant-Gardes, and Post-Avant-Gardes in Yugoslavia, 1918–1991*, edited by Dubravka Djurić and Miško Šuvaković, 376–403. MIT Press, 2003.

Deleuze, Gilles. "He Stuttered." In *Essays Critical and Clinical*, 107–14. Verso, 1998.

Desmond, William. *Beyond Hegel and Dialectics: Speculation, Cult and Comedy*. State University of New York Press, 1992.

Detela, Jure. "Antigonina pesem." In *Moss & Silver*. Translated by Raymond Miller with Tatjana Jamnik as "Antigone's Poem," 40–43. Ugly Duckling Presse, 2018.

Diderot, Denis. *Discours de la poésie dramatique* [Discourse on dramatic poetry]. Nouveaux classiques Larousse, 1975.

Dillon, Matthew. "Tragic Laughter." *The Classical World* 84, no. 5 (1991): 345–55. https://doi.org/10.2307/4350851.

Diogenes Laertius. *Lives of Eminent Philosophers*. Translated by R. D. Hicks. Harvard University Press, 1925.

Dolar, Mladen. "Being and MacGuffin." *Crisis and Critique* 4, issue 1 (2017): 82–101. https://www.crisiscritique.org/storage/app/media/2017-03-01/mladen-dolar.pdf.

Dolar, Mladen. "Beyond Interpellation." *Qui Parle* 6, no. 2 (1993): 75–96. http://www.jstor.org/stable/20685977.

Dolar, Mladen. "Comedy and Its Double. Die Komödie und ihr Double." In *Schluss mit der Komödie! Stop That Comedy!*, edited by Robert Pfaller, 25–59; 181–209. Sonderzahl, 2005.

Dolar, Mladen. "The Comic Mimesis." Paper presented at The Object of Comedy conference at the Jan van Eyck Academie, Maastricht, March 9, 2012.

Dolar, Mladen. "Hegel and Freud." *E-flux Journal* 34 (April 2012): 9–10.

Dolbear, Sam. "Lines That Reduce." In *The Case for Reduction*, edited by Christoph E. H. Holzhey and Jakob Schillinger, 117–33. ICI Berlin Press, 2022.

Dupré, Louis. "The Despair of Religion." *The Owl of Minerva* 16, no. 1 (1984): 21–30.

Eiden-Offe, Patrick. *Hegels Logik Lesen: Ein Selbstversuch* [Hegel's *Logic* lesson: A self-experiment]. Matthes & Seitz Verlag, 2020.

Encamped: The Unliberated Univesity. *Diacritics* 52, no. 1 (2025).

Engels, Friedrich. "Fragments of a Tragicomedy: Horned Siegfried." In *Marx-Engels Collected Works*, vol. 2: *Frederick Engels, 1838–42*, 428–37. International Publishers, 1975.

Engels, Friedrich. Letter to Marie Engels in Barmen. In *Marx-Engels Collected Works*, vol. 2: *Frederick Engels, 1838–42*, 437–42. International Publishers, 1975.

Euripides. *The Bacchae. Iphigenia at Aulis. Rhesus*. Translated by David Kovacs. Loeb Classical Library 495. Harvard University Press, 2003.

Euripides. *Suppliant Women. Electra.* Translated by David Kovacs. Loeb Classical Library 9. Harvard University Press, 1998.

Feuerbach, Ludwig. *Das Wesen des Christentums* [Essence of Christianity]. Otto Wigand, 1841.

Fontana-Giusti, Gordana Korolija. "Bogdan Bogdanović: Dissident in Life, Architecture and Writing." In *Architecture and the Paradox of Dissidence*, edited by Ines Weizman, 33–44. Routledge, 2014.

Freud, Sigmund. *Beyond the Pleasure Principle.* In *The Standard Edition of the Complete Psychological Works of Sigmund Freud*, vol. 18, edited and translated by James Strachey, 1–64. Hogarth Press, 1955.

Freud, Sigmund. *Jokes and Their Relation to the Unconscious.* W. W. Norton, 1990.

Freud, Sigmund. "The 'Uncanny.'" In *The Standard Edition of the Complete Psychological Works of Sigmund Freud*, vol. 17, edited and translated by James Strachey, 217–56. Vintage Books, 1999.

George, Theodore D. *Tragedies of Spirit: Tracing Finitude in Hegel's Phenomenology.* State University of New York Press, 2006.

Geronimi, Clyde, Wilfred Jackson, and Hamilton Luske, dirs. *Alice in Wonderland.* Walt Disney Productions, 1951.

Göschel, Carl Friedrich. *Aphorismen über Nichtwissen und absolutes Wissen im Verhältnisse zur christlichen Glaubenserkenntniss: ein Beytrag zum Verständisse der Philosophie unserer Zeit* [Aphorisms on ignorance and absolute knowledge in relation to Christian theological knowledge: A contribution to understanding the philosophy of our time]. E. Franklin, 1829.

Halliwell, Stephen. *Greek Laughter: A Study of Cultural Psychology from Homer to Early Christianity.* Cambridge University Press, 2008.

Hartley, Daniel. *The Politics of Style: Towards a Marxist Poetics.* Brill, 2016.

Hegel, G. W. F. *Phänomenologie des Geistes.* Vol. 3 of *Gesamte Werkausgabe*, edited by Eva Moldenhauer and Karl Markus Michel. Suhrkamp Verlag, 1986. Translated by A. V. Miller as *Phenomenology of Spirit*. Oxford University Press, 1977.

Hegel, G. W. F. *Vorlesungen über die Ästhetik III.* Vol. 15 of *Gesamte Werkausgabe*, edited by Eva Moldenhauer and Karl Markus Michel. Suhrkamp Verlag, 1970. Translated by T. M. Knox as *Hegel's Aesthetics: Lectures on Fine Art*. Vol. 2. Oxford University Press, 1975.

Hegel, G. W. F. *Vorlesungen über die Philosophie der Religion. Teil 2: Die bestimmte Religion. Teil 3: Die vollendete Religion.* Edited by Walter Jaeschke. Felix Meiner Verlag, 1994; *Vorlesungen über die Philosophie der Religion.* 2 vols. Edited by Philipp Marheineke, Duncker und Humblot, 1840. Translated by Robert F. Brown, Michael Stewart, and Peter C. Hodgson as *Lectures on the Philosophy of Religion: The Lectures of 1827*, edited by Peter C. Hodgson. Oxford University Press, 2007.

Hegel, G. W. F. *Wissenschaft der Logik.* Vols. 5–6 of *Gesamte Werkausgabe*, edited by Eva Moldenhauer and Karl Markus Michel. Suhrkamp Verlag, 1986. Translated by George di Giovanni as *The Science of Logic*. Cambridge University Press, 2010.

Heidegger, Martin. *Being and Time.* Translated by J. Stambaugh and D. J. Schmidt. State University of New York Press, 2010.

References

Hobbes, Thomas. *Leviathan*. Cambridge University Press, 2003.
Homeric Hymns. Homeric Apocrypha. Lives of Homer. Edited and translated by Martin L. West. Loeb Classical Library 496. Harvard University Press, 2003.
Husserl, Edmund. *Ideas Pertaining to a Pure Phenomenology and to a Phenomenological Philosophy*, vol. 2. Translated by Richard Rojcewicz and André Schuwer. Kluwer Academic Publishers, 1989.
Jay, Martin. *War and Remembrance in the Twentieth Century*, edited by Jay Winter and Emmanuel Sivan. Cambridge University Press, 1999.
Kant, Immanuel. *Kritik der Urteilskraft* [Critique of Judgment]. Vol. 5 of *Kants Gesammelte Schriften*. Reimer, 1908. Reprint of the 1790 edition.
Kempenaers, Jan. *Spomenik*. Roma Publications, 2015.
Khatib, Sami. "Melancholia and Destruction: Brushing Walter Benjamin's 'Angel of History' against the Grain." "Politics and Melancholia," ed. Dominiek Hoens and Justin Clemens, special issue, *Crisis and Critique* 3, no. 2 (2016): 21–39. https://www.crisiscritique.org/storage/app/media/2016-09-05/sami-ka.pdf.
Kierkegaard, Søren. *The Concept of Anxiety: A Simple Psychologically Oriented Deliberation in View of the Dogmatic Problem of Hereditary Sin*. Translated by Alastair Hannay. Liveright Publishing, 2014.
Kirn, Gal. "Transformation of Memorial Sites in the Post-Yugoslav Context." In *Retracing Images: Visual Culture after Yugoslavia*, edited by Daniel Šuber and Slobodan Karamanić, 251–81. Brill, 2012.
Kirn, Gal, and Robert Burghardt. "Yugoslavian Partisan Memorials: Between Memorial Genre, Revolutionary Aesthetics and Ideological Recuperation." *Manifesta Journal: Journal of Contemporary Curatorship* 16 (2011): 66–75.
Kocbek, Edvard. *Strah in pogum: Štiri novele* [Fear and courage: Four short stories]. Državna založba Slovenije, 1951.
Kolenc, Bara. *Ponavljanje in uprizoritev: Kierkegaard, psihoanaliza, gledališče* [Repetition and enactment: Kierkegaard, psychoanalysis, theater]. DTP Analecta, 2014.
Kubrick, Stanley, dir. *The Shining*. Los Angeles: Warner Bros. Pictures, 1980.
Lacan, Jacques. *Écrits: A Selection*. Translated by Alan Sheridan. Routledge, 2001.
Lacan, Jacques. *The Seminar of Jacques Lacan: Book VII: The Ethics of Psychoanalysis*. Edited by Jacques-Alain Miller. Translated by Dennis Porter. W. W. Norton, 1997.
Lacan, Jacques. *The Seminar of Jacques Lacan: Book VIII: Transference*. Edited by Jacques-Alain Miller. Translated by Bruce Fink. Polity Press, 2015.
Lacan, Jacques. *The Seminar of Jacques Lacan: Book XI: The Four Fundamental Concepts of Psychoanalysis*. Edited by Jacques-Alain Miller. Translated by Alan Sheridan. W. W. Norton, 1998.
Lear, Jonathan. *Happiness, Death, and the Remainder of Life*. Harvard University Press, 2000.
Marder, Elissa. *Dead Time: Temporal Disorders in the Wake of Modernity*. Stanford University Press, 2002.
Marx, Karl. *Der achtzehnte Brumaire des Louis Bonaparte*. In *Marx-Engels-Werke 8*, edited by Institut für Marxismus-Leninismus beim ZK der SED, 111–207. Dietz Verlag, 1960. Translated as *The Eighteenth Brumaire of Louis*

Bonaparte in *Marx-Engels Collected Works*, vol 11, *Marx and Engels: 1851–53*, 103–97. International Publishers, 1979.

Marx, Karl. "Bemerkungen über die neueste preußische Zensurinstruktion." In *Marx-Engels-Werke 1*, edited by Institut für Marxismus-Leninismus beim ZK der SED, 3–24. Dietz Verlag, 1956. Translated as "Comments on the Latest Prussian Censorship Instruction" in *Marx-Engels Collected Works*, vol. 1, *Karl Marx: 1835–43*, 109–212. International Publishers, 1975.

Marx, Karl. "Zur Kritik der Hegelschen Rechtsphilosophie. Einleitung." In *Marx-Engels-Werke 1*, edited by Institut für Marxismus-Leninismus beim ZK der SED, 378–91. Dietz Verlag, 1956. Translated as "Contribution to the Critique of Hegel's Philosophy of Law. Introduction." in *Marx-Engels Collected Works*, vol. 3, *Karl Marx: March 1843–August 1844*, 175–87. International Publishers, 1979.

Marx, Karl, and Friedrich Engels. *Die heilige Familie*. In *Marx-Engels-Werke 2*, edited by Institut für Marxismus-Leninismus beim ZK der SED, 3–223. Dietz Verlag, 1962. Translated as *The Holy Family, or Critique of Critical Criticism* in *Marx-Engels Collected Works*, vol. 4, *Marx and Engels: 1844–45*, 103–97. International Publishers, 1975.

Marx, Karl, and Friedrich Engels. *Das Kapital: Kritik der politischen Ökonomie. Erster Band*. Vol. 23 of *Marx-Engels-Werke*, edited by Institut für Marxismus-Leninismus beim ZK der SED. Dietz Verlag, 1890. Translated as *Capital: A Critique of Political Economy, Volume 1*. Vol. 35 of *Marx-Engels Collected Works*. International Publishers, 1996.

Mascat, Jamila M. H., and Gregor Moder, eds. *The Object of Comedy*. Palgrave Macmillan, 2020.

Michelet, Karl Ludwig. *Geschichte der letzten Systeme der Philosophie in Deutschland von Kant bis Hegel* [History of the latest systems of philosophy in Germany from Kant to Hegel]. Nabu Press, 2012.

Močnik, Rastko. *Meščevo zlato: Prešeren v označevalcu* [Moon's gold: Prešeren in the signifier]. Analecta, 1981.

Muñoz, José Esteban. *Cruising Utopia: The Then and There of Queer Futurity*. New York University Press, 2009.

Nelson, Gary, dir. *Freaky Friday*, Walt Disney Productions, 1976.

Nietzsche, Friedrich. *Beyond Good and Evil*. Translated by R. J. Hollingdale. Penguin Classics, 2003.

Nietzsche, Friedrich. *Thus Spoke Zarathustra*. Translated by Adrian Del Caro. Cambridge University Press, 2006.

Nuzzo, Angelica. *Approaching Hegel's Logic Obliquely: Melville, Molière, Beckett*. State University of New York Press, 2018.

Parrott, James, dir. *Brats*. Hal Roach Studios, 1930.

Parrott, James, dir. *Twice Two*. Hal Roach Studios, 1933.

Pinkard, Terry. *Hegel's Phenomenology: Sociality of Reason*. Cambridge University Press, 1996.

Plato. *Plato: Five Dialogues: Euthyphro, Apology, Crito, Meno, Phaedo*. Translated by John M. Cooper and G. M. A. Grube. Hackett, 2002.

Plato. *Symposium*. Translated by W. R. M. Lamb. Harvard University Press, 1925.

Plato. *The Theaetetus of Plato*. Translated by M. J. Levett and Myles Burnyeat. Hackett, 1990.

Plato. *Theaetetus and Sophist.* Edited and translated by Christopher Rowe. Cambridge, 2015.
Pluth, Ed, and Cindy Zeiher. *On Silence: Holding the Voice Hostage.* Palgrave Pivot, 2019.
Rose, Gillian. *Love's Work: A Reckoning with Life.* New York Review Books, 2011.
Ruge, Arnold. "Hegels Rechtsphilosophie und die Politik unserer Zeit." *Deutsche Jahrbücher* (189, 190) 1842. Translated by James A. Massey as "Hegel's 'Philosophy of Right' and the Politics of Our Times." In *The Young Hegelians: An Anthology,* edited by Lawrence S. Stepelevich, 211–36. Cambridge University Press, 1983.
Santner, Eric L. *The Royal Remains: The People's Two Bodies and the Endgames of Sovereignty.* University of Chicago Press, 2011.
Sartre, Jean-Paul. *Being and Nothingness: An Essay on Phenomenological Ontology.* Translated by Hazel E. Barns. Philosophical Library, 1956.
Scholem, Gershom. *Walter Benjamin: The Story of a Friendship.* Translated by Harry Zohn. Faber and Faber, 1982.
Scholem, Gershom. "Walter Benjamin and His Angel." In *On Walter Benjamin: Critical Essays and Recollections,* edited by Gary Smith, 51–89. MIT Press, 1988.
Schroeder, Barbet, dir. *Single White Female.* Columbia Pictures, 1997.
Seiter, Williams A., dir. *Sons of the Desert.* Hal Roach Studios, 1933.
Sextus Empiricus. *Outlines of Scepticism.* Edited by Julia Annas and Jonathan Barnes. Cambridge University Press, 2000.
Shakespeare, William. *The Comedy of Errors.* Cambridge University Press, 1988.
Smole, Dominik. *Antigona.* In *Antigone Adapted: Sophocles' "Antigone" in Classic Drama and Modern Adaptation, Translation, and Transformation,* translated and edited by Robert Cardullo, 91–172. Academic Press, 2011.
Sophocles. *Antigone.* Translated by Reginald Gibbons and Charles Segal. Oxford University Press, 2003.
Sorenson, Kaitlyn Tucker. "Experience as Device: Encountering Russian Formalism in the Ljubljana School." *Slavic Review* 79, no. 1 (2020): 93–114. https://www.jstor.org/stable/27059228.
Sorenson, Kaitlyn Tucker. "Razpor: On Slavoj Žižek's First Break." *European Review* 29, no. 6 (December 2021): 752–61.
Speight, C. Allen. *Hegel, Literature and the Problem of Agency.* Cambridge University Press, 2001.
Spinoza, Benedictus de. *Ethics.* In *The Collected Works of Spinoza,* vol. 1, edited by Edwin M. Curley, 408–617. Princeton University Press, 1988.
Stepelevich, Lawrence S., ed. *The Young Hegelians: An Anthology.* Cambridge University Press, 1983.
Strauss, David Friedrich. *The Life of Jesus, Critically Examined.* Translated by George Eliot. Cambridge University Press, 2010.
Stirner, Max. *Der Einzige und sein Eigentum.* Reclam, 1991. Translated as an excerpt by Steven T. Byington as "The Ego and Its Own: All Things Are Nothing to Me" in *The Young Hegelians: An Anthology,* 327–34. Cambridge University Press, 1983.
Stirner, Max. "Kunst und Religion." In *Max Stirner's kleiner Schriften und Entgegnungen auf die Kritik seines Werkes: Der Einzige und sein Eigenthum'aus*

den Jahren 1842–1848, edited by John Henry Mackay, 258–68. Bernhard Zack's Verlag, 1914. Translated by Lawrence S. Stepelevich as "Art and Religion" in *The Young Hegelians: An Anthology*, 327–34. Cambridge University Press, 1983.

Sturges, Preston, dir. *The Miracle of Morgan's Creek*. Paramount Studios, 1944.

Suchting, W. A. "Marx, Hegel and 'Contradiction.'" In *Marx and Philosophy: Three Studies*, 81–103. Palgrave Macmillan, 1986.

Swift, David, dir. *The Parent Trap*. Walt Disney Home Entertainment, 1961.

Tomšič, Samo. "Laughter and Capitalism." *S: Journal of the Circle for Lacanian Ideology Critique* 8 (2015): 22–37.

Vurnik, Blaž. "Kabinet čudes: Ljubljana v žičnem obroču" [Cabinet of curiosities: Ljubljana in the barbed-wire ring] *Delo.si*, April 22, 2016. http://www.delo.si/znanje/izobrazevanje/kabinet-cudes-ljubljana-v-zicnem-obrocu.html.

Vranešević, Goran. "The Extimate Essence of Speculation." *Psychoanalysis, Culture, and Society* 29 (2024): 396–411. https://doi.org/10.1057/s41282-024-00443-7.

Weatherill, Rob. *The Death Drive: New Life for a Dead Subject?* Encyclopedia of Psychoanalysis, vol 3. Rebus Press, 1999.

Williams, Robert. "Overcoming the Kantian Frame: Tragedy, Recognition, and the Death of God." *The Owl of Minerva* 45, nos. 1–2 (2013–14): 91–111.

Wolff, Charlotte. *Hindsight: An Autobiography*. Quartet Books, 1980.

Wolff, Charlotte. *Love between Women*. Duckworth, 1971.

Wolff, Charlotte. *Studies in Hand-Reading*. Chatto & Windus, 1936.

Yarbrough, Jean, dir. *The Naughty Nineties*. Universal Studios, 1945.

Žižek, Slavoj. *Antigone*. Bloomsbury Academic, 2016.

Žižek, Slavoj. *Bolečina razlike* [The pain of difference]. Obzorja, 1972.

Žižek, Slavoj. *Hegel in označevalec: Poskusi "materialističnega obrata Hegla" v sodobni psihoanalitični teoriji in njihov pomen za historični materializem* [Hegel and the signifier: attempts at a "materialist Hegelian turn" in contemporary psychoanalytic theory and their relevance for historical materialism]. Univerzum, 1980.

Žižek, Slavoj. "Laugh Yourself to Death: The New Wave of Holocaust Comedies!" *Lacan.com*, December 14, 2005. https://www.lacan.com/zizekholocaust.htm.

Žižek, Slavoj. *Less Than Nothing: Hegel and the Shadow of Dialectical Materialism*. Verso Books, 2012.

Žižek, Slavoj. *The Sublime Object of Ideology*. Verso Books, 1989.

Žižek, Slavoj. "Why Should a Dialectician Learn to Count to Four?" *Radical Philosophy* 58 (1991): 3–9. https://www.radicalphilosophy.com/article/why-should-a-dialectician-learn-to-count-to-four

Žižek, Slavoj, ed. *Everything You Always Wanted to Know about Lacan (but Were Afraid to Ask Hitchcock)*. Verso Books, 1988.

Zupančič, Alenka. *The Ethics of the Real: Kant and Lacan*. Verso Books, 1995.

Zupančič, Alenka. *Let Them Rot: Antigone's Parallax*. Fordham University Press, 2022.

Zupančič, Alenka. *The Odd One In: On Comedy*. MIT Press, 2008.

INDEX

abortion, abortionist, 6, 155; life/death and, 131, 133–34; philosophy and, 46–55, 58–60, 133–34; of revealed religion, 66–67, 80, 85; of revolution, 128; self/subject and, 50, 57–60, 85, 125. *See also* midwife

absence, 18, 118, 124–25, 128–32, 141–46. *See also* silence

Absolute: individual and, 67–73, 75–82; negativity and, 8–10, 60, 132–33, 153, 155; power and, 155–57, 160–62; religion and, 67–73, 75–82, 89, 130–31

academy: censorship and, 5, 9–10, 16–17, 86–90, 103–5, 154–57; seriousness and, 5, 98, 121

Adorno, Gretel, 115

Aeschylus, *Eumenides*, 71–72, 76

aesthetics: comedy and, 46, 49–50, 104–5; double and, 22–24, 27–28, 31–43, 101–2, 105–6; ethics and, 15, 34, 49–50, 66, 69–71, 136–40, 158; history and, 2–3, 86–88, 118; negativity and, 8–9, 46–47, 49, 63, 101–2; politics and, 1–3, 87–88, 103–5, 118–19, 136–43, 153; religion and, 48–49, 63–83, 85–86, 101–3, 105–6; self/subject and, 46, 50, 101–3, 105–7; tragedy and, 49

affect: censorship and, 3–4, 16–17, 86–88, 91–95, 97–100, 102, 107, 154–55; comedy and, 3–4, 7, 24–25, 65, 70, 74–76, 78–82, 85, 87–88, 91–95, 109, 113–14, 149–50; community and, 6, 15–16, 65, 80–83, 85, 87–88, 91–92, 94–95, 105–6, 108–9; dialectics and, 22–24, 107; negativity and, 64, 74, 80–82, 97–99, 107, 150, 153, 156; philosophy and, 102–3, 107; politics and, 3–4, 7, 87–88, 91–95, 97–100, 107, 113–14, 155–56; religion and, 100, 102–3, 105–6, 108; tragedy and, 70–71, 74

Agamben, Giorgio, 115, 122

Agathon, 74–75

agency: comedy and, 2–3, 72–73, 79–80, 119; negativity and, 2–3, 17–20, 129–31, 144–48, 153; self/subject and, 17–20, 49, 72–73, 76–77, 79–80, 119, 125, 129–30, 140, 144–45, 153–54, 161; tragedy and, 2–3, 49, 70–71, 76–77, 117–18, 125

Ahmed, Sara, 17–18, 127–28, 156–57

Allen, Gracie, 36–37

American Dialect Society, 37–38

angels, 114–16, 124–27. *See also* phantoms

anguish, 15–16, 64, 66–67, 69–71, 73–76, 78–82, 94–95, 158

Anouilh, Jean, 18, 137

anxiety, 7, 93–95, 125, 158–62

Apuleius, *Golden Ass*, 10–12

Aristophanes, 10–12, 34–35, 46, 72, 74–75, 85–86; *Clouds*, 15, 46–47, 50–54; *Frogs*, 73, 78, 92–93

Aristotle, 92–93, 122–23; *Rhetoric*, 93

Artaud, Antonin, 34

Art-Religion: comedy and, 1–3, 15, 45–46, 48–49, 59–60, 63–64, 72, 75–76, 80–82, 100–103; history and, 3, 15, 21–22, 100, 102–3; hymn and, 48–49, 72; object of, 48–50, 101, 105–6; self/subject and, 59–60, 63–64, 72, 75–76, 100–103, 158. *See also* Revealed Religion

ass, 10–12. *See also* crack; negativity

Athens, Athenians, 51, 53, 86, 88, 91–93, 95. *See also* censorship

Aufhebung. *See* suspension *under* dialectic

197

Baudelaire, Charles, 114–15, 121; "The Essence of Laughter," 123–27
Beckett, Samuel, *Waiting for Godot*, 122
Becoming, 11, 45; Being and, 22, 55–58, 63, 133
Being: Becoming and, 22, 55–58, 63, 133; law and, 150; negativity and, 10–12, 14, 37–39, 42–43, 45–48, 56–58, 60–61, 63–66, 80–82, 101–2, 126–27, 130–31, 143–44, 153, 156; Nothing and, 8, 10–12, 14, 21–22, 37–43, 45–48, 58–61, 63–65, 80–82, 101–2, 104, 110–11, 125–27, 132–33, 150, 153, 156; pure Being, 14, 21–22, 37–39, 58, 60–61, 66, 126–27
Benjamin, Walter, 5–6, 17–18, 71, 114, 123–25, 147–49, 154; *Arcades Project*, 114–15, 122; "Fate and Character," 119–20, 150–51, 153; "The Metaphysics of Youth," 122–23; "On the Concept of History," 114–15; *The Origin of German Tragic Drama*, 120–21; suicide, 118–19; "World and Time," 120
Bergman, Ingmar, *The Seventh Seal*, 41–42
Bogdanović, Bogdan, 142–43; *Stone Flower*, 134–35
Brecht, Bertolt, 18, 118, 137
Broz, Josip. *See* Tito
Burns, George, 36–37
Butler, Judith, 26

cancel culture, 160–62
capitalism, 7, 87, 157
censorship, 7, 19–20; academy and, 5, 9–10, 16–17, 86–90, 103–5, 154–57; affect and, 3–4, 16–17, 86–88, 91–95, 97–100, 102, 107, 154–55; in ancient Athens, 91–95; audience and, 99–100; comedy and, 16–17, 86–88, 91–95, 154–55, 160–62; in Prussia, 3–6, 9–10, 16–17, 86–92, 95, 97–100, 102–5, 107, 154; self-censorship, 127–28, 149; violence and, 92, 157, 161
Chaplin, Charlie, 40, 114–15; *The Circus*, 116, 119–20; *The Great Dictator*, 118–19
character, 8–9; comedy and, 2–3, 71–72, 116, 119–20, 150; double and, 18, 69, 129–30, 139–40, 143–44, 151; fate and, 2–3, 119–20, 150–51, 153; individual and, 2–3, 119–20, 139–40, 150–51; tragedy and, 2–3, 119–20, 150
Christ, 8–9, 126–27; negativity and, 9, 11, 15, 60, 63–67, 74–82, 130–31; as tragic hero, 3, 15, 64–67, 74–82, 89. *See also* crucifixion; incarnation
Christianity, 1–2, 88–90; censorship and, 101–2, 105–6; as divine drama, 3, 5–6, 21–22, 60–61, 63–67, 74–82, 101. *See also* religion
Church, 8, 16–17, 86–88, 90, 98, 102, 105–6. *See also* state
Cixous, Hélène, "The Laugh of the Medusa," 161–62
class, 92–93, 154–55, 158
cleavage, 1, 10–12. *See also* crack; negativity
cock, 1–2, 13–14, 114, 118–19. *See also* owl
Columbia University, 156
Comay, Rebecca, 132, 149–50
comedy: aesthetics and, 46, 49–50, 104–5; affect and, 3–4, 7, 24–25, 65, 70, 74–76, 78–82, 85, 87–88, 91–95, 109, 113–14, 149–50; agency and, 2–3, 72–73, 79–80, 119; censorship and, 16–17, 86–88, 91–95, 154–55, 160–62; character and, 2–3, 71–72, 116, 119–20, 150; community and, 2–3, 5–6, 15–16, 73, 75, 79–83, 85–87, 93–95, 110–11, 116–17, 158–59; conflict and, 2–3, 15, 65–67, 71–72, 75, 77, 80–82; critique and, 3–4, 88, 90–91, 95, 100, 102–5, 107–8, 118, 121; damned and, 123–28, 147–48; as destructive, 2–5, 17, 46–47, 49–50, 52–53, 59, 66–67, 72–74, 78–80, 82–83, 86–87, 92–93, 100, 102–3, 105–6, 120; double and, 4–5, 15–16, 21–43, 47, 59–60, 63–67, 72, 74–75, 78–80, 87–88, 100–103, 107–8, 116, 118–19, 121, 124–25; ethics and, 49–50, 63–64, 66, 71, 79–80, 119; freedom and, 37, 72–74, 79–80, 82, 92, 101–2, 117–20, 150–51, 153–54, 158, 160; history and, 3–7, 10–12, 15–17, 19–22, 29–30, 72–74, 80–82, 86–88, 91,

Index

100, 102–3, 106–11, 113–20, 122–25, 128, 154, 158, 161–62; horror and, 15, 19, 22–23, 26, 46–47, 53–54, 66, 80–82, 102–3, 113–19, 123–25; life/death and, 73–83, 92–94, 107, 125–26, 129–31, 147–48; negativity and, 2–5, 8–10, 15–16, 18, 24–27, 43, 45–46, 49–50, 59–60, 67, 74, 80–82, 102–3, 107–8, 115–16, 122, 125, 129–31, 133, 154; philosophy and, 5–8, 10–12, 14–15, 49–51, 53–54, 86; politics and, 3–7, 9–10, 14, 17–19, 87–88, 91–95, 100, 104–6, 118–20, 154, 158; religion and, 1–3, 15, 21–22, 45–46, 48–49, 59–60, 63–67, 71–82, 86–88, 90–91, 100–103; self/subject and, 3–6, 26–27, 63–64, 85, 100–103, 110–11, 119–20, 125; skepticism and, 47–50, 59–60, 63–64, 86, 102–3; Spirit and, 5–6, 16–17, 26, 70, 91, 99–100, 104–7, 122–23, 147–48; tragedy and, 15, 34–37, 65–67, 72–75, 77, 80–83, 119, 129; violence and, 159–60. *See also* negation, negativity; tragedy
comic genius, 150–51, 158
community: affect and, 6, 15–16, 65, 80–83, 85, 87–88, 91–92, 94–95, 105–6, 108–9; comedy and, 2–3, 5–6, 15–16, 73, 75, 79–83, 85–87, 93–95, 110–11, 116–17, 158–59; ethics and, 15, 79–80, 89, 136–40, 157–58, 161–62; history and, 80, 105; individual and, 15–16, 66–69, 72, 75–82, 85, 139, 155, 157; negativity and, 8, 15–16, 22, 66, 85, 110–11; self/subject and, 10–12, 15, 80–82, 85, 89, 92, 99, 105, 109–11, 122–23, 157–62
concept, 7, 8–9, 11–13, 22, 28–29, 119–20, 151; knowledge and, 46–48, 53, 54–55, 58–59, 132–33
count, counting, 13–14, 21–23, 25–29, 38–43, 60–61, 101, 104, 132, 151, 154, 161–62
crack, 1–18. *See also* negation, negativity
Critical Generation, 135–36, 138–39
critique: comedy and, 3–4, 88, 90–91, 95, 100, 102–5, 107–8, 118, 121; as destruction, 90–91, 102–3, 109–10; community and, 105; history and, 108–9; philosophy and, 90–91, 98, 108–10; politics and, 98–100, 104–5, 110–11; religion and, 98, 105, 108; self/subject and, 109–11; Spirit and, 104–5
Croatia, 139
crucifixion, 15, 21–22, 60, 63–68, 74–83, 89, 130–31. *See also* incarnation
cut, 10–12. *See also* crack; negativity

damned, 2–3, 17–18, 65, 92–93, 115–16, 119–20, 122–28, 130–31, 147–48, 154–56, 158–59
death, 133–34, 138; comedy and, 73–83, 92–94, 107, 125–26, 129–31, 147–48; of Christ, 60, 64–67, 74–83, 89; of individual, 69–71, 75–83, 109–10, 125–26, 130–31; social, 69, 123–25, 130–31; tragedy and, 69–71, 74–83, 130–31. *See also* crucifixion; life
death drive, 131
Debenjak, Božidar, 24
Deleuze, Gilles, 30
Demeter, 48–49, 72
Derrida, Jacques, 25
Desmond, William, 82
despair, 6, 10–12, 19, 45, 65, 123–24, 133, 150, 156
Deutsche Jahrbücher, 90–91
Deutsch-Französische Jahrbücher, 91
dialectic, 24–28, 40, 45–46, 75, 80–82; doubles/triads/tetrads and, 12–15, 21–43, 63–64, 67, 69, 80–82, 90–91, 102–3, 107, 151, 153; history and, 3, 7–8, 10–13; master-slave, 142–43; suspension (*Aufhebung*) and, 3, 7–8, 11–15, 24–29, 45–46, 63–66, 107–8, 122, 132–33; triangles/circles and, 132–33, 154
Diderot, Denis, 85–86
Dionysus, 48–49, 51–52, 72–73, 78, 92–95
divinity, 9, 60–61, 64–69, 71–73, 75–82, 126–27. *See also* humanity
Dolar, Mladen, 22, 24, 30, 40–41, 74–75, 132; "Being and MacGuffin," 14, 38–39

Dolbear, Sam, "Lines That Reduce," 151, 153
double, doubling of double: aesthetics of, 22–24, 27–28, 31–43, 101–2, 105–6; affect and, 22–24, 97–98, 107, 156; Being/Nothing as, 14, 21–22, 37–39, 42–43, 47–48, 58, 60, 63–66, 126, 153, 156; character/fate and, 18, 69, 129–30, 139–40, 143–44, 151; comedy and, 4–5, 15–16, 21–43, 47, 59–60, 63–67, 72, 74–75, 78–80, 87–88, 100–103, 107–8, 116, 118–19, 121, 124–25; critique and, 100–107, 111; dialectic and, 12–15, 21–43, 63, 67, 69, 107, 132, 153, 156; grasping and, 10–13, 27–28, 56–57; history and, 4–6, 15–16, 18, 21–22, 30, 72, 74–75, 87–88, 102–3, 107–8, 116, 118–19, 121, 124–25, 140, 147, 155; horror and, 22–23, 34–36; incarnation/crucifixion as, 15, 63–67, 74–75, 78–80; National Feeling/Public Spirit as, 3–4; negativity and, 4–6, 13–15, 21–22, 27–30, 33–34, 37–39, 42–43, 47–48, 50–51, 58–60, 63–67, 69, 72, 107, 116, 118, 121, 129–30, 140, 153, 155–56, 161; odd couple and, 23–24, 36–38, 40–43, 63; religion and, 15, 21–22, 78–80, 86–88, 90–91, 101–8; self/subject and, 15, 27–28, 33, 47–48, 56–60, 63–67, 69, 75, 101–3, 105–6, 111, 139–40, 143–44, 161; Spirit/Matter as, 12–13, 161; tragedy and, 21–22, 34–37, 72, 74–75, 119; twins and, 23–24, 31–36, 38–39, 47–48, 56–57, 74–75, 101–2, 107, 155. *See also* odd couple; twins
drama: audience and, 2–3, 65, 72, 85–87, 91–95, 105–6; character and, 18, 119–20, 139, 150; divine, 3, 5–6, 21–22, 60–61, 63–67, 74–82, 101; history and, 2–3, 5, 11, 17, 21–23, 29–30, 71–75, 85–87, 118, 150; laughter and, 91–95, 123–24; religion and, 3, 5–6, 11, 15, 21–22, 59–61, 63–67, 71–75, 77–82, 90, 101, 105–6; self/subject and, 3, 5–6, 11, 15, 18, 47, 59–61, 63–64, 85, 101–2. *See also* comedy; tragedy
Dupré, Louis, 79–80

egg, 10–12. *See also* negation, negativity
Engels, Friedrich, 87, 91; *The Holy Family* (with Marx), 87
ethics: aesthetics and, 15, 34, 49–50, 66, 69–71, 136–40, 158; comedy and, 49–50, 63–64, 66, 71, 79–80, 119; community and, 15, 79–80, 89, 136–40, 157–58, 161–62; negativity and, 2–3, 14–15, 157; philosophy and, 15, 49–50; religion and, 3, 66, 68–71, 79–80, 89; self/subject and, 63–64, 68–71, 79–80, 119, 158, 161–62; tragedy and, 34, 66, 69–71
Euripides, *The Bacchae*, 94–95; *Electra*, 94–95
event (nonevent), 6, 19–20, 124–25, 130–32, 136, 140, 144–45, 147; revolution and, 113–14, 117–18
excretion, 10–12. *See also* negation, negativity

farce, 21–24, 34–35, 113–14. *See also* comedy; tragedy
fart, fart joke, 51–54
fate, 2–3, 119–20, 150–51, 153. *See also* character; tragedy
fault line, 10–12. *See also* negation, negativity
feminism, 5–6, 17–18, 127–28, 161
fort-da, 40–41, 133, 146–47
fortune-telling, 119, 150–51
Frankfurt School, 24, 118
Freaky Friday, 27–28
freedom: abstract, 37, 66–67, 70–72, 74, 82; comedy and, 37, 72–74, 79–80, 82, 92, 101–2, 117–20, 150–51, 153–54, 158, 160; concrete, 66–67, 70–71, 79–80, 92; of speech, 3–4, 91–93, 154–57, 159–60; tragedy and, 70–71, 76–77, 117–18
Freud, Sigmund, 22–23, 127–29, 133

gap, 10–12. *See also* negation, negativity
gender: comedy and, 154–55, 158–59; negativity and, 8, 10–12, 129–30; politics and, 8, 129–30, 138; society and, 67–68, 129–30
gender affirmation surgery, 155
ghosts, 22–23, 113–14, 116, 125–28, 138, 146–47. *See also* phantoms

Index

glitch, 117
Göschel, Carl Friedrich, 88–89
grasp, grasping. See under double, doubling of double

Hallische Jahrbücher, 90
Halliwell, Stephen, 78, 92
Hardy, Oliver. See Laurel and Hardy
Hegel, G. W. F., 136–37, 139–40; on ancient drama, 1–3, 5–6, 10–12, 15, 17, 21–22, 37, 47–50, 59–61, 63–67, 71–75, 77–82, 85–87, 90–92, 101; Lectures on Aesthetics, 63–64; Lectures on the Philosophy of Religion, 3, 8–9, 63–71, 74–77, 79; Phenomenology of Spirit, 2–3, 8–9, 15, 45–50, 59–60, 63–72, 75–76, 113–14, 116, 132–33; Science of Logic, 8–9, 14, 21–22, 24, 28–30, 37–38, 63, 132–33; split in scholarship of, 1–2, 5, 8–13, 86–91, 100–111, 158, 160
Heidegger, Martin, 125
Heraclitus, 55–59
hiccup, 3, 17, 123, 128. See also stutter
hiss, 10–12, 63–64, 123, 153–54. See also negation, negativity
historical materialism, 7–8
history: aesthetics and, 2–3, 86–88, 118; angel of, 114–15, 124–25; comedy and, 3–7, 10–12, 15–17, 19–22, 29–30, 72–74, 80–82, 86–88, 91, 100, 102–3, 106–11, 113–20, 122–25, 128, 154, 158, 161–62; community and, 80, 105; conflict and, 136, 140–41, 153; critique and, 108–9; dialectic and, 3, 7–8, 10–13; double and, 4–6, 15–16, 18, 21–22, 30, 72, 74–75, 87–88, 102–3, 107–8, 116, 118–19, 121, 124–25, 140, 147, 155; drama and, 2–3, 5, 11, 17, 21–23, 29–30, 71–75, 85–87, 118, 150; memorials and, 134–37, 141, 147–48, 154; negativity and, 1–12, 14, 17–20, 29–30, 80–82, 114, 116, 118, 121–23, 131–34, 137–38, 140, 147–48, 151, 153–54; race and, 155; religion and, 72, 88, 90–91, 105–6, 108; repetition and, 29–30, 107, 117–18, 122, 154; revolution and, 3–5, 16–17, 86–87, 106–7, 113–14, 116–18, 120, 122–25, 128, 161–62; self/subject and, 73, 80, 104, 108–9, 113, 125, 149, 151, 153–55; Spirit and, 12, 17, 65, 106–7, 122–23, 133, 147–48; tragedy and, 5, 7, 17, 19–23, 29–30, 80–82, 108–11, 118–25, 150
Homeric Hymn to Demeter, 92–93
horror: comedy and, 15, 19, 22–23, 26, 46–47, 53–54, 66, 80–82, 102–3, 113–19, 123–25; double and, 22–23, 34–36
Hribar, Spomenka, 139
Hribar, Tine, 139
humanity, 47–49: divinity and, 9, 60–61, 64–65, 67–73, 75–82, 89, 126–27; history and, 2–3; Spirit and, 12; society and, 67–73, 76–82, 110–11, 120–21, 125–27; sovereign and, 141–42. See also divinity

idealism, 22, 57–58
incarnation, 15, 21–22, 60, 63–65, 67, 74–78, 80–82, 85, 130–31. See also crucifixion
individual, individuality, 119; Absolute and, 69–73, 75–82; character and, 150; comedy and, 71–72; community and, 15–16, 66–69, 72, 75–82, 85, 139, 155, 157; ethics and, 70–71; religion and, 69–72, 76–77, 79–82, 88–89; tragedy and, 70–72, 76–77, 105–6. See also self, subjectivity
it is (I am) / it is not (I am not), 37–38, 41–42, 63–64, 70–71, 73–74, 80–82, 101, 108–11, 125, 132, 140–42, 145–46

Kant, Immanuel, 16, 103–4
Kempenaers, Jan, 134–35
Kermauner, Taras, 135–36
Kierkegaard, Søren, 27–28, 91
Klee, Paul, 115
Krajger, Boris, 138–39
Kraus, Karl, 114–15

Lacan, Jacques, 14, 22, 24, 28–29, 33, 57–58, 129–30, 133–34
lamella, 57–58

language: materiality and, 122–23; mother tongue and, 116–18, 121–23, 128; negativity and, 117–18, 128; Reason and, 120–23, 151; revolution and, 116–18; stutter and, 117–18; tragedy and, 120–21
laugh lines, 149–51, 154. See also wrinkles
laughter, 22–23, 129; body and, 12, 149–50; censorship and, 85–88, 91–95, 99–100, 158, 160–62; class and, 92–93; community and, 82–83, 85, 94–95; critical, 3–4, 53–54, 87, 90–91, 99–100, 102–3, 118–19; defeat and, 17–18, 123–28; despair and, 10–12; detached, 15, 50, 64, 66–67, 82; as destructive, 72–73, 90–95, 102–3; feminine, 122, 126–28; history and, 3–7, 15–17, 86–87, 113–15, 122–25; politics and, 3–4, 92–95, 99–100, 119–20, 122–24, 127–28, 158, 160–62; seriousness and, 74–75, 78, 87, 93; Spirit and, 16–17, 70, 99–100, 122–23, 147–48
Laurel, Stan. See Laurel and Hardy
Laurel and Hardy, 21; *Brats*, 41–43; *Twice Two*, 23, 40–41
Lear, Jonathan, 133
Left Hegelians, 9, 86–90
Ljubljana School of Psychoanalysis, 14, 22, 24–30, 139
Looney Tunes, 25
Luther, Martin, 10–12, 89
Lutheranism, 64, 75–76, 86, 89

Marx, Karl, 3–6, 14, 16–19, 22, 67, 69, 87–88, 91, 95, 100, 105–6, 120–21, 123–24, 149, 155; *Capital*, 87; "Comments on the Latest Prussian Censorship Instruction," 97–100; "Contribution to the Critique of Hegel's Philosophy of Law," 87, 107–11; *The Eighteenth Brumaire of Louis Bonaparte*, 17, 21, 29–30, 87, 113–14, 116–18, 122, 124–25, 128; *The Holy Family* (with Engels), 87
Marx Brothers, 40
Matter, 8; language and, 122–23; Spirit and, 12–13, 16–17, 67, 110–11, 122–23, 147–48, 155

melodrama, 71, 120, 123–24
memorials, memorialization, 134–37, 141–43, 147–48, 154
Michelet, Karl, 13–14
midwife: negativity and, 47–48, 55, 59–60, 66, 109–10, 127–28, 133–34, 161; philosophy and, 46–48, 50, 53–55, 58–59, 109–10, 133–34; self/subject and, 50, 58–60, 133–34, 161. See also abortion, abortionist
mirror stage, 33, 38, 116
Močnik, Rastko, *Mesčevo zlato: Prešeren v označevalcu* (Moon's Gold: Prešeren in the Signifier), 24, 28–29
modernism, 25
monsters, "monstrous compound," 48, 55, 64, 66, 76–77, 113, 117, 127
mother tongue. See under language
Mr. Magoo, 26–27
Muñoz, José Esteban, 157

Nabokov, Vladimir, 40
names, naming, 115–16, 156–57
National Feeling (Nationalgefühl), 3–4, 8, 99–100, 105–6, 155
negation, negativity: aesthetics and, 8–9, 46–47, 49, 63, 101–2; affect and, 64, 74, 80–82, 97–99, 107, 150, 153, 156; agency and, 2–3, 17–20, 129–31, 144–48, 153; Being/Nothing and, 10–12, 37–39, 42–43, 45–48, 56–58, 60–61, 63–66, 80–82, 116, 126–27, 130–33, 143–44, 153, 156; comedy and, 2–5, 8–10, 15–16, 18, 24–27, 43, 45–46, 49–50, 59–60, 67, 74, 80–82, 102–3, 107–8, 115–16, 122, 125, 130–31, 133, 154; community, 8, 15–16, 22, 66, 85, 110–11; determinate, 45–48, 59–60, 129–30, 133–34; double and, 4–6, 13–15, 21–22, 27–30, 33–34, 37–39, 42–43, 47–48, 50–51, 58–60, 63–67, 69, 72, 107, 116, 118, 121, 129–30, 140, 153, 155–56, 161; ethics and, 2–3, 14–15, 157; history and, 1–12, 14, 17–20, 29–30, 80–82, 116, 118, 121–23, 131–34, 140, 147, 151, 153–54; indeterminate, 39, 47–48, 59, 63, 133–34; language and, 117–18, 128; religion and, 8–12, 15, 60, 63–67, 74–82, 85, 130–31; self/

Index

subject and, 10–12, 15, 19–20, 22–23, 26–28, 30, 33–34, 45–48, 50, 57–61, 63–65, 69, 80–82, 85, 101–11, 113, 116, 125–28, 129–30, 133–34, 143–46, 150, 153–59, 161–62; Spirit and, 1, 5, 110–11, 125, 130–31, 133–34, 147–48, 155; tragedy and, 34–35, 74, 76–77. *See also* comedy; double, doubling of double
Nietzsche, Friedrich, 10–12, 27–28, 153
NOT!, 37–38
Nothing: Absolute and, 60–61; Being and, 8, 10–12, 14–15, 21–22, 37–43, 45–48, 58–61, 63–65, 80–82, 101–2, 104, 110–11, 132–33, 150, 153, 156; Becoming and, 22, 133; history and, 17–20, 80–82, 104–8, 110–11, 113, 116, 125–26, 128, 140–41, 143–46, 153, 155; negativity and, 8, 10–12, 19–20, 26–28, 38–39, 42–43, 45–48, 58–61, 63–65, 80–82, 101–2, 107–8, 116, 125–26, 128, 132–33, 140–41, 143–46, 150, 153; pure Nothingness, 14–15, 21–22, 37–39, 45–46, 58–60; self/subject and, 10–12, 15, 19–20, 22–23, 27–28, 33–34, 45–48, 58, 60–61, 63–65, 80–82, 85, 101–2, 104–5, 109–11, 113, 116, 125–26, 128, 129–30, 133, 140, 143–46, 155–56, 161. *See also* Being
nothing more/no more, 13–14, 69
Nuzzo, Angelica, 132

odd couple, 13, 23–24, 31, 36–43, 45–48, 56–57, 63, 75, 100, 114–15, 139, 151. *See also* twins
Old Hegelians, 1–2, 5, 13–14, 65, 80–82, 103, 160
owl, 1–2, 13–14, 114. *See also* cock

Palestine, 8, 155–56
parabasis, 52–53
The Parent Trap, 34–35
Persephone, 92–93
Perspektive, 138–39
phantoms, 46–48, 50, 54–55, 58–60, 64, 108, 113–16, 124–25, 153–55
philosophy: affect and, 102–3, 107; censorship and, 103–4; comedy and, 5–8, 10–12, 14–15, 49–51, 53–54, 86; critique and, 90–91, 104–5, 108–10; double and, 30, 37–39, 56–58; ethics and, 15, 49–50; midwife-abortionist and, 46–60, 109–10, 133–34; negativity and, 8–9, 13–14, 46–47; politics and, 89–90, 103–7; religion and, 9–10, 88–91, 105–7; self/subject and, 50, 104, 106–7; Spirit and, 104–5; tragedy and, 5–6, 18, 104. *See also* critique
Pinkard, Terry, 68
Plato, 49; *Apology*, 53–54; *Symposium*, 34–35, 46–48, 54–55, 57–58; *Theaetetus*, 46–48, 53–59
Plutarch, 92–93
Pohod po Poti okoli Ljubljane (The Walk along the Path around Ljubljana), 135–36
politics: aesthetics and, 1–3, 87–88, 103–5, 118–19, 136–43, 153; affect and, 3–4, 7, 87–88, 91–95, 97–100, 107, 113–14, 119–20, 122–24, 127–28, 155–56, 158, 160–62; comedy and, 3–7, 9–10, 14, 17–19, 87–88, 91–95, 100, 104–6, 118–20, 154, 158; critique and, 99–100, 104–5, 110–11; negativity and, 8–12, 17–20, 106–7; philosophy and, 89–90, 103–7; religion and, 1–2, 87–91, 98, 100, 102, 105–8; revolutionary, 87–88, 95, 100, 103–7; self/subject and, 102–11
postmodernism, 25–26
Prešeren, France, 24, 28–29
proletariat, 8, 17–19, 29–30, 106–7, 110–11, 113–14, 116–18, 122, 128
prostitute, 126–27
Protagoras, 55–56, 58–59
Prussia: Carlsbad Decrees, 86; Laws on the Freedom of the Press, 97–100. *See also* censorship
psychoanalysis, 5–6, 14, 22–23, 33, 57–58
Public Spirit, 3–6, 8, 99–100, 155

queerness, 155–56, 159–60

race, 19–20, 154–55, 158
Reason: language and, 120–23, 151; laughter and, 122–23; negativity and, 122–23, 125–27; self/subject and, 125, 127

reconciliation, 9, 12, 18, 37, 63, 66–67, 69–72, 74, 78–83, 157
relativism, 55–57
release, 15–16, 22–23, 45–46, 65–66, 74, 81, 113–14, 149
relief, 15, 25, 26–27, 33–34, 45, 74–75, 81–82, 124–25, 150, 158
religion: aesthetics and, 48–49, 63–83, 85–86, 101–3, 105–6; affect and, 100, 102–3, 105–6, 108; comedy and, 1–3, 15, 21–22, 45–46, 48–49, 59–60, 63–67, 71–82, 86–88, 90–91, 100–103; community and, 85–86; double and, 15, 21–22, 78–80, 86–88, 90–91, 101–8; drama and, 3, 5–6, 11, 15, 21–22, 59–61, 63–67, 71–75, 77–82, 90, 101, 105–6; ethics and, 3, 66, 68–71, 79–80, 89; history and, 72, 88, 90–91, 105–6, 108; individual and, 69–72, 76–77, 79–82, 88–89; negativity and, 8–12, 15, 60, 63–67, 74–82, 85, 90–91, 126–27, 130–31; philosophy and, 9–10, 88–91, 105–7; politics and, 1–2, 87–91, 98, 100, 102, 105–8; self/subject and, 46, 59–60, 63–64, 72, 75–76, 100–103, 105–7, 158; tragedy and, 21–22, 64–65, 67–68, 70–72, 76–77, 80–82. *See also* Christ; Christianity
Revealed Religion, 21–22, 45–46, 50, 60, 63–66, 75–76, 80–82, 85, 88. *See also* Art-Religion
revolution, 1–2, 6, 91; failed, 17, 19–20, 113–14, 116–18, 122–23, 128; history and, 3–5, 16–17, 86–87, 106–7, 113–14, 116–18, 120, 122–25, 128, 161–62; politics and, 87–88, 95, 100, 103–7
Rheinische Zeitung, 91, 97–98
Right Hegelians, 9–10, 86–90
Rose, Gillian, 123–24, 128
Ruge, Arnold, 4–5, 16–17, 90–91, 120, 157; "Hegel's 'Philosophy of Right' and the Politics of Our Times," 103–7

Sartre, Jean-Paul, 27–28
Saturday Night Live, "Wayne's World," 37–38
Schelling, Friedrich, 89–91
Scholem, Gershom, 114–15

self, subjectivity: aesthetics and, 46, 50, 101–3, 105–7; agency and, 17–20, 49, 72–73, 76–77, 79–80, 119, 125, 129–30, 140, 144–45, 153–54, 161; body and, 10–2, 64–65, 75, 80–82, 122–23, 155, 157, 161–62; comedy and, 3–6, 26–27, 63–64, 85, 100–103, 110–11, 119–20, 125; community and, 10–12, 15, 80–82, 85, 89, 92, 99, 105, 109–11, 122–23, 157–62; double and, 15, 27–28, 33, 47–48, 56–60, 63–67, 69, 75, 101–3, 105–6, 111, 139–40, 143–44, 161; ethics and, 63–64, 68–71, 79–80, 119, 158, 161–62; history and, 73, 80, 104, 108–9, 113, 125, 149, 151, 153–55; negativity and, 4, 10–12, 15, 18–20, 22–23, 26–28, 30, 33–34, 45–48, 50, 57–61, 63–65, 69, 80–82, 85, 101–11, 113, 116, 125–28, 129–30, 133–34, 139–48, 150–51, 153–59, 161–62; politics and, 102–11; religion and, 46, 59–60, 63–64, 72, 75–76, 100–103, 105–7, 158; tragedy and, 108–9, 125, 157
seriousness, 5, 16–17, 24–25, 37–38, 40–43, 67–70, 74–75, 78, 81–83, 87–89, 92–93, 97–100, 102–3, 105–6, 121, 158, 160
sexuality, 154–56, 158
Shakespeare, William, *The Comedy of Errors*, 33–34
Shining, The, 34–35
silence, 18, 103–4, 122–23, 127–30, 138–39, 142–48, 154, 157, 160–62. *See also* absence
Single White Female, 35–36
skepticism, 15, 45, 47–50, 59–60, 63–64, 80, 86, 102–3
slit, 10–12. *See also* negation, negativity
Slovenia, 131–32; Critical Generation, 135–36, 138–39; Kočevski Rog massacre, 138–39; Nazi occupation of, 135; Yugoslavia and, 28–29, 139
Smole, Dominik, *Antigona*, 18, 129–32, 135–48
Socrates, 15, 46–48, 50–59, 74–75
Sophocles, *Antigone*, 5, 8, 15, 18, 64–65, 67–70, 76–77, 129–32, 135–47
Sparta, Spartans, 92–93, 95
Spinoza, Baruch, 74

Index

Spirit, 8; comedy and, 5–6, 16–17, 26, 70, 91, 99–100, 104–7, 122–23, 147–48; Critical, 104–5, 107; history, 12, 17, 65, 106–7, 122–23, 133, 147–48; Matter and, 12–13, 16–17, 67, 110–11, 122–23, 147–48, 155; negativity and, 1, 5, 110–11, 125, 130–31, 133–34, 147–48, 155; tragedy and, 26, 111
split, 1–12. *See also* negation, negativity
Stage '57, 135–36, 138–39
state, 8–10, 16–18, 67–69, 86–90, 95, 97–100, 104–8, 110–11, 134–39, 141, 157
Stepelevich, Lawrence, 88–89
Stirner, Max, 91, 100; "Art and Religion," 101–3; *Ego and Its Own*, 102
Strauss, David Friedrich, 9, 88–90
stutter, 10–12, 17, 38–39, 45, 60–61, 113–14, 117–18, 123, 125–26, 128, 151, 153–54. *See also* language
suffering, 66–67, 69–75, 77, 80, 82–83, 108, 117, 155, 157–58
suicide, 118–19, 128–31, 147
suspension. *See under* dialectic

tarot, 119–20, 151
Three Stooges, 40
TikTok, 159
Tito (Josip Broz), 8, 18, 135–36, 138–41
Tom and Jerry, 26–27
tragedy, 1, 8–9, 49, 113–14; affect and, 70–71, 74; agency and, 2–3, 49, 70–71, 76–77, 117–18, 125; audience and, 93–94; character and, 2–3, 119–20, 150; comedy and, 15, 34–37, 65–67, 72–75, 77, 80–83, 119, 129; conflict and, 2–3, 34, 65–72, 76–77, 80–82, 120–21, 129; double and, 21–22, 34–37, 72, 74–75, 119; ethics and, 34, 66, 69–71; history and, 5, 7, 17, 19–23, 29–30, 80–82, 108–11, 118–25, 150; individual and, 70–72, 76–77, 105–6; life/death and, 69–71, 74–83, 130–31; language and, 120–21; negativity and, 18, 34–35, 74, 76–77; philosophy and, 5–6, 18, 104; religion and, 21–22, 64–65, 67–68, 70–72, 76–77, 80–82; self/subject and, 108–9, 125, 157; Spirit and, 26, 111. *See also* comedy; farce
tragic hero, 49, 64–65, 67–71, 73–77, 80–82, 85, 93–94, 103–4, 108, 120–21, 130–31, 158. *See also* Christ
trauma, 149–50
twins, 13, 21, 23–24, 31–43, 45, 47–48, 55–60, 64, 101–4, 107, 109, 113–15, 126–27, 151, 155. *See also* odd couple

unborn, 133–34
uncanny (*Unheimliche*), 22–23, 33–36, 38
undead, 123–24, 131, 133–34, 147

violence, 19, 137, 155–60; comedy and, 73, 78–80, 92–95, 158–60
Virgin, 126–27

war: memorialization and, 134–37; peace and, 137–43, 146–47
Wile E. Coyote and Road Runner, 26–27
Williams, Robert, 70–71
Wolff, Charlotte ("Lotte"), 151
Wrigley's Doublemint gum, 31–34
wrinkles, 149–51, 153–54, 161–62

Young Hegelians, 1–6, 13–17, 21, 73–74, 86–92, 95, 97–98, 100, 102–3, 106–8, 113–14, 116–18, 120–21, 124–25, 149, 154, 156–57, 160. *See also* Old Hegelians
Yugoslavia, 6, 18, 28–29, 129, 131–32; Hegelian-Lacanianism in, 24–25; memorials in, 134–36, 141–43; staging of *Antigone* in, 137–43, 147–48

Žižek, Slavoj, 14, 22, 24–25; *Antigone*, 130–31; *Hegel and the Signifier*, 24; *The Sublime Object of Ideology*, 26–27; "Why Should a Dialectician Count to Four?," 28–30
zombies, 22–23, 113–14
Zupančič, Alenka, 22, 24–27; *The Odd One In*, 14, 29–30, 77